# Totally
# cocktails

Dear Nick,

Happy Birthday! Hope it's a good'un.

Best wishes —

Nat x

# totally
# cocktails

Maria Costantino

**D&S**
BOOKS

First published in 2007 by D&S Books Ltd

D&S Books Ltd
Kerswell, Parkham Ash,
Bideford
Devon, England
EX39 5PR

e-mail us at:- enquiries@d-sbooks.co.uk

This edition printed 2007

ISBN 13: 978-1-903327-67-8

Book Code: DS0190

material in this book previously appeared in *The Cocktail Handbook* and *Cocktail Deluxe*.

Editorial Director: Sarah King
Project Editor: Justyna Poncyliusz
Photographer: Colin Bowling
Designer: Axis Design

1 3 5 7 9 10 8 6 4 2

# contents

# Introduction

*The word 'cocktail' inevitably conjures up images of the 'speakeasies' of the Prohibition era, of sharp-suited gangsters and elegantly dressed molls, and of the Bright Young Things of the Jazz Age. While the golden age of the cocktail was undoubtedly the 1920s and 1930s, the practice of serving 'mixed drinks' is much older.*

Alcoholic mixed drinks called braggets made of ale and mead (fermented honey) are known to have been popular in the 14th century, while mint julep is believed to have been made first in 18th century Virginia and served as a morning eye-opener.

Over the last 200 years many stories have emerged to explain the origin of the term cocktail. In his 1933 work, *The Cocktail Book – A Sideboard Manual for Gentlemen*, John MacQueen tells the legend of the cock's tail and of the lovely young girl called Daisy who invented it. The story goes that during the American War of Independence, the innkeeper of the Bunch of Grapes and a keen fan of the bloody sport of cock-fighting, discovered that Jupiter, his prize bird, was missing. Some time later, a young officer rode into town with Jupiter under his arm. Squire Allen was delighted to have his bird returned and ordered Daisy to serve the soldier the finest refreshment. A toast was drunk to 'the cock's tail', since the mighty Jupiter had not lost a single feather during his absence.

## Myths and legends

Other stories say that the cocktail was derived from the French word *coquetier* (egg cup). Monsieur Antoine Peychaud, a chemist in New Orleans, is said to have served his guests mixed drinks in egg cups. A mixed drink called a 'coquetel' was taken to America by the Marquis de Lafayette in 1777 and French officers in George Washington's army were said to enjoy the 'concoction' of wines. In 1779, Betsy Flanagan, the widow of a Revolutionary officer and barmaid at Hall's Corner Tavern in New York, is said to have decorated a drink with the feathers of roosters stolen from a loyalist neighbour. A group of French soldiers were served the drink and toasted Betsy with '*Vive le cock-tail*'.

Two further stories place the origins of the cocktail Mexico. One version has English sailors ashore at Campeche in Yucatan. A popular drink was a drac, a mixture of liquors stirred slowly with a wooden spoon. In one bar, the barman stirred the drinks not with a spoon, but with the root of a plant called cola de gallo – in English, a cock's tail. Rather than ask for dracs the English sailors took to asking for 'cock-tails'.

The second version was provided by Harry Craddock, the legendary bartender at the Savoy Hotel in London from 1920 to 1939. Craddock was the first president of the United Kingdom Bartender's Guild and was responsible for introducing the delights of the fashionable American cocktail to Europe. Americans touring Europe often referred to the bar at the Savoy as the '49th state' since it was the finest place to enjoy an American cocktail. In 1930 Craddock published the now highly collectable *Savoy Cocktail Book*. In Craddock's story, the cocktail was invented at the beginning of the 19th century when the American Army of the Southern States was fighting the forces of King Axolotl VIII of Mexico. When a truce was declared, the king offered the American general a drink. A sin-gle cup of liquor was brought in by the king's daughter who, realising that whoever drank first would offend the other, saved everyone's embarrassment by drinking it herself. The king's daughter just happened to be called Coctel and thus, her drink became 'cocktail'.

## Modern masters

While all these stories offer an explanation of the origin of the word 'cocktail' few, if any, offer hints of what went into these remarkable drinks. The earliest mention of the ingredients of cocktails can be found in *The Balance and Columbian Repository*, a newspaper published in Hudson, New York, on 13 May 1806, which described the cocktail as 'a stimulating liquor composed of spirits of any kind, sugar, water, and bit-

ters'.

The American barman 'Professor' Jerry Thomas was the first to produce a book of cocktail recipes in the 1860s, *The Bon Vivant's Guide, or How to Mix Drinks.* The 'Professor' became famous when he was the bartender at the Metropolitan Hotel in New York. Touring Europe, he travelled with a set of silver mixing cups from which he would trail a flame of liquid when he mixed his famous blue blazer cocktail.

The Professor's recipe book was soon followed by many others, but outstanding was Harry Johnson's *Illustrated Bartender's Manual.* Published in 1882, Johnson's book featured an illustration of an ice-filled bar glass with a metal cone – what was to become the modern cocktail shaker.

Today there are thousands of recipes for cocktails and mixed drinks. Some are simple, some elaborate. Some use only a few ingredients, others have so many ingredients that it's amazing they all fit into one glass! Everyone can make a good cocktail: there are no jealously guarded secrets, nor does it require years of toil. In this book you will find a good number of drinks that you can make straight away at home. You won't need to splash out on exotic liqueurs – not yet anyway!

All of the recipes in this book are based on gin, vodka, tequila, rum, brandy, whisky, vermouth, wine (including some champagne and fortified wines like sherry and port) with a few additions such as angostura bitters, grenadine, fruit juices and sparkling minerals. With a few ingredients, you should be able to make a fair proportion of the drinks on offer. A few, however, do use triple sec or a 'branded' ingredient such as Campari or Galliano and it is worthwhile investing in a bottle of each if you enjoy the flavour they impart. You will find more detailed information on each of the spirits in the section on ingredients and at the beginning of each chapter.

The recipes offered in this book are for you to try out for yourself. Choose a cocktail, a highball, a Rickey, a Collins, or a punch – or even a 'mocktail' – that catches your eye and try it. If it's too sweet for your taste, cut down on the sugar or liqueur content. If it's too sour, reduce the lemon or lime juice. Play around with the proportions until you find the 'perfect mix' and have fun!

# Responsible drinking

These – and all alcoholic drinks – are meant to accompany good times with good friends, not be the good time (or good friend) in themselves. Before you begin reading any further, take a moment to consider the responsible use and serving of alcoholic drinks.

Responsible drinking is the key to enjoyment, health and safety – both yours and that of others, especially if you are a driver. Remember, the only person who can safely handle a pint while driving is a milkman!

Do not condone or encourage underage drinking: there are numerous non-alcoholic 'fruity' syrups that can be used to create delicious 'mocktails'. You will find that these are very popular with many people because they are so tasty, so be prepared, when you entertain, to provide them for all your guests!

Do not 'push' an alcoholic drink onto a guest: if they say no, they mean no. Offer delicious juices and sparkling minerals instead, and never, ever, 'spike' anyone's drink: they may be the designated driver that night, be allergic to alcohol, be on medication, have religious beliefs which preclude alcohol or may be 'in recovery'. After all, you invited all your guests because they were friends and you like them, not because they drink!

# The Basics:

The key to making delicious cocktails and mixed drinks involves a couple of simple rules:

Keep your ingredients cool: chill juices and mixers, champagnes and vermouths. Aquavits and vodkas are best if they are very cold.

Wash mixing equipment between making different cocktails to avoid mixing flavours. Rinse spoons and stirrers too!

Have all the equipment – can opener, bottle opener, shaker, jigger, mixing glass, bar spoon, straws, stirrers – ready to hand.

Prepare glasses, fruit juices, fruit garnishes and ingredients like sugar syrup, lemon or lime juices and coconut cream in advance of your guests arriving.

Make sure you have plenty of ice: an ice bucket is ideal and insulation is vital. A well-insulated, capacity ice bucket is better than a 'novelty' design which results in a bucket of melted ice! Tongs are more efficient than a spoon for taking ice from the bucket: you won't get any extra – and unwanted – water.

## Measures

In this book you will see that the recipes call for 1 measure, or ½ measure of a spirit or liqueur. The word measure is used because of the slight variations between metric, British Imperial and US measurements, and because each side of the Atlantic has a variation on the fluid ounce. Since most of the classic cocktails were invented in America, the 'jigger' used in bars in the USA is often a common measurement. It really doesn't matter what 'jigger' you use – you could use a shot glass, or even an egg cup as your 'measure'. As long as you use the same measure throughout, the ratios of one spirit to another in your drink will be correct. It's a good idea, though, to measure – using water – the total quantities of a drink and pour them into the glass to make sure all the contents fit!

# Cocktail essentials

*Many of the stock items you will need may be already in your kitchen cupboards or drinks cabinet. The job of making drinks is much easier – and more pleasurable – when everything is to hand. Consequently, whether the drinks are for an intimate 'dîner à deux', entertaining a few friends, a family get-together at Christmas or Thanksgiving, a summer barbecue or garden party or a more formal celebration, the most important thing is preparation. Lay everything out neatly and keep your utensils and glasses clean. Squeeze enough juice in advance, cut lemons, limes, oranges and other fruit for garnishes and twists and make sure that mixers and fruit juices are well chilled. Ask one or two friends to come around early – that way you can gossip and cut lemon slices at the same time.*

## Bar stock

The drinks in this book are for the most part based on a single base spirit (such as gin, vodka or rum) to which is added a second spirit, liqueur (either Cointreau or Galliano), bitters, juices or minerals. This way, you can choose your favourite spirit and create drinks around it. The exotically named, beautifully bottled and sometimes obscure liqueurs and spirits have been avoided. I leave these for you to discover and enjoy for yourself!

The most essential ingredient: ice, and lots of it!

### Ice

You'll need ice – broken, crushed and cubes – and probably lots of it. Never use the same ice twice. Clean, clear ice cubes are hard to make, especially if you live in a hard-water area. Even bottled waters can make cloudy cubes. If your cubes are cloudy, you could use purified drinking water, available at your chemist, although it is more expensive than bottled. Alternatively, check out the ice on sale at your off license or liquor store. The cubes should be clear. If they're cloudy, you might as well save your money and make your own from tap water.

Keep ice cubes in an ice bucket and use tongs to pick them up. If they get stuck together, a quick squirt of soda water will separate them.

To make broken ice, place some cubes into a plastic bag and hit them with a rolling pin! The aim is to make each piece about one-third the original ice-cube size.

To make crushed ice, you could either carry on hitting the bag or else put the broken ice into a blender. Unless you have a heavy-duty blender, or one that the maker says will crush ice, don't put whole cubes in it. Your blades will never forgive you!

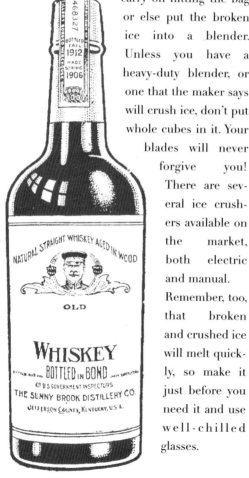

There are several ice crushers available on the market, both electric and manual. Remember, too, that broken and crushed ice will melt quickly, so make it just before you need it and use well-chilled glasses.

## Base spirits

Choose the brand you enjoy most. Quality spirits may be a little more expensive, but a cocktail is no better than its poorest ingredient! The main base spirits are gin, vodka, rum (white and dark, see the section on rum, page 54), tequila, brandy and whisky.

For the sake of simplicity, when referring to whisky in this book, we have adopted the accepted British spelling of the word unless specifically referring to Irish or American whiskey, such as bourbon, rye, corn or Kentucky. Avoid using high-quality Scotch malt unless a recipe demands it. A good blend will be perfect.

## Liqueurs

These are sweetish drinks made from a base spirit which is infused, macerated or redistilled with roots, barks, flowers, fruits or seeds. (In the United States, liqueurs are called cordials. In other English-speaking countries, however, a cordial is a non-alcoholic, concentrated fruit juice.) Some of the drinks in this book require Galliano, triple sec, such as Cointreau, and Campari

Galliano is a sweetish, gold-coloured liqueur from Lombardy in Italy and has a spicy, herbal taste tinged with vanilla. It comes in a very tall bottle and was named after Major Guiseppe Galliano, an Italian war hero from the Abyssinian Wars of 1895. The recipe, containing more than 80 herbs, roots, flowers and berries from Alpine regions, is a closely guarded secret and the method of

production has remained unchanged since it was first made by the distiller Arturo Vaccari.

## Triple sec

One of the most refined forms of Curaçao, triple sec a colourless liqueur made from the peel of small, green oranges native to the island of Curaçao in the Caribbean. Triple sec means ' triple dry', but the liqueur is not as dry as it sounds, and is a major ingredient in many of the most famous cocktails and mixed drinks. The world's best-known brand of triple sec is Cointreau, first made in 1849 at Angers, France, by brothers Edouard and Adolphe Cointreau. Curaçao can also come in different colours – blue, green, yellow and red – and is used mainly to produce many of the more vividly coloured modern cocktails and mixed drinks.

The corkscrew, an essential bar tool.

Campari really comes somewhere in between a bitters and a liqueur. It is a patent Italian aperitif (from the Latin *aperire*, 'to open', and thus an alcoholic drink taken before a meal to stimulate and sharpen the appetite). It is red and very dry, with a pronounced quinine taste, and can either be drunk 'on the rocks' with soda or used as the ingredient in a cocktail. Campari is the basis of two of the most famous cocktails, the Americano (page 186 ) and the Negroni (page 199).

## Wines, aromatised wines and fortified wines

Vermouths are properly aromatised wines. The best-known French vermouth is Noilly Prat, made in Marseilles. It is very dry and is made with two white wines and 40 herbs which are steeped for 18 months. Turin, Italy, is the biggest vermouth-producing city and is the home of both Martini and Cinzano which produce excellent dry, extra dry and sweet vermouths, which can be either red or white.

Despite its red (Italian: *rosso*) colour, sweet vermouth is also made with white wine, albeit with sweeter grapes to which sweeteners, quinine and caramel are added.

### Sherry and port

These two wonderful fortified wines are so often ignored or simply offered either 'straight' as an aperitif (in the case of sherry) or as a digestif (in the case of port). There are a number of delicious cocktails and mixed drinks which use these as their base and which offer an opportunity to be a little different. A good sherry choice for cocktails would be a fino, while for port, select a tawny. For more on these two wines, see pages 182–83.

### Wines

Entire books have been written on the relative merits of individual wines. It really comes down to a simple matter of taste. The choice of wine or champagne is entirely up to you.

### Beer

No matter what you have lovingly created, there will always be one person at the party who will want a beer – and nothing else. Take as much trouble with beer as you would with any spirit. Each has its own unique colour and flavour. Check out 'real ales' and those available from micro-breweries. Beer and ale are also the basis of some interesting cocktails and punches.

Stout is a very dark – almost black - ale and is used in a black velvet (page 189). Bitter amber ale is used in the punch called brown Betty (page 210).

## Angostura bitters

In the recipes in this book you will frequently see in the ingredients '1 or 2 dashes bitters'. Bitters are an essential ingredient of a large number of cocktails. Oddly enough, bitters are bitter if you taste them straight, but their effect in a cocktail is almost the exact opposite. Bitters essences are alcoholic drinks made from roots, flowers, fruits and peels macerated in neutral spirit. The most famous patent bitters are angostura bitters

Originally made in the town of Angostura, (now Cuidad Bolivar), Venezuela, it is now produced in Trinidad. Angostura has over 40 ingredients, including gentian root and the bark from the cusparia tree. In this book, when you see bitters specified, use angostura bitters.

*Even though you will only add one or two dashes of angostura bitters to a drink, they do have an alcohol content of 45 per cent, so don't be tempted to add them to 'mocktails' (non-alcoholic drinks) for teetotallers, youngsters or 'designated drivers'.

This handy little gadget makes zest from citrus fruit and can also be used to make twists and spirals.

## Grenadine

Grenadine is a sweet syrup flavoured with pomegranate juice, which gives it its rich, rosy-pink colour. Prolonged exposure to the air once the bottle has been opened will make the syrup ferment and mould, so keep an eye on it. To stop the fermentation, you could add about 10 per cent vodka – but remember, your grenadine should not then be used in mocktails! You could perhaps decant some grenadine into another bottle, add vodka to 10 per cent of the volume, label it and keep the remainder as 'unadulterated'. Keep the grenadine in a cool place, but don't refrigerate it as this can cause the sugar to crystallise, or at least harden, which prevents it from mixing easily with other drinks.

## Minerals and juices

If you've purchased a good-quality spirit, why spoil it with poor-quality minerals and juices? Squeeze your own citrus juices or buy the best you can find and serve chilled. A comprehensive selection includes: soda water, cola, tonic water, ginger ale, lemonade, lemon-lime soda (such as 7-Up), tomato juice, cranberry juice, grape juice, pineapple juice, orange juice, apple juice, grapefruit juice, lemon juice, lime juice and Rose's Lime Juice. it is also worth trying some of the more 'exotic' juices, such as passionfruit, mango, peach and tangerine

## Fresh fruit

Freshly squeezed citrus fruits will produce the best juice. Citrus fruits other than lemons turn soft and show spots as they age, while lemons turn hard. While the flesh inside might be OK, it may have an peculiar taste. Choose fruits with bright skins and remember to wash them before using the skin for twists. Once squeezed, fruit juices will slowly start to ferment. Refrigeration will slow the process, but my advice is 'buy 'em fresh, squeeze 'em fresh and use 'em fresh'.

Strain lemon and lime juice before use to ensure no pips get in the drink. Likewise, you might want to strain other citrus juices. Strain through a fine nylon sieve to ensure that clear drinks remain unclouded by the juice. If you don't have the energy or time to hand-squeeze your fruit and don't have one of those fancy electric juicers, try using a mixer/blender. Peel the fruit (reserving the peel), pulp it at high speed and strain. Peaches and mangos can be 'squeezed' in a blender – and yes, you can even do a pineapple this way, but don't

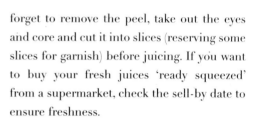

forget to remove the peel, take out the eyes and core and cut it into slices (reserving some slices for garnish) before juicing. If you want to buy your fresh juices 'ready squeezed' from a supermarket, check the sell-by date to ensure freshness.

Although there are many famous and delicious cocktails which use cream or milk, none are included in this book. Yoghurt, however, is a wonderful ingredient in mocktails, and you will find a few 'healthy options' to try in that section.

The famous pina colada, possibly the most popular cocktail in the world, does use coconut cream as one of its ingredients. This is very simple to make and the instructions are given alongside the recipe (see page 73).

Some bartenders also use a teaspoon of raw egg white or egg yolk to give a cocktail a 'silver' and 'frothy' or 'golden' finish. Although the egg cannot be tasted, many people don't like the idea of raw egg in their drink. Furthermore, some people may be advised on medical grounds to avoid raw eggs altogether. In this book, drinks that include egg are omitted.

## Condiments

Drinks with tomato juice, such as the bloody Mary (page 82) can be 'spiced up' according to taste with Worcestershire sauce*, Tabasco sauce, ground black pepper and perhaps a few celery seeds.

\* Vegetarians should note that one of the ingredients of Worcestershire sauce is anchovy essence and they may prefer to avoid this.

## You will also need

**Salt** preferably coarsely ground, if you want to make the tequila-based Margarita (page 142) or the vodka-based salty dog (page 101).

**Sugar** in cube form; granulated sugar and castor sugar (sometimes called 'superfine' in recipe books). Gomme syrup is simply a sugar syrup and is easy to make. The object is to make the sugar syrup as heavy as possible without crystallisation. Gomme syrup is used in place of castor sugar and most bartenders prefer it since there is less risk of there being

a sediment at the bottom of the glass and it also saves time.

**Spices** these are used particularly in punches and hot drinks. Nutmeg, ginger, cinnamon and cloves are probably already in your kitchen cupboard.

**Garnishes:** green cocktail olives, cocktail onions, sprigs of fresh mint. Mint is an easy plant to grow in a garden or on a window sill.

There are many varieties, including pineapple mint, apple mint and variegated (with yellow and green leaves) varieties. Grow mint in a pot even in the garden – that is unless you want your garden full of it as it will spread and overwhelm other plants.

Wedges, slices and twists of orange, lemon slices and lime slices; pineapple and grapefruit slices, maraschino cherries are also useful. Seasonal fruit is always an attractive and delicious garnish for mocktails and party punches: try cool cucumber or apple wedges.

## When you see the term 'garnish with lemon twist',
**follow these steps:**

1. Hold the peel, coloured side down, over the top of the drink.
2. Twist the peel. This releases the volatile oil into the drink.
3. Rub the coloured side of the peel along the rim of the glass and then discard the peel, unless otherwise stated. If, however, you find you like the bitter sharpness of the citrus oil, you can drop the twist into the drink.

## To make gomme syrup:

Add three cups of granulated sugar to one cup of cold water. Bring to the boil and reduce the heat. Allow to simmer for two minutes. Skim the surface and allow to cool. Then pour off into a bottle and store in a cool place. Don't keep it in the fridge as the sugar may crystallise.

## To make orange/lemon/lime slices:

1. Cut the 'knobs' off the top and tail of the fruit. Cut deep enough to expose the pulp.
2. Cut the orange in half lengthways from top to tail.
3. Put each orange half cut side down and cut crosswise into ¼ inch-thick slices.
4 Cut into the centre of each slice – start at the flat fruit edge and go just up to, but not into, the peel.
5. Slip the cut onto the rim of the glass so that it hangs half-in, half-out.

## Preparing garnishes

Don't just slice fruit – try cutting citrus peel into shapes such as stars, crescents or hearts, that can be speared on a cocktail stick and used to decorate drinks. Remember to wash the fruit before you use it.

## To make wedges:

1. Cut the 'knobs' off the top and tail of the fruit.
2. Slice the fruit in half from top to bottom, and then again across the 'equator'.
3. Cut each piece into four equal wedges.
4. When you squeeze a wedge, hold it over the glass and squeeze it downwards into the drink. Try shielding the glass with your other hand: by some unexplained phenomenon of physics, lemon juice will always hit you in the eye! Drop the wedge into the drink.

## To make twists:

Twists are usually made of lemon, but sometimes limes and oranges are used.

1. Cut a slice from the top and tail of the fruit – just thick enough to expose the pulp.
2. Using a sharp knife, cut through the peel into the fruit from top to tail.
3. Insert a small spoon through the cut. The idea is to separate the fruit from the peel: work the spoon up and down and around the inside of the peel.
4. Once the fruit is separated from the peel, take it out and use it for juice.
5  Cut the peel into thin strips – as thin as possible – cutting lengthways from top to tail.

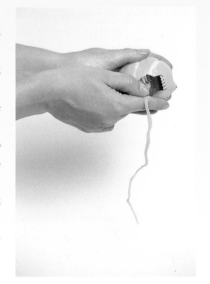

# The Well-stocked Bar

*The basis for many cocktails, no matter how exotic, remains a spirit. These are mixed with each other, with liqueurs, with fruit juices, with eggs, with cream or coconut cream to produce the thousands of exciting combinations available today. Look through the recipes and find the 'flavours' that interest you: then look at the ingredients to see what you need. Don't forget that you can also get many of these spirits and liqueurs in 'miniatures': tiny, but perfectly formed, single measures that are ideal if you want to try out a cocktail without splashing out on a big bottle!*

## Spirits

**Bitters:** The term bitters refers to a number of spirits flavoured with bitter herbs and roots. These range from products like Campari – which can be drunk in whole measures like any other spirit or mixed with other ingredients like Fernet-Branca and Amer Picon – to bitters that are added in drops to 'season' a drink. The most famous of these 'dropping' bitters are undoubtedly angostura bitters, made from a secret Trinidadian recipe; Peychaud bitters made in New Orleans; and Abbot's Aged bitters made in Baltimore, Maryland since 1865. There are also orange bitters made by numerous companies.

**Brandy and Cognac:** Both are spirits made from distilled grape wine. Brandy can be made in any country where vines are grown –

Pisco is a clear brandy from Peru and Chile – but Cognac can only come from the Cognac region in France, where the brandy is made from white wines and distilled in traditional pot stills before maturing in oak casks. Cognacs are labelled: VSO (Very Superior Old) VSOP (Very Superior Old Pale) VVSOP (Very, Very Superior Old Pale) and XO (Extremely Old).

**Armagnac:** This is a grape brandy produced in this region in southwest France and which uses only three specified white wines: Haut Armagnac (white), Tenareze and Bas Armagnac (black). If the spirit is described simply as 'Armagnac' it is a blend of these three types.

**Calvados:** This is an apple brandy made in Normandy, France; Applejack is an American apple brandy – sometimes known as Jersey Lightning – after the state where it is produced. It is sold straight or blended with neutral spirits.

**Eau de Vie:** This is a spirit produced from fruit other than grapes and apples: it is a colourless (because it has not been aged in wooden casks) fruit brandy, most often made from soft berries such as raspberries, strawberries, pears and cherries. Eau de vie is not sweetened and should not be confused with it syrupy liqueur cousin, (often made using one of the same fruits) although this tends to be coloured anyway!

**Whisky:** (Scotch and Canadian) and whiskey (Irish, American and Japanese).

**Bourbon:** This is a generic term for a bourbon-style American whiskey, distilled in a continuous still method from fermented cereal mash containing a minimum of 51% corn and aged for 6 to 8 years in oak casks.

**Canadian Whisky:** This is made from cereal grains such as barley, corn, rye and wheat in varying proportions depending on the manufacturer, in a continuous still method and aged for six years.

**Irish Whiskey:** Similar to Scotch, the difference here is that the barley is dried in a kiln rather than over a peat fire.

**Rye Whiskey:** Produced in both Canada and the USA, rye is distilled from a mixture of cereals but no less than 51% rye.

**Scotch:** Blended Scotch is a mixture of grain spirit – usually maize – and one or more malt whiskies. The malt whisky is made from barley which has germinated, been dried over smoky peat fires, mashed, fermented, distilled and aged in wooden casks for 10 to 12 years or more.

**Vodka:** This is an almost neutral spirit distilled from a fermented mash of grain, which is filtered through charcoal. There are colourless and odourless varieties as well as subtly flavoured and aromamtised versions such as bison grass vodka, cherry vodka, lemon vodka, and pepper vodka.

**Gin:** London dry gin is made form a distillate of unmalted grain. The spirit is infused with juniper and other 'botanicals' before and during distillation to produce a gin with a subtle flavour and aroma. London dry gin is therefore a 'style' of gin as there are many famous brands to choose from such as Gordon's, Bombay Sapphire and Beefeater. Plymouth Gin is made only in Plymouth, England and is the traditional gin used for a 'pink gin'. This is produced by Coates at the Blackfriar's distillery in the city. Sloe gin – and its French equivalent prunelle – is not a spirit but a liqueur made of sweetened gin in which the fruit (sloes) of the blackthorn bush have been steeped and then strained out after they have stained the spirit a deep red. (Prunelle is green however!).

Dutch genever sometimes called 'Hollanders gin' is very different to English gin because it uses a more pungent grain mash that is quite heavily malted. There are two grades: *'oude'* (old) and *'jonge'* (young), the latter looking a little less beer-coloured and more like English gin.

**Rum:** This is the distilled spirit of fermented sugar cane sap. The cane is crushed to remove the sap, the water allowed to evaporate off, and the resulting syrup is spun in a centrifuge to separate out the molasses which are extracted, reduced by boiling, then fermented and distilled. The exceptions to this method are rums from Haiti and Martinique, which are made from reduced but otherwise unprocessed sugar cane sap.

Dark rum is matured for about five years in barrels previously used for bourbon. The rum is then blended and sometimes caramel is added to darken the colour. White rum is a clear, colourless, light-bodied rum: the molasses are fermented then distilled in a column still to produce the spirit, which is aged for just one year before bottling. Golden rum is produced in the same way as white rum, but is aged for around three years in charred barrels which give the rum its golden hue and mellow flavour.

**Tequila and Mescal:** Tequila is a spirit distilled in the region of the same name in Mexico from the cactus-like plant *agave tequilana*. The heart of the cactus is harvested, steam-cooked and crushed to remove the juice, which is then fermented and double distilled. Silver tequila is matured briefly in stainless-steel or wax-lined vats so it remains colourless – and a little coarse. Gold tequila is matured in oak vats for three or more years where it develops a more mellow flavour and a golden colour. Mescal is the juice or pulque of the agave cactus which is distilled only once (not twice as in tequila). It is often sold bottled with an accompanying pickled, white, agave worm – which is supposed to be eaten! If you can stomach mescal, you can probably stomach the worm as well!

**Kirsch:** This is the original 'cherry spirit' – a true brandy or eau de vie – made from cherries, and is normally regarded as a 'separate' product to other fruit brandies/eau de vie. It is a particular speciality of Bavaria in western Germany: '*Kirsch*' means 'cherry'. But remember, Kirsch is colourless, and is not related to the bright red and sweet, syrupy 'cherry brandy' liqueurs (see below).

**Aquavit or Akavit:** This is a grain- and/or potato-based spirit that has been aromatised with fragrant spices like caraway seeds, fennel, cumin, dill and bitter oranges. The Scandinavian countries and Germany produce the true 'aquavits' which are often called 'schnapps', a name derived from the old Nordic word '*snappen*', meaning to snatch or seize, and denotes the traditional way of drinking – down in one gulp! In Denmark Aalborg produces a premium high-strength (42% ABV) aquavit, while Archers produces a well-known range of less strong (around 23% ABV) fruit-flavoured schnapps.

# Liqueurs

**Advocaat:** A liqueur that originated in the Netherlands made of a base spirit and sweetened egg yolks.

**Amaretto:** An almond-flavoured liqueur. The most famous brand is Disaronno amaretto, but other amaretto's are also available.

**Anisette:** A french, sweetened and aniseed-flavoured liqueur, the most famous brand of which is Marie Brizard.

**Baileys Irish Cream:** A sweet, cream liqueur (as distinct from a creme liqueur, see below) made with whiskey and cream and flavoured with coffee. Baileys is the most well-known proprietary brand.

**Benedictine:** A bright, golden, aged liqueur using a secret recipe of 75 herbs.

**Chartreuse:** An ancient French liqueur made by monks. There are two colours: green Chartreuse, which is intensely powerful and aromatic, and yellow Chartreuse, which is sweeter and slightly minty in flavour.

**Coconut Rum:** This is a sweet, white rum-based liqueur flavoured with coconut. The most well-known proprietary brand is Malibu, but coconut rum is made throughout the Caribbean rum-producing countries. Rum tree is also based on white rum but is a sweet, citrus-flavoured liqueur.

**Cointreau:** Properly speaking, this very popular branded liqueur is a form of Curaçao (see below): a brandy-based spirit, flavoured with the peel of bitter oranges. It can be served straight up, on the rocks and in mixed drinks where it is used in place of triple sec (see below).

**Creme Liqueurs:** These are sweetened liqueurs – as distinct from dry spirits like whisky or cognac – and consist of one dominant flavour, often, but not always, fruit: there are also nut-flavoured liqueurs. The most commonly used creme liqueurs are:

**Creme de Banane:** a sweet clear, yellow banana liqueur. A banana liqueur made from green bananas is pisang ambon, a product of Indonesia.

**Creme de Cacao:** Chocolate flavoured and available in two varieties: Dark (a distillate of cocoa beans and, sometimes, vanilla, macerated in alcohol, diluted and sweetened, and light, which has a more subtle flavour and is colourless because the cocoa remains are absent.

**Creme de Cassis:** A blackcurrant-flavoured liqueur.

**Creme de Menthe:** White and green liqueurs distilled from a concentrate of mint leaves. The white version is more subtle than the green which gets its colour from and added colorant.

**Creme de Fraise:** A strawberry-flavoured liqueur.

**Creme de Framboise:** A raspberry-flavoured liqueur.

**Curaçao:** Originally, a white-rum-based liqueur flavoured with the peel of bitter green oranges found on the island of Curaçao. Today it is made by a number of companies with brandy as the base spirit. A variant name was triple sec (the most famous being Cointreau) but, confusingly, Curaçao is not sec (dry) but always sweet. Curaçao comes in a range of colours as well as the clear version: orange, red, yellow, green and blue. Whatever the colour they all taste of orange and they do add a wonderful colour to mixed drinks and cocktails.

**Drambuie:** A Scotch-whisky-based liqueur flavoured with heather, honey and herbs.

**Galliano:** This is a golden yellow liqueur from Italy made to a secret recipe of some 80 herbs, roots and berries, with the principal flavourings being liquorice, anise and vanilla.

**Glayva:** Like Drambuie (see above) Glayva is a Scotch-whisky-based liqueur, flavoured with honey and herbs.

**Grand Marnier:** The is France's Cognac-based Curaçao (see above), made with the juice of Caribbean oranges and top-quality Cognac, and cask aged.

**Kahlua:** A dark-brown coffee-flavoured liqueur from Mexico.

**Kümmel:** A pure grain distillate – effectively a type of vodka – in which caraway seeds are infused to produce a spearmint-flavoured liqueur made in Latvia, Poland, Germany, Denmark, the Netherlands and in the USA. Goldwasser, made in Gdansk, Poland, has flakes of real gold in it.

**Liqueur Brandies:** There are essentially three fruit brandies: cherry, apricot and peach (although this last is not often seen). These are not 'true' brandies, but sweetened and coloured liqueurs based on simple grape brandy that has been flavoured with the relevant fruit – as opposed to being distillates of the fruit itself.

**Mandarine Napoleon:** This is also a type of Curaçao (see above), but this time made with skins of tangerines steeped in Cognac and other French brandies before being coloured to a vivid yellow-orange with carotene and matured for several months. Mandarine Napoleon, the leading brand, is in fact made in Belgium.

**Maraschino:** This is a clear, colourless liqueur derived from an infusion of pressed cherries and cherrystone distillate and aged for several years. Originally, marasca cherries grown in Dalmatia were used but when this area became part of the Venetian 'empire' plantings of the marasca cherry trees were established in the Veneto area of Italy. A number of Italian companies produce maraschino including Luxardo (in straw covered flasks), Drioli and Stock.

**Melon Liqueur:** A bright green, sweet and syrupy liqueur, the most famous of which is the Japanese brand Midori. The flavouring agent is melon, but the bright green is achieved through the use of vegetable dyes. First devised in the 1980s, Midori is one of the most recent 'inventions' in liqueurs to hit the cocktail scene.

**Pastis:** A traditional drink of the Mediterranean countries from Spain to Greece and beyond, and where it is known by a variety of names, pastis is an old French word meaning 'muddled', 'hazy' or 'unclear'. Pernod and Ricard are the most well-known brands, and there is also anise (which is dry); Spain has ojen (pronounced 'oh-hen'), and anis, which can be both sweet and dry; Greece has ouzo. The principal flavouring agent in these is either liquorice or aniseed, along with other herbal ingredients, which are steeped in a neutral alcohol base. Arak, (or raki, in Turkey, Greece and the Balkan countries) which can be found in Java, Borneo, and Sumatra is not a liqueur, but a spirit that can be up to 50% alcohol by volume distilled from a variety of different 'sources' (depending on the raki's country of origin) including sugar cane, rice, figs and plums. Sambuca is an Italian aniseed-flavoured liqueur made from anise, herbs and roots.

**Ratafia:** This was the 'forerunner' of the liqueur: nuts and fruits steeped in a sweetened spirit base. Today the term ratafia has come to mean a brandy mixed with fresh fruit juices, and made in France. Pineau des Charentes – which comes in both white and rosé varieties – is made in the Cognac region; in Armagnac, they make their own version called Floc de Gascogne, while in the Calvados region of Normandy, fresh apple juice is fortified with the local apple brandy and called Pommeau.

**Southern Comfort:** America's foremost liqueur using American whiskey and peaches in a recipe that is a closely guarded secret. The practice of blending peach juice and whiskey was common in the bars of the southern states of America in the 19th century and this no doubt played its part in the creation of one of the most popular liqueurs. Unusually for a liqueur, Southern Comfort has a high bottled strength – 40% ABV.

**Tia Maria:** A dark, sweet, coffee-flavoured liqueur from Jamaica based on dark Jamaican rum that's at least five years old, Blue Mountain coffee and local spices. As well as mixing well in many cocktails, Tia Maria is also popular 'straight up' – or drizzled over chocolate desserts!

**Van der Hum:** This is the South African equivalent of Curaçao (see above) which used Cape brandy and tangerine-like oranges, known locally as *naartjies*.

The liqueurs listed above are just a few of the most well known, but why not look out for some of the more 'obscure' types such as: La Vielle Cure ('The Old Rectory'); Verveine du Velay ( a little like Chartreuse in that it comes in green and yellow varieties); Trappistine, made by Trappist monks in the convent of the Abbaye de Grace de Dieu in Doubs, eastern France, near the border with Switzerland; Fiori d'Alpi made in northern Italy with a little gnarled tree in each bottle!; Curant y Tres from eastern Spain; and Cynar from Italy and made with artichokes!

# Wines and Fortified Wines

Fortified wines are wines that have been strengthened by the addition of a spirit - usually a grape spirit. The world's classic fortified wines such as Madeira, Marsala, muscat and muscatel each have their own method of production and the majority are made from white grapes – the most notable exception however is port. Sherry contains only wine and grape spirit, but vermouth – and related products – contain a number of aromatising ingredients.

**Vermouth:** The cocktail bar would be nothing without vermouth. There are French vermouths and Italian vermouths, and there are dry and sweet vermouths, as well as white or 'bianco', rosé and rosso vermouths. The most well-known brands of dry, white vermouths are from Martini from Italy, and Noilly Prat and Lillet from France. Cinzano produce the well-known bianco vermouth which is sweet. Red vermouths are produced by Cinzano, Martini and by Carpano, who make Punt e Mes, a deep-red bitter vermouth from Turin. Dubonnet from France – which can be either red or white – is also a version of vermouth.

Some recipes have been created using a particular brand of spirit, fortified wine, or liqueur. You will find these specified in some recipes, but don't feel obliged to use them! However, the ingenious bartenders who created the drinks in the first place selected these named products specifically for their individual qualities of flavour and aroma.

In the recipes in this book, only one wine is included: champagne. True champagne must be made by the champagne method – the sparkle is made by secondary fermentation in the bottle, not in a vat or by artificially carbonating it. To be called champagne, it must be made using the prescribed method and be produced in the Champagne region of France, a region about 100 miles (160 km) northeast of Paris around the towns of Rheims and Epernay. Champagne cocktails are not only elegant and delicious, but are a very good way of extending this king of wines among more thirsty revellers! Once again, if you want to add sparkle, but are on a budget, there are many fine sparkling wines, *vins moussex*, available to choose from.

## Juices and Mixers

In addition to your selected spirits, liqueurs, fortified wines and champagne, a well-stocked bar needs fresh fruit juices, and 'mixers' such as cola, lemonade, ginger ale, tonic and soda water. Like your spirituous ingredients, buy the best quality for the best tastes and flavours. If you can squeeze your own fruit juices, these will be even tastier than juices in cartons or cans, but its a good idea to pass the squeezed fruit juices through a fine sieve to remove any 'pips and bits' that might spoil the finished drink.

The bar staples in this department are lemon (and lime) juice, grenadine, and a simple sugar syrup, sometimes called gomme syrup.

You can squeeze lemons and limes by hand with a reamer, but if you have to make up a quantity, the best way is to peel the fruits, pop them in a blender or food processor and blitz them. Then strain the juice through a very fine sieve to remove any 'impurities'.

Grenadine is a sweet syrup, flavoured with pomegranate juice which gives it a rich, pink colour. It is used to add colour, flavour and sweetness to many cocktails. Grenadine is non-alcoholic – or has a very low alcohol content, so once the bottle is opened, the syrup will being to ferment and mould. Keep it in a cool place – but not in the fridge as this can cause the sugar to crystallise or harden, making it harder to mix with other ingredients. Other non-alcoholic syrups used include pineapple and orgeat (an almond-flavoured syrup). These are widely available because they are used in making ice-cream desserts, 'posh' milkshakes and smoothies! If you don't have any don't worry: a purée of fresh pineapple – mashed and rubbed through a fine sieve to remove lumps – works just as well. In the case of orgeat, you can substitute with an equal measure of amaretto!

A number of drinks call for sweetening to offset the 'tartness' of some juices. Granulated sugar doesn't dissolve that easily in cold 'solutions' so a sugar, or gomme syrup, being liquid – and colourless – is a simple but effective alternative.

## To make a sugar/gomme syrup:

Dissolve equal volumes of water and sugar – say 8 oz (200 gms) sugar in 8 fl oz (250 ml) of water – and simmer in a saucepan over a very low heat until all the sugar is dissolved. You may need to 'skim' the syrup to make it clear. Allow the syrup to cool and then decant it into a handy-sized bottle that pours well. Store in a cool place.

## Coconut Cream

Some recipes call for coconut cream: you can buy it ready-made in cans, but this is usually for culinary use, for preparing dishes like curriy and, until it is cooked with the other ingredients, it tastes pretty disgusting! On the other hand, specially prepared coconut cream made for drinks is usually hyper-sweet and is full of preservatives. It is very easy to make your own:

Take a chilled, hard block of pure creamed coconut and grate it up to break down the grainy texture. Use 1 tablespoon of the grated coconut cream with slightly less than 1 tablespoon of caster sugar (you can adjust the sweetness to suit your own taste) and mix together with the absolute minimum of hot water. Stir until you have a smooth, creamy paste that is slightly runny, but coats the back of a spoon. When it's cool, it's ready for use. Use it the same day: if you try to store it it will separate, become grainy and, worse, turn rancid!

## Garnishes

Some cocktails and mixed drinks are served 'unadorned' – without fruit garnishes, straws or stirrers. This will be specified for each recipe. However, fresh fruit garnishes not only add visual excitement but are edible too! If an olive is called for, don't use one stuffed with anchovy unless you want a fish flavour added to your drink! It's a good idea to rinse off olives before you use them so that any excess oil or brine is removed. Garnishes are your golden opportunity to display artistic skill, so be bold and be adventurous and, most of all, enjoy yourself. You can prepare garnishes in advance so that they are ready to be popped into the drink, onto the glass or onto a cocktail stick or speared with other fruits to create a veritable 'Carmen Miranda' hat! Make sure the fruit is fresh and all skins have been washed.

# Gadgets & gizmos

*In many books and bartender's guides, the lists of 'necessary equipment' can be off-putting. Once again, you will probably already have some items, such as a sharp paring knife, a strainer, and a can and bottle opener. Most of the specially designed 'gadgets' that are the tools of the trade are widely available in kitchen shops and department stores. The following items are really essential for mixing drinks and cocktails.*

**Shaker** This is fundamental tool of the cocktail bartender. A shaker is used in making drinks that contain fruit juices, syrups, thick liqueurs or any ingredients that need a thorough mix. Because the ice gets shaken about, there will be some dilution and clear drinks cannot easily be produced.

The capacity of the shaker should be enough to hold two drinks and ice – around 400g (14 oz) or so. There are two types of shaker to choose from.

The familiar stainless-steel shaker has a strainer built into the lid and a cap which doubles as a measure – usually around 60g(2 oz). It is essential that the shaker does not leak from the main seal when pouring into the glass. If it does develop a drip, wrap a cloth around the seal when you shake.

The second type of shaker is the Boston shaker (sometimes called an American shaker). The Boston shaker has one glass flat-bottomed cone which slots into larger steel flat-bottomed cone. When you shake, make sure that the metal half is on the bottom. While a Boston shaker is easier to 'break open', it can be harder to pour and you will need a strainer.

**Hawthorn strainer** A stray piece of ice or a lemon pip entering a drink will spoil its taste and look. A Hawthorn strainer is the classic bartender's model. The name of the maker, Hawthorn, is spelled out in strainer holes and around the edge is a coil which fits neat-

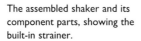

The assembled shaker and its component parts, showing the built-in strainer.

ly in the glass cone of the Boston shaker. You have to hold the Hawthorn tightly in place with your fingers, which can be tricky at first. If you prefer, look for a strainer that clips onto the rim of the mixing glass.

**Paring knife** As sharp as possible. Keep it sharp and keep it safe.

**Cutting board** This doesn't have to be big or elaborate. You'll need it for cutting citrus slices, twists and decorative spirals of peel.

**Lemon squeezer** This can be any style or the style that you are most comfortable with. The traditional glass citrus reamer – with the raised dome in the middle of a bowl – is fine, but I recommend passing the juice through a fine nylon sieve to remove pips and stray 'teardrops' of fruit pulp. If you've invited a number of guests for drinks, you'll have to squeeze plenty of juice in advance.

**Mixing glass** This glass is used for mixing most drinks that don't have fruit juices – drinks that are clear, not cloudy. Use a mixing glass with a pouring spout to stop the ice from falling into the drinking glass when you pour. A mixing glass should hold around 16 oz of liquid. (See also glass pitcher/jug.)

**Jigger** America and Britain each have their own ideas about what constitutes a 'fluid ounce'. Continental Europe prefers metric measurements in centilitre/millilitre form. The 'classic' jigger, the little metal measuring cup, that is used in bars in the United States measures 1½ US oz. The measure in a British jigger (1 imperial oz) contains 0.96 US fluid oz. In effect, there's little very little difference: 1 imperial fl oz = 28.4 ml and 1 US fl oz = 29.6 ml. The recipes in this book use the term measure and assumes 1 measure = 25 ml.

**Confused? Don't worry!**

It doesn't matter how big the 'jigger' is, just as long as you use the same measure throughout the recipe. You could use a shot glass (these measure about 2 fl oz or 57 ml), the measure on top of your shaker; or you could splash out on your own personal set. A useful tip, however, is to see how many measures (use water to test!) will fit into each glass and adjust the quantities to fit the glass exactly.

Soon you will be able to judge by eye, and tasting will help you to add more or less of an ingredient to achieve the perfect mix.

**Measuring spoons** Two teaspoons are helpful, one for dry substances and one for liquids. A tablespoon is also useful. All measures are level spoons unless otherwise stated.

**Ice bucket** Size and insulation are important. Don't be tempted by a pleasing design if it doesn't function well.

**Tongs** Tongs are better than an ice scoop: shaking and mixing with ice will dilute drinks sufficiently without adding a scoop of melted ice water as well! Use a scoop, or even a slotted spoon, for crushed ice.

**Long-handled bar spoon** This is a long, flat-headed spoon with a twisted shaft that is used to stir drinks in a mixing glass. An ordinary long-handled spoon works just as well.

**Muddler** Muddlers come in various shapes and sizes. Large ones are used with the mixing glass, smaller ones are for the drinkers to fiddle with. They have a 'bulb' at the end and are intended to crush sugar or pound mint in a drink. You could use a mortar and pestle for crushing mint for your mint julep (page 117) or a long-handled wooden spoon in the mixing glass/pitcher. As long as it reaches the bottom, it will do and it won't scratch.

**Swizzlers** Similar to a muddler, but with a 'paddle' on the end. You place the shaft between the palms of your hand and rub them together so that the paddle agitates the drink. Like muddlers, swizzle sticks are often used simply for decoration.

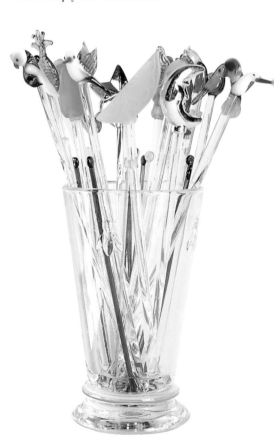

**Glass pitcher/jug** For iced water or fruit juices. Choose one with an involuted pourer (a turned-over lip). This will keep back the ice cubes and you can use it instead of a mixing glass.

**Glass-cleaning cloth** You need a glass cloth to keep your glassware sparkling and free from the bits of lint that ordinary 'linens' leave behind. They're easy to spot – they have the word 'Glass' woven into them.

**Corkscrew** Go for the Bartender's Friend, an all-in-one opener for corked and crown-topped bottles, as well as cans.

**Cocktail sticks** Wooden and coloured plastic ones are readily available.

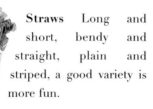

**Straws** Long and short, bendy and straight, plain and striped, a good variety is more fun.

**Napkins and coasters** Somewhere to place the cocktail stick after you've eaten the garnish.

**Paper parasols** Why not? Decoration is a personal thing, but a cocktail should be pleasing to the eye, as well as to the palate. Some diehards do, however, think that the only good decoration is an edible one.

**Blender/food processor** Although not essential, a blender or food processor is ideal for making juices and frozen daiquiris. You can also make many other 'shaken' cocktails in a blender and they are particularly useful if you are making a large number of the same drinks for a party.

**Glassware**

All glasses must be spotless! After washing, polish them completely dry with a clean glass cloth to avoid stains. A beautiful glass will give maximum visual impact. There are, naturally, 'classic' glasses for particular drinks, but there are infinite designs to choose from. Nevertheless it's worth looking for glasses with a fine rim; a slender stem (when appropriate), long enough so that the cool drink is not warmed by the hand's heat; a glass that suits the drink it will hold – the right size and the right shape, and, if necessary, heat-proof for hot toddies. The recipes in this book advise you which type of glass to use. Useful glasses include the following.

**Cocktail glass** Elegant and essential, around 120-150ml (4–5 fl oz), with a stem long enough to protect the bowl from the heat of the hand and the opening wide enough to display a garnish.

**Old fashioned** Also called a rocks glass This is used for any cocktails served 'on the rocks'; 170-230g (6-8 oz) capacity is a good size.

**Highball** This is a tallish glass, between 230-280g (8-10 oz). A useful glass, it can serve many purposes.

**Collins** This is for long drinks – the taller the better. Collins glasses, unlike highballs, always have perfectly straight sides. Around 280-380g (10-12 oz) capacity.

**Sour** This is a stemmed glass which is used for drinks that aren't strictly cocktails, but aren't 'long' either. A good-looking 'white-wine glass' will do very well.

**Ballon** A 'balloon' is basically a red-wine glass, of 240-300ml (8–10fl oz) capacity. Choose a well-rounded ballon with plenty of room for ice and garnish. Coloured drinks look particularly attractive in these glasses. A large ballon can be used as a goblet.

**Champagne saucer and champagne flute**
The traditional champagne saucer (said to have been modelled on Marie-Antoinette's bosom) was used when Madeira cake was dunked in the champagne. Although elegant and unmistakable, the open saucer shape lets the bubbles dissipate quickly. Nevertheless, some cocktails are traditionally served in a champagne saucer. Champagne flutes are stemmed, narrow, tulip-shaped glasses. Not only do they look pleasing, flutes also retain the bubbles in a drink for longer. But not even a flute will protect a sparkling drink from the ravages of lipstick. It may look glamorous, but the chemicals in the 'lippie' make fizzy drinks (beer included) loose their sparkle.

**Toddy** For hot drinks you'll need heat-proof glasses with handles.

Glasses need to be chilled, ready to receive the drink (except for toddies, which should be warm). There are a number of ways to chill

glasses. Either put them in the freezer for 20 to 30 minutes. (Warning: Don't put crystal glasses in the freezer! They may shatter) or place an ice cube in the bottom of the glass, swirl it around and discard.

To really give a glass a good, frosted look, fill each glass with crushed ice and put it in the refrigerator. Throw away the crushed ice just before the drink is poured in.

Some drinks, like Margaritas, have a frosted effect on the rims. This is done with either sugar or salt (depending on the drink). Dampen the rim of the pre-chilled glass with a slice of lemon (or lime) and dip the rim into a saucer of castor sugar or salt. Remember to pick up glasses by the stems or by the bottom of the glass so the frost is not disturbed or the glass marked by finger prints.

## Cocktail terminology

**BUILD** Pour the ingredients directly into the drinking glass.

**DASH** A tiny amount, a drop.

**GARNISH** Decorate or attach to the rim of the glass.

**LONG** A drink with five measures or more of liquid.

**MUDDLE** Mashing or grinding herbs, such as mint, into a smooth paste in the bottom of a glass.

**ON THE ROCKS** Poured over ice.

**SHAKE** In a cocktail shaker, shake for 8 to 10 seconds: the whole shaker should feel cold.

**SHORT** Less than five measures of liquid before shaking.

**STRAIGHT UP** Mixed and served without ice.

**STRAIN** Pour out, leaving behind the ice and any other solids.

**SHOOTER** A short drink, usually downed 'in one'.

**TWIST** 1–2 inches (3–6 cm) length of pith-free citrus peel, held 'skin side' over a drink and twisted in the middle to release the essential oil. The peel is usually discarded but can, if preferred, be dropped in the drink.

# A Word on Methods

## Chilling and Frosting Glasses

The simple rule of cocktails is 'chill before you fill'! There are three ways to make a glass cold:

1) Put the glasses in the fridge or freezer for a couple of hours before using them – but don't do this with fine crystal glasses because they can shatter.

2) Fill the glasses with crushed ice before using them. Discard the ice and shake out any water before pouring in the drink.

3) Fill the glasses with cracked ice and 'stir' it round a little before discarding it and pouring in the drink.

There are two types of 'frosted' glasses. For frosted drinks, the glasses should be stored in the fridge or better, buried in shaved ice, to give them a white, frosted and ice-cold appearance. A 'sugar', 'salt' or 'coconut' frosted glass is prepared by moistening the rim with a little lemon or lime juice and then dipping the rim into the condiment.

When a recipes tells you to 'add the ingredients' to a shaker, glass or blender, get into the habit of putting the 'cheapest' ingredients in first! Put lemon or lime juice, sugar syrup and fruit juices in first, then the more valuable spirits and liqueurs. This means that if you make a mistake, chances are it will be with the less expensive ingredients!

Don't, whatever you do, shake a drink with carbonated mixers – ginger ale, tonic or soda water, or even champagne! This type of ingredient is left right until the last and is used to 'finish' a drink.

Where a method says 'shake and strain', half fill the shaker with clean ice cubes, add the ingredients and shake briskly – until the outside of your shaker is very cold! Pour immediately through the strainer, leaving the ice behind. The volume of liquid will have increased because some of the ice will have melted and blended with the other ingredients. Remember this, so you don't produce more drink than your glass will hold.

Don't shake and strain with crushed ice: the crushed ice will just get stuck in the strainer holes and clog them up. Drinks shaken with crushed ice are poured 'unstrained' into the glass.

Where a method says 'shake and pour unstrained', add a glassful of ice to the shaker, pour in the ingredients and shake. Pour the drink into the same-size glass that you used to measure the ice.

Where a recipe instructs you to 'stir and strain', half fill the mixing glass, or the bottom half of your shaker with ice cubes, add the ingredients and stir with the long-handled bar spoon for 10 to 15 seconds. Use a Hawthorn strainer, the strainer part of your shaker or even a mesh sieve and pour the drink through it into the glass.

Where you are instructed to 'stir and pour unstrained', prepare as above, but only use a glassful of ice and don't strain. Add all the contents to a same-size glass as the one you used to measure the ice.

A streamlined cocktail shaker

To 'build' a drink means that you are creating the drink directly in the glass in which it will be served. Some drinks are built 'over ice' – the ice cubes are added to the glass first and the liquors added – other are made as a 'pousse-café'. A pousse-café makes use of the difference in the 'weights' of liqueurs and spirits so that one sits on top of the other forming separate, often coloured, layers. This can be a little fiddly to do at first, but the results can be spectacular. The trick is to pour the liquors very slowly over the back (the rounded side) of a small spoon, so that it very gently sits on top of the layer before it.

# Planning a Party

The recipes offered in this book give measurements sufficient to make ONE drink, unless otherwise specified. If you are planning on serving a number of mixed drinks at a party, use the table below to help you calculate roughly just how many bottles you will need:

   How many drinks in a bottle? If you use a measure of 1.5 fl oz (37.5 ml), you can get approximately this number of measures from each of the different size bottles:

| | 1.5 fl oz (37.5 ml) measure | | | | | | |
|---|---|---|---|---|---|---|---|
| Bottles | 1 | 2 | 4 | 6 | 8 | 10 | 12 |
| 27 fl oz (75 cl) measures | 16 | 33 | 67 | 101 | 135 | 169 | 203 |
| 36 fl oz (1 litre) | 22 | 45 | 90 | 135 | 180 | 225 | 270 |
| 54 fl oz (1.5 litre) | 39 | 78 | 157 | 236 | 315 | 394 | 473 |

   So, two 27 fl oz (75 cl) bottles of whisky will yield you 33 measures (of 1.5 oz/37.5 ml); two x 1 litre bottles of whisky will yield 45 measures and so on.

# Dos and don'ts

**Do** get into the habit of adding the cheapest ingredients – such as juices – first to the shaker or mixing glass. If you make a mistake, you won't have wasted too much valuable spirit.

**Do** serve drinks with a mixer in a highball glass. Fill the glass two-thirds full with ice and add the ingredients.

**Do** use a mixing glass for cocktails containing only alcoholic products.

**Do** shake sharply for about 8 to 10 seconds.

**Do** serve cocktails immediately. If you leave them to stand they will separate.

**Do** wash the shaker or mixing glass after each 'batch'. Sugar/syrup needs attention as it will make the join in the shaker sticky.

**Don't** shake fizzy drinks!

**Don't** use ice cubes twice. Always use clean ice.

**Don't** add alcoholic bitters or syrups to non-alcoholic mocktails.

**Don't** force an alcoholic drink on anyone. Offer a mocktail instead.

**Don't** forget that the volume of a drink mixed with ice will increase. Make sure the glass is large enough to hold it.

**Don't** forget the teetotallers and drivers. Do not encourage under-age drinking, drink-driving, drunkenness, or anti-social behaviour.

## Remember

Cocktails and mixed drinks are delicious, and they are alcoholic. If you're thirsty, drink water or juice. A cocktail is for sipping and enjoying with friends. Think of American humorist and playwright George Ade's words from his play *The Sultan of Sula* (1903):

## R-E-M-O-R-S-E!

*Those dry Martinis did the work for me;*

*Last night at twelve I felt immense,*

*Today I feel like thirty cents.*

# Gin cocktails

martini
see page 66.

The word gin is believed to have come about from the mispronunciation of foreign names for the juniper berry from which the liquor is distilled. Some believe that the word gin is derived from the Dutch word *jenever*: Dr Sylvius de la Boe first formulated the liquor as a treatment for kidney complaints at the university medical school in Leyden in the mid-16th century. Others say that it comes from the French word *genièvre*, while a few maintain that it was Italy that gave us *ginepro*, since Tuscany continues to be the main producer of the juniper berries which give gin its perfume and taste.

Gin became widely popular in Britain in the 17th century when the Dutch William III (who married Mary II and became king of England in 1689) raised the excise duties on French wines and brandies as a measure of revenge for French hostilities in Holland. Gin's comparatively low cost, coupled with its potency, meant that it soon found its way into most people's lives and into popular culture. By the 18th century gin

pink pussycat
see page 69.

was the 'poor man's tea' (tea was so expensive that it was kept under lock and key in specially designed caddies). Soldiers drank gin before battle to give them 'Dutch courage'; juniper berries were falsely believed to induce miscarriages and gin became known as 'mother's ruin'.

By the 1740s, gin consumption had reached 20 million gallons annually. Sale was virtually unrestricted, so anyone could set up a still and open a gin shop. Advertisements promised 'Drunk for a penny. Dead drunk for tuppence'. Contemporaries estimated that there was one gin shop for every six houses in London. The Gin Act of 1736 was an attempt by Parliament to limit the appalling scenes of public drunkenness as portrayed in Hogarth's famous engraving *Gin Lane* (1751) and to curb the rising mortality rate. Distillers were taxed, but the act was impossible to enforce and illegal

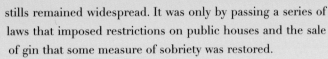

gentlemen's
club
see page 56.

stills remained widespread. It was only by passing a series of laws that imposed restrictions on public houses and the sale of gin that some measure of sobriety was restored.

In the 20th century, during Prohibition in America (1919–33), the alternative to expensive smuggled, bootlegged spirits was an illicit still. By 1929 there were more than a hundred recipes for 'bathtub' gin and hundreds more recipes for cocktails to disguise the taste!

Today's gin is made by infusing juniper berries and other flavourings into a high-quality, neutral grain spirit, usually corn, malted barley and sometimes a small amount of another grain. Coriander is a flavouring (known as a botanical) in both Dutch jenevers and London Dry gin. London Dry gin is a style of gin: it can be made anywhere as long as the base spirit is rectified to neutrality before being redistilled with the botanical flavourings. Dutch jenevers, in contrast, retain the flavour of the grain in the spirit. Plymouth gin is made in only in Plymouth, Devon, with the natural water from Dartmoor. It was apparently the Royal Navy who first mixed gin with angostura bitters to make a 'pink gin', which, even today, is still properly made with Plymouth gin.

# Bennet cocktail

*This lime-flavour cocktail was invented in the 1920s.*
*Originally it was served 'straight up' without the sugar. It is also*
*sometimes served in an old-fashioned glass filled with broken ice.*
*Try the variations for yourself.*

## Ingredients:

ice cubes

2 measures gin

⅔ measure lime juice

⅓ measure sugar syrup

1 dash bitters

## Gin

## Method:

Half-fill the shaker with ice
cubes.

Add the gin, lime juice, sugar
syrup and bitters.

Shake and strain into a
cocktail glass.

# Bernardo

*A delicious and sophisticated drink – ideal for unwinding after a long day!*

## Ingredients:

ice cubes
2 measures gin
½ measure triple sec or
Cointreau
2 teaspoons lemon juice
2 dashes bitters
1 lemon twist

## Gin

## Method:

Half-fill the shaker with ice cubes.
Add the gin, Cointreau, lemon juice and bitters.
Shake well and then strain into a cocktail glass.
Garnish with the lemon twist.

| method: | SHAKER |
|---|---|
| glass: | COCKTAIL |

# Bronx cocktail

*This cocktail was devised in 1906 by Johnny Solon, the celebrated barman at the Waldorf Astoria Hotel in New York. Johnny was apparently inspired following a trip to the Bronx Zoo. Originally served straight up in a cocktail glass, it's just as nice in an old-fashioned glass three-quarters filled with broken ice.*

## Ingredients:

ice cubes
1½ measures gin
¾ measure rosso vermouth
¾ measure dry vermouth
¾ measure orange juice

# Gin

## Method:

Half-fill the shaker with ice cubes.
Add the gin, two vermouths and the orange juice and shake well.
Strain into a cocktail glass.

## Variations:

### Bloody Bronx

use blood orange juice.

### Dry Bronx

replace the sweet, rosso vermouth with dry
(1½ measures dry vermouth in total).

# Captain's table

*This cocktail includes Campari, Italy's most famous aperitif.*

## Ingredients:

ice cubes
2 measures gin
½ measure Campari
1 teaspoon grenadine
1 measure orange juice
4 measures ginger ale
1 maraschino cherry

## Gin

## Method:

Half-fill the shaker with ice cubes.
Add the gin, Campari, grenadine and orange juice. Shake well and strain into a highball glass almost filled with ice cubes.
Top up with the ginger ale and garnish with the cherry.

| method: | SHAKER |
|---------|--------|
| glass: | COCKTAIL |

# Crimson sunset

*Tastes wonderful and looks lovely – but it may require a little practice!*

## Ingredients:

ice cubes

2 measures gin

½ measures tawny port

2 teaspoons lemon juice

½ teaspoon grenadine

# Gin

## Method:

Half-fill the shaker with ice cubes.

Add the gin and lemon juice only and shake well.

Strain into a cocktail glass.

Drop the grenadine into the centre of the drink and float the port on top.

# The Collins

*The tallest of the mixed drinks, the original Collins was, in fact, John Collins.*
*He was a well-known head waiter at Limmer's, a popular coffee house and hotel in*
*London's Conduit Street between 1790 and 1817. His original recipe called for Dutch*
*jenever and never really caught on until someone*
*used Old Tom gin and the Tom Collins was*
*born.*

## Ingredients:

ice cubes
2 measures gin
1 measure lemon juice
¾ measure sugar syrup
5 measure soda water

Old Tom gin is a sweet gin, now rarely
produced, and was supposedly first
distilled by Captain Dudley Bradstreet
in London in 1738. Taking advantage of
a loophole in the prohibitionist 1736
Gin Act, Bradstreet used a wooden
carving of a tom cat as his shop sign.
Customers placed a sum of money into
the mouth and an appropriate amount
of gin would be dispensed from its paw
– via a tube – into the buyer's glass.
Now a Tom Collins is made with
London gin, but you can use any spirit
of your choice. In America, the John
Collins lives on and is made with
bourbon or whisky, while cousins Mike
Collins (made with Irish whiskey), Jack
Collins (apple brandy), Pierre Collins
(cognac), Pedro Collins (rum) and Juan
Collins (tequila) make up the family.
Sadly, all the relatives are male and the
only Joan Collins is the popular actress.
Whatever spirit is used, they are usually
served in their own Collins glass – but a
highball is just fine.

# Gin

## Method:

Fill a frosted glass two-thirds
full with ice, add the lemon
juice, sugar syrup and gin.
Top with soda water and
stir.
Garnish with lemon slice and
serve with straws.

| method: | MIXING GLASS |
|---|---|
| glass: | COCKTAIL |
| garnish: | LEMON TWIST |

# Delmonico cocktail

*A classy cocktail for a relaxing evening.*

## Ingredients:

ice cubes

1 measure gin

½ measure brandy

½ measure sweet vermouth

½ measure dry vermouth

1 dash angostura bitters

1 lemon twist

# Gin

## Method:

Half-fill a mixing glass with ice cubes.
Add the gin, brandy, two vermouths and the bitters.
Stir well and strain into a cocktail glass.
Garnish with the lemon twist.

## Variations:

If you use orange bitters in place of angostura, you will make a Harvard.

# Dragonfly

*A very simple drink to mix and a refreshing*
*change from the usual 'gin and tonic'.*

## Ingredients:

ice cubes

½ measures gin

4 measures ginger ale

1 lime wedge

# Gin

## Method:

Fill a highball glass almost to
the top with ice cubes.
Add the gin and the ginger
ale and then garnish with the
wedge of lime.

| method: | MIXING GLASS |
| --- | --- |
| glass: | COCKTAIL |
| garnish: | COCKTAIL OLIVE |

# Fifty-fifty

*An easy recipe to remember, but a drink not easily forgotten.*

## Ingredients:

ice cubes

1½ measures gin

1½ measures dry vermouth

1 cocktail olive

# Gin

## Method:

Half-fill the mixing glass with ice cubes.

Add the gin and vermouth.

Stir well and strain into a cocktail glass.

Garnish with the olive.

# Flying Dutchman

*The name of this drink probably stems from the fact
that it was made with Dutch jenever and triple sec, the
orange liqueur Curaçao from the island of the same
name in the former Dutch West Indies.*

## Ingredients:

ice cubes

2 measures gin

½ measure triple sec or Cointreau

# Gin

## Method:

Almost fill an old-fashioned
glass with ice cubes.
Add the gin and the
Cointreau and stir well.

| method: | BUILD |
| --- | --- |
| glass: | OLD FASHIONED |

# Gentlemen's club

*This is the ideal drink for any man who thinks cocktails are for girls!*

## Ingredients:

ice cubes

1½ measures gin

1 measure brandy

1 measure sweet vermouth

1 measure club soda

# Gin

## Method:

Almost fill an old-fashioned
glass with ice cubes.
Add the gin, brandy and
vermouth.
Add the soda and stir well.

# Gibson

*This variation on the dry Martini was created at the
Player's Club in New York in the 1940s for the American
artist and illustrator Charles Dana Gibson. One story has it that
Gibson didn't like olives, so asked for a cocktail onion instead. The
barman, thinking of the shapely 'Gibson Girls' the illustrator had
made famous, added two onions in their honour!*

## Ingredients:

ice cubes
2½ measures gin
1½ teaspoons dry vermouth
2 cocktail onions

## Gin

## Method:

Half-fill the mixing glass with
ice cubes.
Add the gin and vermouth.
Stir well and strain into a
cocktail glass.
Add the two cocktail onions.

| method: | BUILD |
| --- | --- |
| glass: | OLD FASHIONED |
| garnish: | WEDGE OF LIME |

# Gimlet

*A gimlet is a small, pointed hand tool used to bore holes in wood. They were often used in bars to tap into barrels, and soon the word gimlet came to mean a small, sharp cocktail. Gimlets seem to have been concocted originally by British residents in the Far East after the First World War. Gin and lime juice are the two ingredients. Some say that freshly squeezed lime juice was used, but others believe that Rose's Lime Juice, which is concentrated and sweetened, was preferred. Although limes were probably plentiful, the British may well have used the cordial since it predates the gimlet recipes.*

## Ingredients:

ice cubes
2 measures gin (some insist on Plymouth gin)
¾ measure Rose's Lime Juice
1 measure cold soda water (optional)

# Gin

## Method:

Pour the gin and the lime cordial into an old-fashioned glass filled with ice and stir.
Add the soda (if desired) and garnish with the lime wedge.

## Variations:

Rum, tequila or vodka can replace the gin if you prefer. Whatever the spirit, lime juice cordial is the 'correct' accompaniment.

# Gin daisy

*'Daisies' were invented in America and have been around since the 1850s. Originally they were served in a tankard and straight up, but today an old-fashioned glass with plenty of broken or crushed ice is more usual. A small amount of fruit syrup is always used and can be complemented by using a little seasonal fruit as garnish. If any soda is added, it should never be more than half the quantity of the spirit.*

## Ingredients:

ice cubes
broken ice
2 measures gin
1 measure lemon juice
½ level teaspoon castor sugar
1 teaspoon grenadine
1 measure soda water
(optional)
1 maraschino cherry
1 orange slice
1 sprig mint

# Gin

## Method:

Half-fill the shaker with ice cubes.
Add the gin, lemon juice, sugar and grenadine.
Shake well and strain into an old-fashioned glass filled with broken ice.
Top up with soda if desired.
Garnish with the cherry and orange slice.

## Variations:

Any spirit base can be used to make a daisy. Try substituting the gin with brandy or vodka. For a rum daisy, leave out the sugar and use 1½ measure white rum, 1 measure lime juice, 1 teaspoon grenadine and garnish with twists of lime and orange. See also the golden daisy (page 114).

| method: | SHAKER OR BLENDER |
|---|---|
| glass: | HIGHBALL |

## Gin fizz

*The fizz was first mentioned in the 1870s, and although it is similar to the Collins, a fizz is always shaken before adding the soda and was traditionally served at around 11.30 am. Whatever time you prefer your drink, a fizz should be served immediately after preparation.*

*Beware ordering some of the beautifully named fizzes in a bar, as some classic recipes use raw egg to give more froth at the finish. If you're not happy with the idea of egg in your drink, let the barman know.*

## Ingredients:

ice cubes
2 measures gin
1 measure lemon juice
1 teaspoon castor sugar
(or 1 dash of gomme syrup)
5 measures soda water –
preferably dispensed from a
soda siphon, but still very
chilled!

# Gin

## Method:

Half-fill the shaker with ice cubes.
Add the gin, sugar and lemon juice and shake as hard as you can. (Alternatively, use crushed ice and an electric blender.)
Strain into a frosted highball glass half-filled with ice.
Add the soda while simultane-ously stirring with a swizzle stick or muddler.
Drink immediately through a straw while the fizz fizzes!

# Gin Rickey

*A close cousin of the fizz and the Collins, the Rickey contains no sugar, however. The cocktail of gin, lime juice and soda water was first made in around 1893 in Shoemakers Restaurant in Washington, DC, for a Congressional lobbyist from Kentucky, Joe 'Colonel Jim' Rickey.*

## Ingredients:

ice cubes
2 measures gin
juice of 1 lime
4 measures soda water

## Variations:

A Rickey can be made using any spirit as its base: replace the gin with 2 measures of either bourbon, brandy, rum or vodka.

# Gin

## Method:

Into a highball glass half-filled with ice, squeeze the juice of the lime.
Add the gin and stir.
Add the soda water and garnish with the wedge of lime. (Alternatively, drop half of the spent lime shell into the glass after squeezing!)

| method: | SHAKER |
|---|---|
| glass: | HIGHBALL |
| garnish: | TWIST OF LEMON, SPRINKLING OF NUTMEG (OPTIONAL) |

## Gin sling

*The sling first appeared in literature as far back as 1759 and appears to have been derived from the German word* schlingen, *which means 'to swallow quickly'. However, a sling, like a gimlet, is also a bar tool, and was used to handle barrels. Slings are sweetish, long drinks traditionally based on gin and sometimes topped with plain water rather than soda. A true sling should contain lemon or lime juice and sugar/syrup or a sweet liqueur. The Singapore sling, created in 1915 by Ngiam Tong Boon at the Raffles Hotel in Singapore, contains cherry brandy. The basic gin sling, as given in Harry Craddock's 'cocktail bible',* The Savoy Cocktail Book *contains only the base spirit, sugar, water and one lump of ice.*

## Ingredients:

ice cubes
2 measures gin
1 measure lemon juice
⅔ measure gomme syrup
2 measures cold water
nutmeg (optional)

## Gin

## Method:

Half-fill the shaker with ice cubes.
Add the gin, gomme syrup, lemon juice and water and shake well.
Strain into highball glass almost filled with ice cubes.
Garnish with the lemon twist.
Sprinkle with nutmeg (optional).

### Variations:

Any base spirit and any fruit juice can be used to make a sling. Experiment by replacing the gin with either bourbon, brandy, rum, Scotch or vodka.

# Gin swizzle

*Swizzles were devised in the West Indies and first became*
*popular with travellers in the early years of the 19th century.*
*Originally, swizzles were made with rum, lime juice,*
*gomme syrup or a liqueur, crushed ice and sometimes*
*soda water. Other ingredients, such as fruit juices,*
*were added in small quantities to add subtle colour*
*or flavour. Swizzling the drink gives it a foamy*
*appearance and frosts the glass.*
*A great party drink, you can make swizzles in a*
*pitcher, pour into chilled glasses and decorate with*
*sprigs of mint.*

## Ingredients:

ice cubes
2 measures gin
1½ measures lime juice
1 teaspoon castor sugar
1 dash bitters
2–3 measures soda water

## Variations:

To make up a pitcher of gin
swizzles, fill the pitcher two-
thirds full with crushed ice
and add the ingredients. Give
the mix a good, hard swizzle
– put the stick between the
flat palms of your hand and
rub them together – until the
pitcher is frosted. Pour into
chilled glasses, add a swizzle
stick, straws and garnish.

Any spirit can be used to
make a swizzle. Lime juice
works best with gin or rum,
while lemon juice works best
with other spirits.

# Gin

## Method:

Half-fill the shaker with ice
cubes.
Add the lime juice, gin, sugar
and bitters and shake well.
Almost fill a Collins glass
with ice cubes and then stir
them with a swizzle stick
until the glass is frosted.
Strain the mixture in the
shaker into the glass and add
the soda. Serve with a swizzle stick and straws.

| method: | SHAKER |
| --- | --- |
| glass: | OLD FASHIONED |
| garnish: | PINEAPPLE SLICE |

# Grass skirt

*A Polynesian kingdom from the 6th century until 1893, Hawaii became a republic in 1894 and a United States territory in 1900 before becoming a state in 1959. The beautiful islands not only provide its most famous fruit, the pineapple, but hundreds of species of flowers that grow nowhere else in the world. As for the people, Richard Henry Dana Jnr wrote in*
Two Years Before the Mast *(1840):*
*'I would have trusted my life and my fortune in the hands of any one of these people;...had I wished for a favor or act of sacrifice, I would have gone to them all, in turn, before I should have applied to one of my own countrymen...'*

## Ingredients:

ice cubes
1½ measures gin
1 measure triple sec or Cointreau
1 measure pineapple juice
½ teaspoon grenadine
1 pineapple slice

# Gin

## Method:

Half-fill the shaker with ice cubes.
Add the gin, triple sec or Cointreau, pineapple juice and grenadine.
Shake well and pour unstrained into an old-fashioned glass and garnish with the pineapple slice.

# Honolulu cocktail

*This recipe was devised by Victor Bergeron, better known as 'Trader' Vic. In the 1930s he opened a bar called Hinky Dinks in Oakland, California. The bar originally had a 'hunting and shooting' theme, but this was soon changed to a Pacific Island theme. Trader Vic's combination of exotic food and 'tropical' drinks, such as Dr Funk of Tahiti, the suffering bastard and the white witch, soon brought him fame, and today there are a number of his restaurants around the world.*

## Gin

## Ingredients:

ice cubes

1½ measures gin

½ teaspoon castor sugar

¼ teaspoon orange juice

¼ teaspoon pineapple juice

¼ teaspoon lemon juice

1 dash bitters

## Method:

Half-fill the shaker with ice cubes.

Add the gin, sugar, orange, lemon and pineapple juice and the bitter.

Shake well and then strain into a well-chilled cocktail glass.

| method: | MIXING GLASS |
|---|---|
| glass: | COCKTAIL - THOROUGHLY CHILLED |
| garnish: | A GREEN OLIVE (BUT NEVER, EVER A STUFFED OLIVE) OR A TWIST OF LEMON (TO BE DISCARDED) |

# Martini

*'Let's get out of these wet clothes and into a dry Martini'.*
*So goes the line in the 1937 film* Every Day's a Holiday, *starring Mae West. The undoubted king of cocktails, the drink of the rich, glamorous and the famous, the Martini has a long history, which, like the recipe for the 'perfect' or the 'driest' dry Martini, continues to be hotly debated. Some say the Martini was invented for John D Rockefeller by a bartender called Martini di Arma di Taggia at the Knickerbocker Hotel in New York in 1910. In Martinez, California, about 32km (20 miles) from San Francisco, a bronze plaque announces that in 1874, bartender Julio Richelieu created the Martinez Special. A couple of drinks later, the 'z' got lost! For more on the legend, lore, and lure of the Martini, read Barnaby Conrad III's The Martini (Chronicle Books, 1956). Whichever recipe you prefer, remember that a Martini must be stirred and never shaken.*

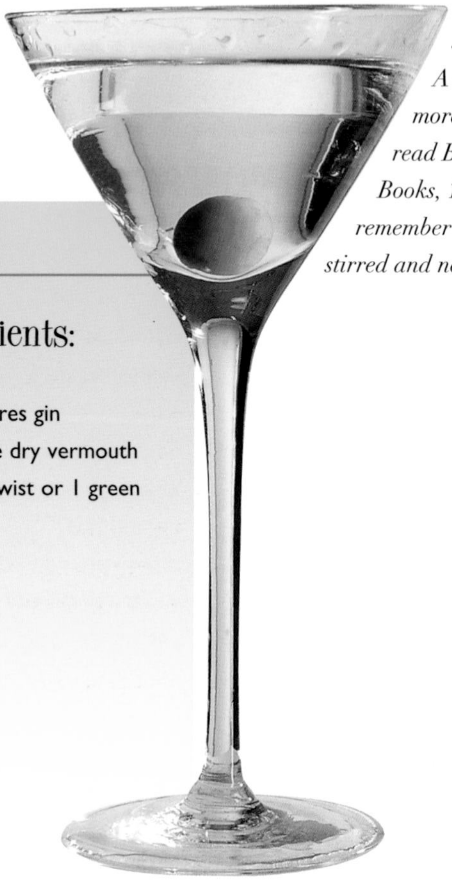

# Gin

## Ingredients:

ice cubes
2½ measures gin
1 measure dry vermouth
1 lemon twist or 1 green olive

## Variations:

This is just one recipe – there are many others, and all vary in the proportion of vermouth used. Why not find the proportion you enjoy the most and make your Martini your very own!

(For a 'vodka variation', see kangaroo in the vodka section, page 95).

# Maiden's prayer

*In the land of cocktails there are a number of maidens*
*– maiden's kiss, maiden's blush and even maiden-no-more.*
*Try this and maybe your prayers will be answered!*

## Ingredients:

ice cubes
2 measures gin
1 measure triple sec or
Cointreau
juice of 1 lemon
3 drops bitters

### Variations:

Maiden-no-more?
Simply add a teaspoon of
brandy to the ingredients.

# Gin

## Method:

Half-fill the shaker with ice
cubes.
Add the bitters, lemon juice,
triple sec or Cointreau and
gin.
Shake well.
Strain and serve in a well-
chilled cocktail glass.
Close your eyes and pray!

| method: | SHAKER |
|---|---|
| glass: | SOUR |
| garnish: | ORANGE SLICE AND A CHERRY |

# Orange blossom

*This drink was born during Prohibition and is sometimes known as an Adirondack. Originally served straight up, it was simply a good slug of gin – probably bathtub gin – with a blush of orange juice to smooth it out. President Roosevelt shook one for Prime Minister Winston Churchill during World War Two.*

*It seems that just one orange blossom was enough for the PM.*

## Gin

### Method:

Half-fill the shaker with ice cubes.
Add the sugar, gin and orange juice.
Shake and then strain into a sour glass with plenty of ice or straight up if preferred.
Garnish with orange slice and cherry.

## Ingredients:

ice cubes
1½ measures gin
1½ measures orange juice
½ teaspoon castor sugar
1 slice orange
1 cherry

| method: | SHAKER |
| glass: | COLLINS |
| garnish: | SLICE OF GRAPEFRUIT AND A CHERRY |

# Pink pussycat

*Grenadine is the ingredient that makes many cocktails pink: pink elephant, pink squirrel and the pink panther. The pink pussycat uses grapefruit juice – a juice that for some unknown reason has been used to torture the tastebuds into waking up at the breakfast table. Try this, and grapefruits will take on a whole new meaning.*

## Ingredients:

ice cubes

2 measures gin

2 measures grapefruit juice

2–3 measures pineapple juice
(depending on how sharp you
want your pussycat's claws!)

⅓ measure grenadine

# Gin

## Method:

Half-fill the shaker with ice cubes.

Add the gin, pineapple and grapefruit juices and the grenadine.

Shake well and strain into an ice-filled Collins glass.

Garnish with a slice of grapefruit (be brave!) and a cherry.

| method: | MIXING GLASS |
|---|---|
| glass: | COCKTAIL |
| garnish: | TWIST OF LEMON |

# Silver bullet

*Many cocktails that have the word silver in their names include raw egg white. A silver bullet, however, is eggless and is a variation of the Martini. Like the Martini, you can vary the proportion of Scotch to your taste.*

## Ingredients:

ice cubes
2½ measures gin
1½ teaspoons Scotch whisky
1 lemon twist

## Gin

## Method:

Half-fill the mixing glass with ice cubes.
Add the gin and Scotch and stir well.
Strain into a chilled cocktail glass and add the twist of lemon.

# White lady

*This fabulous cocktail was invented by legendary bartender Harry MacElhone in 1919 while at Ciro's Club in London. In 1923, at his own Harry's New York Bar in Paris, MacElhone altered the recipe by replacing the original white crème de menthe with gin to create an internationally popular cocktail.*

## Ingredients:

ice cubes
1½ measures gin
1½ measures Cointreau
1½ measures lemon juice

# Gin

## Method:

Half-fill the shaker with ice cubes.
Pour in the lemon juice, Cointreau and gin and shake well.
Strain into a very cold cocktail glass.
Alternatively, you could serve it on the rocks in an old-fashioned glass.

# Bunny Hug

*The Bunny Hug was a risqué, but popular dance in the 1920s danced to a syncopated rhythm – a 'bunny' was a euphemism for a 'bottom'!*

## Ingredients:

1 measure gin

1 measure Scotch whisky

1 measure Pernod or Ricard

# Gin

## Method:

Place all the ingredients in a shaker along with some ice cubes and shake well. Strain into a chilled cocktail glass.

| method: | MIXING GLASS |
| --- | --- |
| glass: | COCKTAIL |
| garnish: | CHERRY SOAKED IN KIRSCH |

## Caesar Ritz

*A subtle fruit-flavoured cocktail created at the Hotel Ritz in Paris that uses a touch of kirsch – a colourless 'eau de vie' (white brandy) distilled from black cherries and their stones.*

## Ingredients:

2 measures gin
⅔ measure dry vermouth
⅓ measure cherry brandy
⅓ measure Kirsch

# Gin

## Method:

Place all the liquors into a mixing glass with some ice cubes and stir well. Strain into a chilled cocktail glass and garnish with the Kirsch-soaked red cherry.

# Dempsey

*Many cocktails were created to mark special events and outstanding achievements. The Dempsey was devised in 1921 to celebrate boxer Jack Dempsey's world championship victory.*

## Ingredients:

1 measure gin
1 measure Calvados
½ teaspoon Pernod
½ teaspoon grenadine

# Gin

## Method:

Place all the ingredients in a shaker with some ice cubes and shake well. Strain into an old-fashioned glass filled three-quarters with broken ice.

# Gloom Raiser

*Devised in 1915 by Robert Vermeire at the Royal Automobile Club, Pall Mall, London, the Gloom Raiser was no doubt intended to raise the spirits during World War I.*

## Ingredients:

2 measures gin

1 measure Noilly Prat
(dry vermouth)

1 teaspoon Pernod

1 teaspoon grenadine

1 twist of lemon

# Gin

## Method:

Place all the ingredients in a mixing glass with some ice cubes and stir. Strain into a champagne saucer, squeeze on the lemon twist and discard.

| method: | BUILD |
| --- | --- |
| glass: | GOBLET OR OVERSIZED GOBLET (LONG FALL), COCKTAIL (SHORT FALL) |
| garnish: | SLICE OF LIME |

# Fallen Angel

*How far you want to fall is up to you: 'long' or 'short' are both delicious descents.*

# Gin

## Method:

To a goblet or oversized wine glass filled three quarters with broken ice, add the ingredients and top with lemonade. Garnish with a slice of lime and serve with straws.

For a 'short fall', add ½ measure of sugar syrup, shake with ice cubes in a shaker, strain into an ice-filled glass and omit the lemonade.

## Ingredients:

1½ measure gin
1 measure lime juice
1 teaspoon white creme de menthe
1 dash angostura bitters
4 measures lemonade

# Harry's Cocktail

*Created in 1910 by the great Harry MacElhone at the Casino Bar,*
*Aix-les-Bains, France.*

## Ingredients:

⅔ measure gin

⅓ measure sweet vermouth

1 dash absinthe (substitute:
   Pernod or Ricard)

2 sprigs of mint

## Gin

## Method:

Shake all the ingredients in a
shaker with some ice cubes.
Strain into a chilled cocktail
glass and serve with a
stuffed olive.

| method: | MIXING GLASS |
|---|---|
| glass: | COCKTAIL |
| garnish: | CHERRY ON A STICK, ORANGE TWIST |

# RAC Cocktail

*The Royal Automobile Club premises in Pall Mall, London, (1908–11) were designed by Arthur J. Davis and Charles Mewes and include a fabulous neo-classical swimming pool. Along with the Ritz Hotel in London, also designed by Davis and Mewes, these buildings, and their sumptuous interiors, are among the jewels of Edwardian architecture. The RAC Cocktail is also a jewel, created in 1914 by Fred Faecks at the RAC.*

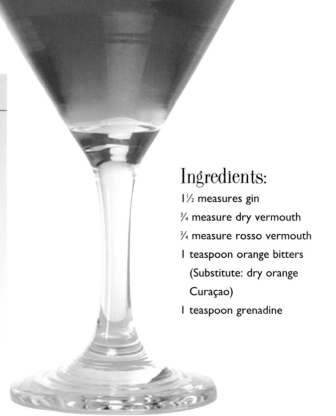

# Gin

## Method:

Place all the ingredients in a mixing glass with some ice cubes. Stir and strain into a cocktail glass and add a cherry on a stick. Squeeze a twist of orange over the drink and discard.

## Ingredients:

1½ measures gin

¾ measure dry vermouth

¾ measure rosso vermouth

1 teaspoon orange bitters (Substitute: dry orange Curaçao)

1 teaspoon grenadine

# Prohibition Cocktail

*The Volstead Act prohibiting the manufacture, distribution and sale of alcohol led to a hugely inventive period in cocktail making – largely because the bootlegged liquor was so awful it had to be mixed to disguise the taste! Why not try this out on December 5 – the day in 1933 that saw the end of Prohibition.*

## Gin

## Ingredients:

2 measures gin

2 measures Lillet (dry vermouth)

½ teaspoon apricot brandy

I teaspoon orange juice

## Method:

While you whistle *Happy Days Are Here Again*, place all the ingredients in a shaker with ice cubes and shake well. Strain into a cocktail glass, squeeze over a twist of lemon and discard.

| method: | SHAKER |
|---|---|
| glass: | COCKTAIL |
| garnish: | SLICE OF ORANGE WRAPPED AROUND A CHERRY |

# Monkey's Gland Cocktail

*This strangely named cocktail was devised by Harry MacElhone around 1920 – at the time when Dr. Serge Voronoff was experimenting with injections of all manner of ingredients which aimed to stop the ageing process! A simpler, and more effective solution is to be found in Harry's rejuvenating elixir.*

## Ingredients:

2 measures gin

2 measures orange juice

I teaspoon Pernod

2 teaspoons grenadine

# Gin

## Method:

Place all the ingredients in a shaker with ice cubes and shake well. Strain into a cocktail glass and garnish with the cherry wrapped in the slice of orange. Feel younger instantly.

# Singapore Sling

*The world famous Singapore Sling was devised at the Raffles Hotel in Singapore, in 1915, by Ngiam Tong Boon. It was originally intended as a 'lady's drink', but it soon became widely enjoyed by both sexes. It was the favourite drink of writers Somerset Maugham, Joseph Conrad and Hollywood actor Douglas Fairbanks. Some 'modern' interpretations use soda water to finish the drink but in this, the Raffles Hotel version, it is never used. Where possible, use a very brightly coloured cherry brandy so the resulting drink is a beautiful pink colour.*

## Gin

## Ingredients:

I measure gin
I measure cherry brandy
½ measure Cointreau
I measure lime juice
I measure pineapple juice
I measure orange juice
¼ measure grenadine
I teaspoon Benedictine
I dash angostura bitters

## Method:

Place all the ingredients except the Benedictine into a shaker with ice cubes and shake well. Strain into a highball glass filled three-quarters with broken ice and sprinkle the Benedictine on top. Garnish with the slice of pineapple and the cherry.

# Caruso

*This minty cocktail was invented and named after the great Italian tenor, Enrico Caruso, when he stayed at the Hotel Sevilla, Cuba in the 1920s.*

## Ingredients:

1 measure gin

1 measure dry vermouth

1 measure green creme de menthe

# Gin

## Method:

In a mixing glass with some ice cubes, stir in the ingredients and strain into a cocktail glass.

If you use white creme de menthe in place of the green, you have a Caruso Blanco.

# Clover Club

*This rich lemon-flavoured cocktail burst onto the scene in 1925 and takes it name from the famous American night-spot.*

## Ingredients:

1½ measures gin
¾ measure lemon juice
½ measure grenadine
1 egg white

## Variations

Add 4 to 5 mint leaves to the shaker and garnish with a sprig of mint and you have a Clover Leaf.

For a Clover Club Royal, reduce the grenadine to ¼ measure and replace the egg white with an egg yolk. Shake well and strain into a double Champagne saucer filled with crushed ice and garnish with a slice of lemon.

# Gin

## Method:

Place all the ingredients in a shaker with some ice cubes and shake vigourously. Strain into a champagne saucer.

# Typhoon
*Create a storm with one of these!*

## Ingredients:
I measure gin
½ measure Pernod or Ricard
I measure lime juice
chilled champagne

# Gin

## Method:
Place all the ingredients, except the champagne, into a shaker with some ice cubes and shake well. Pour into an ice filled collins glass and top up with champagne.

# Wakiki Beachcomber

*Very simple to make – just three ingredients
that washed up on the beach.*

## Ingredients:

1 measure gin
1 measure triple sec/Cointreau
1½ tablespoons pineapple juice

# Gin

## Method:

Place all the ingredients in a
shaker with some ice cubes
and shake well. Strain into a
cocktail glass.

| method: | BUILD |
| glass: | COLLINS |
| garnish: | LEMON SLICE AND MINT SPRIG |

# Oasis

*Cool, blue, refreshing – and very quick to make.*

## Ingredients:

2 measures gin

½ measure blue Curaçao

tonic water

# Gin

## Method:

Fill a collins glass two-thirds full of ice. Pour over the gin and add the Curaçao. Top up with tonic and stir well. Garnish with the lemon slice and mint sprig and serve with a stirrer.

# Alaska Cocktail

## Gin

### Method:
Stir together the ingredients in a mixing glass with some ice cubes. Strain into a cocktail glass.

### Ingredients:
2 dashes orange bitters

1½ measures gin

¾ measure yellow Chartreuse

method: MIXING GLASS

glass: COCKTAIL

# Alfonso Special

*King Alfonso XIII of Spain appears to have drowned the
sorrows of his exile quite well.*

## Ingredients:

1 measure Grand Marnier

¾ measure gin

¾ measure dry vermouth

4 dashes sweet vermouth

1 dash angostura bitters

# Gin

## Method:

Place the ingredients in a
mixing glass with some ice
cubes and stir well. Strain
into a cocktail glass.

# Bijou

*The traditional recipe for this cocktail calls for Plymouth gin,*
*a distinctly smooth gin made with the natural waters from*
*Dartmoor, in the southwest of England.*

## Ingredients:

I measure Plymouth gin
I measure green Chartreuse
I measure sweet red
  vermouth
I dash orange bitters

# Gin

## Method:

Place a few ice cubes in a
mixing glass and pour in the
ingredients. Stir and strain
into a cocktail glass and
garnish with the cherry and
lemon slice.

| method: | SHAKER |
|---|---|
| glass: | COCKTAIL |
| garnish: | LEMON TWIST |

# Green Lady

*This recipe from Harry MacElhone's* Harry's ABC of Mixing Cocktails *is credited to Georges Pesce of Fouquet's Bar in Paris. It's a delightfully elegant drink, and an opportunity to use both green and yellow Chartreuse along with gin.*

## Ingredients:

2 measures gin

⅔ measure green Chartreuse

⅔ measure yellow Chartreuse

## Rich & Elegant

## Method:

Place the ingredients in a shaker with some ice cubes. Shake and strain into a cocktail glass and add the twist of lemon.

# Merry Widow Cocktail No. 1

*One to hum along with to Franz Lehar's operetta
of the same name!*

## Ingredients:

1¼ measures gin

1¼ measures dry vermouth

½ teaspoon Benedictine

½ teaspoon Pernod or Ricard

1 dash orange bitters

# Gin

## Method:

Stir the ingredients in a mixing glass with some ice cubes. Strain into a cocktail glass and garnish with a twist of lemon.

| method: | SHAKER |
| --- | --- |
| glass: | COLLINS |
| garnish: | SLICE OF LEMON AND A CHERRY |

# Shanghai Gin Fizz

*A herb-flavoured delight that's as rich as silk!*

## Ingredients:

⅔ measure gin

⅔ measure Benedictine

⅔ measure yellow Chartreuse

⅔ measure lemon juice

½ measure sugar syrup

4 measures soda water

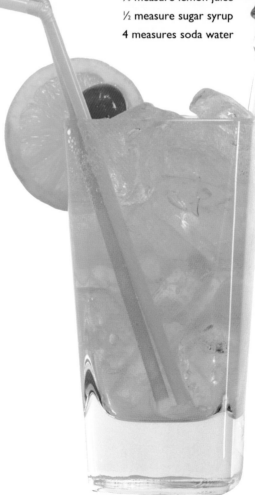

# Gin

## Method:

Place all the ingredients – except the soda water – in a shaker with some ice cubes and shake well. Strain into a collins glass half-filled with ice and top with soda water. Garnish with a slice of lemon and a cherry, and serve with a muddler and straws.

# K.G.B. Cocktail

*Another chance to use the delicious caraway-flavoured kümmel.*

## Ingredients:

½ measure kümmel

1½ measures gin

¼ teaspoon apricot brandy

¼ teaspoon lemon juice

## Gin

## Method:

Place the ingredients in a cocktail shaker with some ice cubes and shake well. Strain into a well-chilled cocktail glass and add the twist of lemon.

method: MIXING GLASS

glass: COCKTAIL

# Xanthia Cocktail

## Ingredients:

I measure gin

I measure yellow Chartreuse

I measure cherry brandy

## Gin

## Method:

Place all the ingredients in a mixing glass with some ice cubes and stir. Strain into a cocktail glass.

# Mule's Hind Leg

*A fruity-herb flavour that packs a kick too!, this drink blends 'old world' gin and Benedictine with 'new world' maple syrup and applejack.*

## Ingredients:

½ measure gin

½ measure applejack (substitute: Calvados, apple brandy)

⅓ measure Benedictine

⅓ measure apricot brandy

⅓ measure maple syrup

# Gin

## Method:

Place all the ingredients in a shaker with some ice cubes and shake. Strain into an old-fashioned glass three-quarter filled with broken ice.

| method: | SHAKER |
|---|---|
| glass: | COCKTAIL |

# Spring Feeling Cocktail

*As soon as the first spring flowers appear, it's a good time to
indulge in one of these and feel your sap start to rise!*

## Gin

### Method:

Shake the ingredients with
some ice cubes and strain
into a cocktail glass.

### Ingredients:

1½ measures gin

¾ measure green Chartreuse

1 tablespoon of lemon juice

# Beef Salad

*The 'beef' comes from Beefeater gin, the 'salad' from its delightful green colour courtesy of the Midori and the green Chartreuse.*

## Ingredients:

1½ measures Beefeater gin
½ measure Midori melon liqueur
1 teaspoon green Chartreuse
4½ measures sparkling bitter lemon

## Gin

## Method:

Add the liquid ingredients to an ice-filled highball glass and garnish with fruits in season. Serve with straws.

How about a Beef Salad on Rye? Just add ½ measure rye whiskey!

| method: | SHAKE |
| --- | --- |
| glass: | GOBLET OR OVERSIZED WINE GLASS |
| garnish: | FRUIT IN SEASON |

# Chaos Calmer

*Orange-flavoured gin makes a very pleasant change from the usual gin-tonic combination.*

## Ingredients:

1½ measures gin
¼ measure triple sec/Cointreau
1½ measures orange juice
¾ measure lime juice
1 teaspoon grenadine

# Gin

## Method:

Place all the ingredients into a shaker with a glassful of broken ice and shake well. Pour, unstrained, into a goblet or oversized wine glass and garnish with fruit in season.

# Codswallop

*Believe it or not, in the 1850s Mr. Hiram Codd patented a soda water-lemonade bottle which was sealed with a glass marble in the neck. The marble was held in place by the pressure of the fizzy drink, and to release the contents you had to 'wallop' (hit) the top of the bottle to break the seal.*

## Gin

## Ingredients:

1½ measures gin

⅓ measure Campari

⅓ measure creme de framboise

⅓ measure lime juice

4 measures lemonade

## Method:

Add all the ingredients to an ice-filled highball glass and top with cold lemonade.

| method: | SHAKER |
|---|---|
| glass: | HIGHBALL |

# Even Pair

*The flavour of this gin-based mixed drink comes from pear liqueur. There are a number on the market including Poire William from France, named after the variety of pear used in its production, Italy's Pera Segnana, and variations from Germany and Switzerland. Never failing to raise an eyebrow and debate as to 'how do they do that' is the 'novelty' Poire Prisonniere (literally, imprisoned pear) where the pears are painstakingly grown in bottles while they are still attached to a tree: each fruit effectively has its own individual green house!*

## Ingredients:

1 measure gin
1 measure dry vermouth
⅓ measure pear liqueur
4 measures tonic water

# Gin

## Method:

Place all the ingredients except the tonic water into a shaker with two or three ice cubes. Shake well and strain into an ice-filled highball glass. Top with tonic.

# Evergreen

*One to make you burst into song!*

## Ingredients:

1 measure creme de banane
½ measure Midori melon
  liqueur
½ measure blue Curaçao
½ measure gin
2 measures white grape juice

# Gin

## Method:

Shake all the ingredients in a
shaker with two or three ice
cubes and strain into a chilled
cocktail glass. Garnish with a
green cherry.

| method: | SHAKER |
| --- | --- |
| glass: | HIGHBALL |
| garnish: | SLICE OF ORANGE AND PINEAPPLE |

# Lady Killer

*Delightful passion fruit flavour.*

## Ingredients:

1 measure gin
¾ measure apricot brandy
¾ measure Cointreau
2 measures passion fruit juice
2 measures pineapple juice

# Gin

## Method:

Place the ingredients in a shaker with two or three ice cubes and shake well. Strain into a highball glass filled with ice and garnish with the orange and pineapple slices.

# Titanic Uplift

*It was said of the enormously expensive, but disastrous box office flop,* Raise the Titanic, *that it would have been cheaper to drain the Atlantic. Here's how to do it yourself!*

## Ingredients:

2 measures Midori melon
   liqueur
1 measure gin
4 measures orange juice

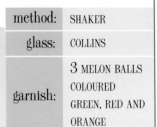

# Gin

## Method:

Place the ingredients in a shaker with some ice cubes and shake vigourously. Strain into a collins glass three-quarters filled with broken ice. Garnish with the three coloured melon balls. Serve with a straw.

| method: | SHAKER |
| glass: | COCKTAIL |
| garnish: | ORANGE AND PINEAPPLE SLICES |

# Marimba

*Like the musical instrument, this tropical-fruit-flavoured cocktail is certain to get you dancing.*

## Ingredients:

1 measure Southern Comfort
½ measure gin
¼ measure amaretto
1 measure pineapple juice
1 measure mango juice
¼ measure lime juice

## Gin

### Method:

Place all the ingredients in a shaker with some ice cubes and shake rhythmically. Strain into a cocktail glass and garnish with pineapple and orange slices.

# Arctic Summer

*A delicious blend of apricot and lemon.*

## Ingredients:

1½ measures gin

¾ measure apricot brandy

1 teaspoon grenadine

4 measures sparkling bitter lemon

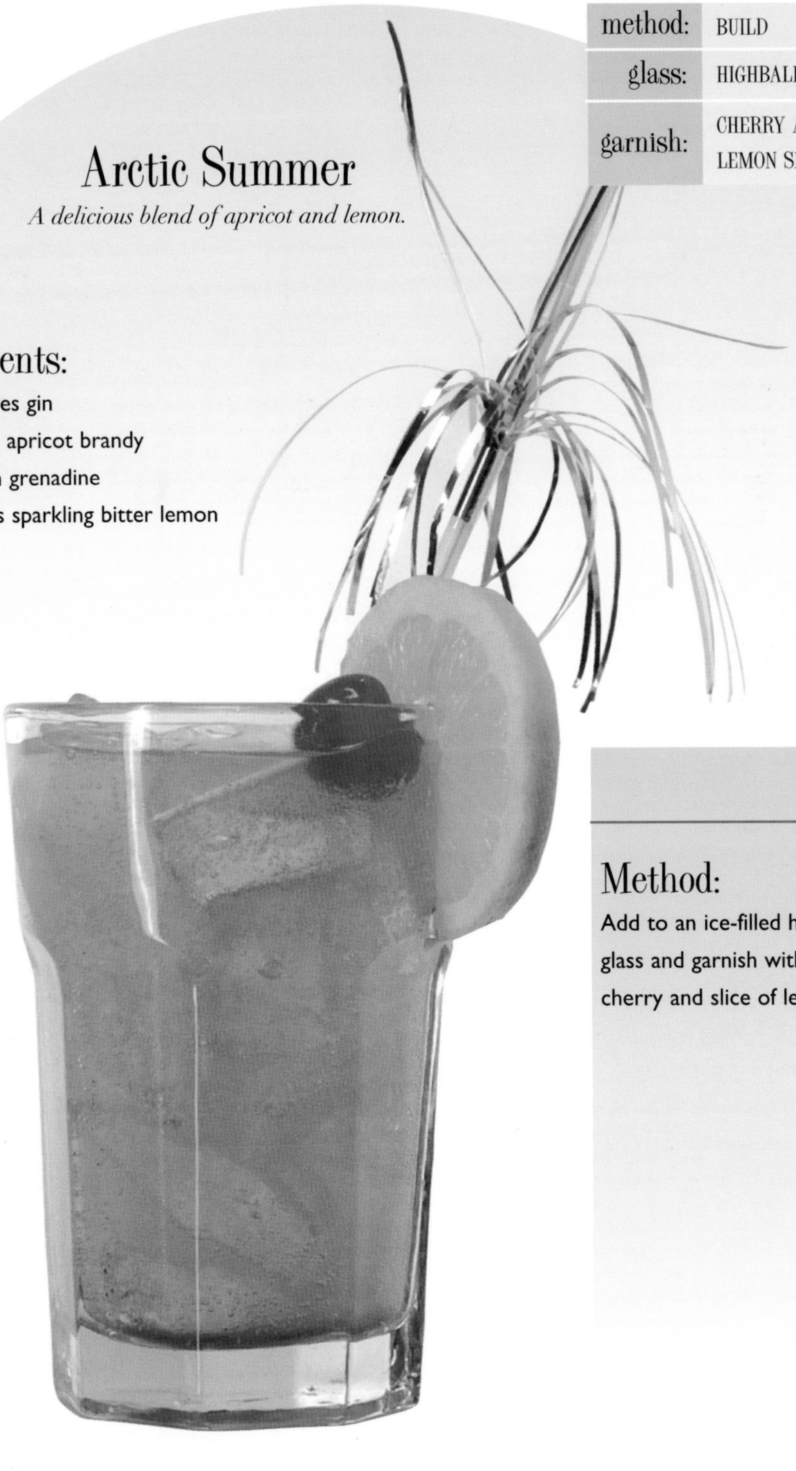

# Gin

## Method:

Add to an ice-filled highball glass and garnish with a cherry and slice of lemon.

| method: | SHAKER |
|---|---|
| glass: | HIGHBALL OR OLD-FASHIONED |
| garnish: | WEDGE OF LIME AND SPRIG OF MINT |

# Ramos Fizz

*The Ramos Fizz was the creation of Henrico C. Ramos in around 1888, when he arrived in New Orleans and bought the Imperial Cabinet Saloon. Ramos created a light, truly mouthwatering cocktail, the recipe for which was a closely guarded secret until the saloon closed in 1920, because of Prohibition, and Henrico's brother Charles Henry Ramos, finally revealed the ingredients. In honour of Henrico Ramos, why not make the Ramos Fizz on December 5th – the date that the Volstead Act (which brought in Prohibition in the USA) was repealed.*

# Gin

## Method:

Pour all of the ingredients except the soda water into a shaker with half a cup of crushed ice. Shake vigourously. Strain and pour into an ice-filled glass – a highball if you want to add the soda, or an old-fashioned if you'd like just a squirt or none at all. Finish with soda water if desired, and garnish with the lime wedge and mint sprig. Serve with a straw and a stirrer.

## Ingredients:

2 measures gin
1 dash sugar syrup
3 drops triple sec/ Cointreau
1 measure lemon juice
¾ measure lime juice
1 egg white
1 measure full cream milk or whipping cream
1 teaspoon powdered/ caster sugar
3 measures soda water (optional)

# Barbary Coast

*The Barbary Coast was the Mediterranean coastline of north Africa from Morocco to Libya and the home of pirates. That they ever drank this confection is highly unlikely: the drink dates from the 1920s, and originally, it was made without the rum.*

## Ingredients:

½ measure gin

½ measure white rum

½ measure Scotch

½ measure white creme de cacao

½ measure double cream

## Gin

## Method:

Place all the ingredients in a shaker with two or three ice cubes and shake vigourously. Strain into old-fashioned glass three-quarters filled with broken ice.

| method: | SHAKER |
|---|---|
| glass: | GOBLET OR OVERSIZED WINE GLASS |
| garnish: | FRUIT IN SEASON |

# Caribbean Sunset

*A fruity flavour and marvellous colour.*

## Ingredients:

1 measure creme de banane
1 measure gin
1 measure blue Curaçao
1 measure whipping cream
¾ measure lemon juice
⅓ measure grenadine

# Gin

## Method:

Place all the ingredients except the grenadine into a shaker with two or three ice cubes and shake well. Strain into a goblet filled with broken ice. Add the grenadine, allowing it to sink to the bottom and garnish with seasonal fruit.

# Strawberry Dawn

*A lovely creamy cocktail with a delicate colour.*

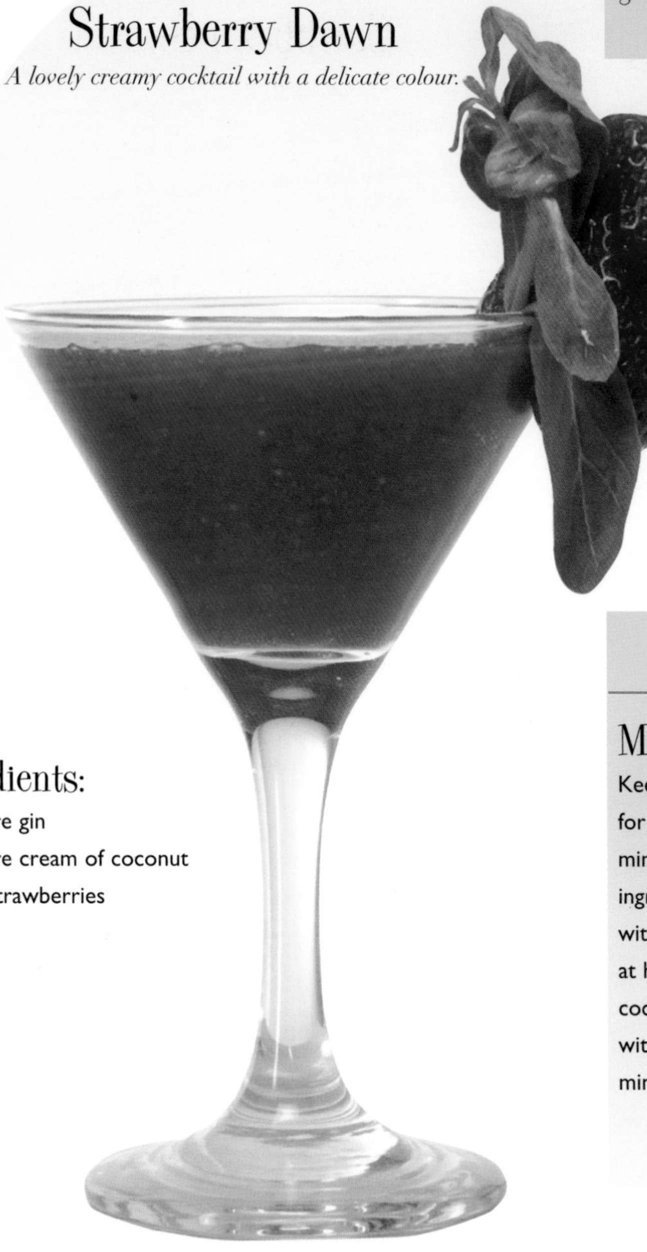

## Gin

## Ingredients:

1 measure gin

1 measure cream of coconut

5 fresh strawberries

## Method:

Keep one strawberry aside for garnish along with the mint sprig. Place all the ingredients into the blender with a glass of ice and blend at high speed. Pour into a cocktail glass and decorate with the strawberry and mint.

| method: | SHAKER |
|---------|--------|
| glass:  | SHOT   |

# Honolulu Shooter

*The delightfully fruity shooter could be made into a longer*
*drink and served on the rocks if you prefer – simply adjust the*
*quantities of the juices to suit your taste and create your own*
*paradise island.*

## Ingredients:

1 measure gin

1 teaspoon pineapple juice

1 teaspoon orange juice

1 teaspoon lemon juice

1 teaspoon of pineapple syrup

1 drop angostura bitters

# Gin

## Method:

Shake all the ingredients vigourously in
a shaker with two or three ice cubes.
Strain into a shot glass.

# Rum cocktails

*'Fifteen men on the dead
man's chest
Yo-ho-ho, and a bottle of
rum!
Drink and the devil had
done for the rest -
Yo-ho-ho, and a bottle of
rum!'*

**Treasure Island,** *by
Robert Louis Stevenson (1883).*

**El presidente**
see page 122.

Rum is traditionally the drink of swash-buckling pirates and, you may be surprised to know, the first national spirit of Australia. Rum is, in effect, the glorious by-product of the manufacture of sugar. It was Christopher Columbus who introduced sugar cane to the Americas, and rum can be made from the fermented juices of the entire sugar cane, a speciality of South America called *aguardiente de caña* (literally 'fire-water from cane'). More familiar is the rum made from molasses, the heavy dark syrup left over after the solid sugar has been crystallised out of the sugar cane.

Raw sugar cane is pressed between rollers to extract the juice, which is then boiled down, clarified and put into machines which spin at high speeds and crystallise the sugar and separate it from the molasses. The molasses is reboiled to make a low-grade sugar and the residue is mixed with water and yeast, allowed to ferment and then distilled to produce rum.

Rums are divided into categories: light, medium, full bodied and aromatic. By law, each bottle must state its country of ori-

Cuba libre
see page 118.

gin. You will also see rum that is called *añejo*: this means 'aged' rum. It generally has a tawny colour and more mellow flavour.

Light rum refers to its body, rather than its colour. A light rum may be colourless (so-called 'white rum') or it may be aged for three years to give more flavour and then be coloured with caramel. This is known as golden rum. Light rums are the style of the Spanish-speaking Caribbean, especially of Cuba, Puerto Rico and the Virgin Islands. Aged for more than six years, Puerto Rican rum may be called vieux or liqueur rum.

Medium-bodied rums are the speciality of the French speaking islands such as Martinique and Haiti, and are distilled from the juice of sugar cane rather than molasses. The juice is con-centrated and distilled in pot stills and the rum is aged in oak casks, from which it takes it colour. From Guyana in Central America comes Demerara rum, made from the sugar produced in the area around the Demerara River. Although a very dark colour, it, too, has a medium body, often with a high alcohol content – 151 per cent proof – although strangely, it doesn't taste strongly alcoholic and can lull you into a false sense of security. Demerara rum is particularly good in hot toddies and grog and was sprinkled on the top of Don Beach's original zom-bie (see page 137).

Full-bodied rums come from Jamaica, where they are naturally fermented (with yeast from the air rather than cultured yeast, which settles on the surface of the 'mash') for about three weeks. It is then double-distilled: once to make a residue called dunder, and again to produce the more pungent rum. (An old insult is to call someone a 'dunderhead' – someone who is 'slow-witted' or whose mind has been dulled by excess rum.) It is then allowed to age in oak casks for no fewer than five years. Its colour is enhanced by the addition of caramel.

The final category of rum, aromatic, is used a great deal in The Netherlands and in Scandinavia. This is Batavia Arak, and comes from the island of Java, Indonesia (formerly the Dutch East Indies). Batavia refers to the town where this very dry and very pungent rum is made. The Arak is made from Javanese molasses into which small cakes of Javanese red rice are placed. This ferments naturally and the distilled rum is then shipped to Europe where it is aged for a further six years before it is blended and bottled.

**Havana beach**
see page 124.

| method: | BUILD |
| --- | --- |
| glass: | HIGHBALL |
| garnish: | HALF LEMON SHELL |

## Ingredients:

ice cubes

2 measures white rum
(preferably Bacardi)

½ measures triple sec
or Cointreau

juice of ½ lemon

4 measures ginger ale

spent shell of ½ lemon
to garnish

# Rum

## Method:

Add the lemon juice to a
highball glass two-thirds filled
with ice.

Drop in the spent shell of
the lemon and add the rum,
triple sec or Cointreau and
top with ginger ale.

# Bacardi buck

*Bucks are tall drinks that are made by 'building' (directly adding all the ingredients to an ice-filled glass). They have been around since the late 19th century and consist of a base spirit, ginger ale and lemon or lime juice. The traditional method is to squeeze half a lemon or lime directly into the glass and then to drop in the spent half shell. As usual, with all rules, there is an exception: bucks made with white rum, such as the Bacardi buck, have a small amount of another ingredient, such as a fruit juice or a liqueur. This is also one of several drinks that uses the famous brand of Bacardi rum.*

| method: | SHAKER |
| --- | --- |
| glass: | TRADITIONALLY, A CHAMPAGNE SAUCER, OR A COCKTAIL GLASS |
| garnish: | CHERRY ON A STICK |

115

# Bacardi cocktail

*The firm of Bacardi y Cia, proprietors of the Bacardi trademark, objected to the use (or misuse) of the name 'Bacardi' as applied to any drink not made with Bacardi rum. A New York Supreme Court Ruling in 1937 decreed in the firm's favour and Bacardi y Cie have exclusive rights to the use of the name.*

## Ingredients:

ice cubes
1½ measures Bacardi
white rum
1 measure lime juice
(or lemon if preferred)
½ measure gomme syrup
1 teaspoon grenadine

# Rum

## Method:

Half-fill the shaker with ice cubes.
Add the lime (or lemon juice), grenadine, gomme syrup and Bacardi rum. Shake well and strain into a champagne saucer/cocktail glass and garnish with a cherry on a stick.

## Variations:

For a Bacardi flyer, make a Bacardi cocktail, strain into a large champagne saucer and top with chilled champagne.

For a Bacardi special, use 2 measures Bacardi rum, ¾ measure gin, 1 measure lime juice, 1 teaspoon grenadine and ½ teaspoon castor sugar. Shake all the ingredients except the rum until cold. Add the rum and shake again. Strain into a cocktail glass.

| method: | BLENDER |
| --- | --- |
| glass: | GOBLET OR LARGE WINE GLASS |

# Batidas

*A batida is a fruity Brazilian drink traditionally made with aguardiente de caña. This is the name given to the rums of South America, which are distilled from fermented and concentrated sugar-cane sap. The best known is Cachaca (pronounced cachasa) and is similar to unmatured white rum – full-bodied and a little 'raw'. Cachaca is available if you want to make a truly authentic batida, or you can use white rum in its place for a slightly 'smoother' taste.*

## Ingredients:

1 glass crushed ice
2 measures Cachaca
(or white rum)
4 oz fresh pineapple
cut into chunks
½ teaspoon granulated sugar

# Rum

## Method:

Place the crushed ice in the blender and add the Cachaca or white rum, pineapple chunks and sugar.
Blend until smooth and then pour into the goblet or wine glass.
Serve with short straws.

## Batida abaci
(Pineapple batida)

# Caipirinha

*Pronounced 'cai-pir-een-i', it means ' 'peasant's drink' in Brazil. This lime-flavoured rum drink traditionally uses the South American rum aguardiente de caña, the best known of which is Cachaca (see also the batidas).*

## Ingredients:

ice cubes
2½ measures Cachaca
(or white rum)
1 fresh lime
1½ teaspoons granulated sugar

# Rum

## Method:

Wash the lime and cut the 'knobs' from the top and tail. Cut the lime into eight wedges. Put the sugar in the glass, add the lime wedges and crush them until the juice is released and the sugar dissolved. Add the Cachaca or white rum and muddle further to ensure all the sugar is fully dissolved. Add the ice cubes to the glass and muddle some more. Decorate with a slice of lime if desired.

| method: | BUILD |
|---|---|
| glass: | HIGHBALL |
| garnish: | SPENT SHELL OF ½ LIME |

# Cuba libre

*According to legend, an army officer in Havana, Cuba, invented this drink when he mixed Bacardi white rum with the newly arrived soft drink Coca Cola. If you ask a barman for a 'Bacardi and coke' you will be served exactly with these two registered brands. Ask for a Cuba libre and he will ask you which light rum you'd prefer!*

## Ingredients:

ice cubes
2 measures white rum
juice of ½ lime
4–5 measures cold cola
spent shell of the lime
for garnish

# Rum

## Method:

Into a highball glass squeeze the juice of ½ lime.
Drop the spent shell of the lime into the glass and then fill the glass two-thirds full with ice cubes.
Add the rum and top with cold cola.
Serve with straws.

## Variations:
### Cuba libre supreme:

replace the rum with Southern Comfort.

### Cuba libre Espana:

½ measure of white rum, ½ measure dark rum, 1 measure sweet sherry, juice 1/2 lime, cold cola. Build into a highball glass as for a Cuba libre.

| method: | BUILD |
| glass: | HIGHBALL |
| garnish: | ORANGE SLICE, CHERRY AND A PAPER PARASOL |

---

| method: | SHAKER |
| glass: | COCKTAIL |
| garnish: | SLICE OF LIME |

# Daiquiri

*The original Daiquiri, consisting of rum, lime and sugar, was created in Cuba in 1896 by an American mining engineer called Jennings Cox, who named the drink after the town of Daiquiri. Some say he ran out of gin and had to 'make do' with rum. Others say the rum was the only available 'medicine' to ward off malaria and the other ingredients were added by American workers to make it more palatable. The 'frozen' version of the classic Daiquiri cocktail was made famous in 1912 by Constantino 'Constante' Ribalagua at La Florida restaurant in Havana, Cuba.*

Original
Daiquiri.

# Rum

## Method:

Half-fill the shaker with ice cubes.
Add the lime juice, castor sugar and rum.
Shake well and strain into a well-chilled cocktail glass.
Garnish with a lime slice.

## Ingredients:

ice cubes
2 measures white rum
⅔ measure lime juice
1 teaspoon castor sugar
1 slice lime

## Variations:

For a frozen Daquiri, add crushed ice to give it the consistency of a sherbet or sorbet. Shake and strain the ingredients into a glass filled with crushed ice

# Diabolo

*There is another devilish drink called a 'diablo' made with dry white port (see page 193). There is nothing hellish about either drink, however!*

## Ingredients:

crushed ice
2 measures rum
(of your choice)
½ measure triple sec
or Cointreau
½ measure dry vermouth
2 drops bitters
orange twist

# Rum

## Method:

Put some crushed ice in the shaker and pour on the vermouth, triple sec or Cointreau and rum. Add the bitters and shake. Strain and pour into a cocktail glass with a little crushed ice and garnish with the orange twist.

| method: | SHAKER |
|---|---|
| glass: | OLD FASHIONED |
| garnish: | SLICE OF ORANGE AND A CHERRY |

# El Presidente

*There are probably as many variations of the Presidente
cocktail as there have been Latin American presidents.
Some can be traced to an actual president, others go by the more
general name of 'El Presidente'. The recipe offered here is for the
Presidente created in around 1920 at the
Vista Alegre Bar in Havana, Cuba, for President
General Mario Menocal.*

## Ingredients:

ice cubes

crushed ice

2 measures white rum

1 measure rosso vermouth

⅓ measure dry vermouth

1 teaspoon grenadine

1 slice orange

1 cherry

# Rum

## Method:

Half-fill the shaker with ice
cubes.

Add the grenadine, dry
vermouth, rosso vermouth
and white rum.

Shake well and strain into an
old-fashioned glass almost
filled with crushed ice, or, as
the original version, straight
up.

Garnish with the orange slice
and cherry.

# Grenada

*This orange-and-cinnamon-flavoured drink is named after Grenada, one of the Windward Islands in the West Indies.*

## Ingredients:

ice cubes

3 measures dark rum

1 measure rosso vermouth

1½ measures orange juice

ground cinnamon

## Rum

## Method:

Put some ice cubes in the mixing glass and add the orange juice, vermouth and dark rum.

Stir well and strain into a chilled cocktail glass.

Sprinkle a little ground cinnamon on the top.

# Havana Beach

*A great party drink, it's also easy to make in large quantities*
*using a blender or food processor. The lime is chopped up and*
*distributed through the drink to form tiny green specks.*

## Ingredients:

ice cubes

1 measure white rum

2 measures pineapple
juice

½ lime

1 teaspoon sugar

4 measures ginger ale

1 lime slice

# Rum

## Method:

Cut the half-lime into four
pieces and put them in the
blender or food processor
with the pineapple juice,
sugar and rum.

Blend until smooth.

Put 3–4 ice cubes in a large
goblet and pour in the
mixture.

Top up with ginger ale and
decorate with the lime slice.
Serve with straws.

# Jamaica Sunday

*The full-bodied and aromatic rums of Jamaica are aged in oak vats for a minimum of five years. Some are still shipped to England for ageing and blending in bonded warehouses at ports in London and Liverpool and are known as London or Liverpool 'dock rums'. This recipe has an interesting ingredient – honey.*

## Ingredients:

broken ice
2 measures dark rum –
preferably Jamaican
1 teaspoon clear honey
½ measure lime juice
2 measures lemonade

# Rum

## Method:

Dissolve the honey in the rum and then pour into an old-fashioned glass filled with broken ice.
Top with lemonade and relax!

| method: | MUDDLE AND SHAKER |
|---|---|
| glass: | COCKTAIL |
| garnish: | CHOPPED, FRESH MINT |

# Maison Charles

*A perfect, mint-flavoured cocktail for a hot, summer evening.*

## Ingredients:

crushed ice

2 measures white rum

¼ measure lime juice

¼ measure gomme syrup

fresh mint

castor sugar

# Rum

## Method:

Gently crush one or two sprigs of mint in a mixing glass and cover with the rum. Let it stand for 20 minutes. Using a sharp knife, cut a few leaves of mint very finely – avoid using the central stem of the leaf. Mix a small amount of the chopped mint into the castor sugar to 'frost' the rim of the glass. Run the lime peel around the rim of the glass and dip it in the sugar-mint mix. Put a glass of crushed ice into the shaker. Pour the 'infused' rum into the shaker, along with the lime juice and gomme syrup. Shake well and strain into the frosted cocktail glass. Sprinkle a tiny amount of chopped mint on the top as a final decoration.

## Variations:

For a Madison Avenue, replace the gomme syrup with Cointreau and make in the same manner as the Maison Charles.

# Mojito

*This is basically a Collins (see page 33), but made with rum and sprigs of mint – sometimes called the Cuban mint julep. The drink became popular in Cuba with Americans visiting the island during the Prohibition years.*

## Ingredients:

ice cubes

broken ice

2½ measures white rum

⅔ measure gomme syrup

1 dash bitters

juice of half a lime

2 measures soda water

3–4 sprigs mint

# Rum

## Method:

Gently crush the mint in the bottom of the glass.

Put the spent shell of the lime in the glass and fill with broken ice.

Half-fill the shaker with ice cubes.

Add the rum, lime juice, bitters and gomme syrup.

Shake well and strain into the glass.

Add the soda and gently muddle together.

Add straws.

| method: | BUILD |
|---|---|
| glass: | COLLINS |
| garnish: | SLICE OF GRAPEFRUIT AND A CHERRY |

# Monkey wrench

*A refreshing, long drink that makes grapefruit juice taste wonderful. The lemonade cuts the sharpness of the juice. The cherry also helps!*

## Ingredients:

ice cubes

1¾ measures white rum

3 measures grapefruit juice

3 measures lemonade

slice of grapefruit

1 maraschino cherry

# Rum

## Method:

Fill a Collins glass two-thirds full with ice cubes.

Pour on the rum and grapefruit juice and top with lemonade.

Garnish with the grapefruit slice and cherry and add straws.

# Northside special

*This fruity drink was created at the Myrtle Bank Hotel in Kingston, Jamaica, in the 1930s.*

## Ingredients:

broken ice

2 measures dark rum – preferably Jamaican

3 measures orange juice

½ measure lemon juice

2 teaspoons castor sugar

2 measures soda water

1 slice lemon

1 slice orange

1 cherry

# Rum

## Method:

In a Collins glass, dissolve the sugar in the orange and lemon juice.

Add the rum.

Fill the glass with broken ice and top with soda.

Garnish with the orange and lemon slices and the cherry.

Add straws.

| method: | SHAKER |
| glass: | COCKTAIL |
| garnish: | CHERRY ON A STICK |

# Petite fleur

*Both the name, meaning 'little flower', and the addition of Cointreau suggest that this drink originated in the French-speaking islands of the Caribbean.*

## Ingredients:

ice cubes
1 measure white rum
1⅓ measures Cointreau
1⅓ measures grapefruit juice
1 maraschino cherry

## Rum

## Method:

Half-fill the shaker with ice cubes.
Pour in the grapefruit juice, Cointreau and rum.
Shake well, strain into a cocktail glass and add a cherry on a stick.

| method: | BLENDER |
| glass: | GOBLET |
| garnish: | ¼ SLICE OF PINEAPPLE SKEWERED WITH A MARASCHINO CHERRY |

# Pina colada

*One of the most popular drinks in the world, the pina colada was invented on the island of Puerto Rico and means 'strained pineapple'. Coconut cream is a vital ingredient of the pina colada: there are some pre-prepared brands available, but the best way is to make your own, since pure creamed coconut is easily obtained.*

## Ingredients:

crushed ice
2 measures light rum
5 measures pineapple juice (or 5 slices of tinned pineapple in its own juice, crushed in a blender)
1 measure coconut cream (made to above recipe)
¼ slice pineapple
1 maraschino cherry

# Rum

## To make coconut cream

Take a chilled, hard block of pure creamed coconut and grate it to break down the grainy texture. To make 1 pina colada, take 1 tablespoon of grated creamed coconut and 1 tablespoon of castor sugar and dissolve them in the smallest amount of hot water. Stir until the texture is a smooth, runny paste. Taste to check on the sweetness and adjust as desired. Once cool, it's ready for use. Use the coconut cream the same day – don't store it as it will go off, taste absolutely disgusting and turn into a grainy mess!

## Method:

Pour the pineapple juice into the blender (or crush 5 slices of tinned pineapple in its own juice in a blender) and add the coconut cream and the rum.
Blend for a few seconds.
Add the crushed ice and blend for 5 seconds.
Pour into the goblet and garnish with the fruit.
Serve with a straw.

| method: | BUILD |
|---|---|
| glass: | HIGHBALL |
| garnish: | LIME SLICE |

# Pink rum

*A wonderful flavour and a gorgeous colour – drink it while wearing a hibiscus flower behind your ear!*

## Ingredients:

ice cubes

2 measures white rum

2 measures cranberry juice

1 measure soda water

3 drops bitters

1 slice lime

# Rum

## Method:

Put three drops of bitters into a highball glass and swirl them around so they coat the inside of the glass.
Add some ice cubes and pour in the rum and cranberry juice.
Top with soda water and decorate with the lime slice.

| method: | SHAKER |
|---|---|
| glass: | HIGHBALL |
| garnish: | SLICE OF ORANGE, A CHERRY, PINEAPPLE WEDGE AND LIME WEDGE |

133

# Planter's punch

*This famous drink was created to celebrate Fred L Myers'
founding of the Myer's Rum Distillery in Jamaica in 1879. There
are now several variations of the original recipe.*

## Ingredients:

ice cubes
1 measure dark rum
(preferably Myer's!)
1 measure light rum
1 measure añejo rum
1 measure orange juice
1 measure pineapple juice
½ measure grapefruit juice
1 teaspoon lime juice
1 teaspoon lemon juice
1 teaspoon grenadine
1 slice orange
1 pineapple wedge
1 lime wedge
1 maraschino sherry

# Rum

## Method:

Half-fill the shaker with ice
cubes.
Pour in the rums, lime and
lemon juice, orange juice,
pineapple and grapefruit
juices and the grenadine.
Shake well and strain into an
ice-filled highball glass and
garnish with the fruit.

| method: | MIXING GLASS |
|---|---|
| glass: | OLD FASHIONED |
| garnish: | SPENT SHELL OF $\frac{1}{4}$ LIME |

# Rum Ramsay

*This drink was created around 1930 by barman Albert Martin at the Bon Ton Bar in New Orleans. The recipe was a secret for many years until he passed it on to Victor 'Trader Vic' Bergeron. Martin originally served his Ramsay 'straight up' but it was later popular served with broken ice.*

## Ingredients:

ice cubes
broken ice
1½ measures white rum
1 teaspoon bourbon
juice of ¼ lime
⅓ measure gomme syrup
1 dash bitters

# Rum

## Method:

Put some ice cubes in the mixing glass and squeeze the lime juice into it.
Drop in the spent shell. Add the rum, bourbon and gomme syrup and stir well. Strain into an old-fashioned glass filled with broken ice (or serve straight up if preferred).

# Santiago

## Ingredients:

ice cubes
broken ice
1½ measures white rum
½ measure triple sec or Cointreau
1 teaspoon grenadine
½ measure gomme syrup
1 maraschino cherry

## Rum

## Method:

Half-fill the shaker with ice cubes. Pour in the rum, triple sec or Cointreau, grenadine and gomme syrup. Shake well and strain into an old-fashioned glass filled with broken ice.
Garnish with a maraschino cherry on a stick.

| method: | SHAKER |
|---|---|
| glass: | HIGHBALL |
| garnish: | HALF A SPENT LIME SHELL |

# Scorpion

*Definitely a drink with a sting in its tail!*

## Ingredients:

crushed ice
1 measure dark rum
¾ measure white rum
¾ measure brandy
¼ measure triple sec or
Cointreau
1½ measures orange juice
juice ½ lime

# Rum

## Method:

Put a glass of crushed ice in a
shaker.
Pour in the orange and lime
juice, white and dark rum,
brandy, triple sec or
Cointreau.
Shake well and strain into a
highball glass half-filled with
crushed ice.
Drop in the spent shell of
the lime.

# Zombie prince

*The original zombie was created in 1934 by legendary bartender Don Beach at the 'Don the Beachcomber' restaurant in Hollywood. It was made especially for a guest suffering from a hangover who reportedly said he felt 'like a zombie'. The object seems to have been to get as many different rums as possible into one drink: white rum, golden rum, dark rum and overproof dark rum, as well as cherry brandy and apricot brandy. The original zombie recipe has undergone various permutations from bar to bar. If you like rum, you'll love this 'regal' variation.*

## Ingredients:

crushed ice
1 measure white rum
1 measure golden rum
1 measure dark rum
3 drops bitters
1 teaspoon soft brown sugar
juice of 1 lemon
juice of 1 orange
juice of ½ grapefruit
lime slices
orange slices

# Rum

## Method:

Put just under a highball glassful of crushed ice into the mixing glass.
Pour on the lemon, orange and grapefruit juices.
Add the bitters and the sugar. Pour in the three rums and stir vigorously.
Pour unstrained into a highball glass and garnish with the lime and orange slices.

| method: | SHAKER |
|---|---|
| glass: | COLLINS |
| garnish: | MINT SPRIG & SPENT LIME SHELL |

# Mai Tai

*Victor 'Trader Vic' Bergeron (1901–91) was one of the most creative restaurateurs of the 20th century and became famous for his combinations of exotic foods and tropically inspired drinks. In 1944 Trader Vic invented the Mai Tai – Tahitian for 'the best' – using the finest ingredients he could find: a mix of 17-year-old J. Wray & Nephew rum, triple sec, orgeat (a non-alcoholic almond-flavoured syrup), sugar syrup and lime juice. When the Mai Tai was introduced to Hawaii in 1953, it was so popular that, within a year, all the stocks of 17-year-old rum in the world were exhausted, and the cocktail had to be reinvented using a blend of rums. What follows is the 'standard' bar recipe for a classic Mai Tai.*

# Rum

## Method:

Place all the ingredients into a shaker with a glass of crushed ice and shake briefly. Pour into the collins glass. Add the spent lime shell and garnish with the mint sprig. Serve with a straw and a stirrer.

## Ingredients:

1 measure white rum
1 measure dark rum
⅔ measure triple sec/Cointreau
⅓ measure orgeat (substitute: amaretto)
⅓ measure sugar syrup
¼ measure grenadine
juice of 1 lime

# Vanderbilt

*This cocktail was devised by 'Guido' of the Kursaal Bar in Ostend, Belgium, in 1912 to mark the visit of American millionaire, Colonel Corneluis Vanderbilt. Shortly afterwards the Colonel drowned when the Lusitania was sunk, and the cocktail became internationally famous.*

## Ingredients:

1½ measures cognac

1 measure cherry brandy

1 teaspoon sugar syrup

1 dash angostura bitters

# Rum

## Method:

Into an old fashioned glass filled with broken ice, add the ingredients. Add the lemon twist.

| method: | SHAKER |
| --- | --- |
| glass: | HIGHBALL |
| garnish: | SPRIG OF MINT, SLICES OF LIME AND PINEAPPLE |

## Zombie

*This incredible rum drink was invented in 1934 by Don Beach at Don the Beachcomber Restaurant in Hollywood, California. Bar-lore tells how Don Beach produced this drink for a guest who, suffering from a hangover, said he felt like a zombie. This is just one of Don Beach's 63 exotic cocktail recipes where, it appears, the aim was to get as much alcohol in one glass as possible! If you don't feel like a zombie before, you may just well feel like one afterwards!*

# Rum

## Method:

Place all the ingredients except the over-proof dark rum in a shaker with a glass worth of crushed ice. Shake briefly and strain into a highball glass filled with crushed ice. Garnish with a sprig of mint and slices of lime and pineapple. Add straws and dribble the over-proof dark rum on top with a long-handled bar spoon.

## Ingredients:

½ measure light rum
1 measure golden rum
½ measure dark rum
½ measure cherry brandy
½ measure apricot brandy
2 measures pineapple juice
1 measure orange juice
¾ measure lime juice
½ measure papaya juice
¼ measure orgeat
⅓ measure over-proof dark rum

# St. Lucia

*One to recall the tropical paradise of the beautiful island of St. Lucia.*

## Ingredients:

2 measures white or golden rum

I measure dry vermouth

I measure Curaçao

juice of ½ orange

I teaspoon grenadine

# Rum

## Method:

Place the ingredients in a shaker with some ice cubes and shake vigourously. Pour, without straining, into a highball glass and decorate with the orange peel spiral and the cherry.

| method: | SHAKER |
|---|---|
| glass: | COCKTAIL |
| garnish: | VERY THIN SLICE OF LEMON |

# Bahamas

*A peachy-banana delight.*

## Rum

### Method:

Put some ice cubes in the shaker, pour in the ingredients and shake well. Strain into a chilled cocktail glass and drop in a very thin slice of lemon.

## Ingredients:

I measure white rum
I measure Southern Comfort
I measure lemon juice
I dash creme de banane

# Bali Punch

## Ingredients:

1½ measures white rum

½ measure coconut rum (such as
   Malibu or Batida de Coco)

1 measure lime juice

2 measures passion fruit juice

2 measures orangeade

½ measure pineapple syrup

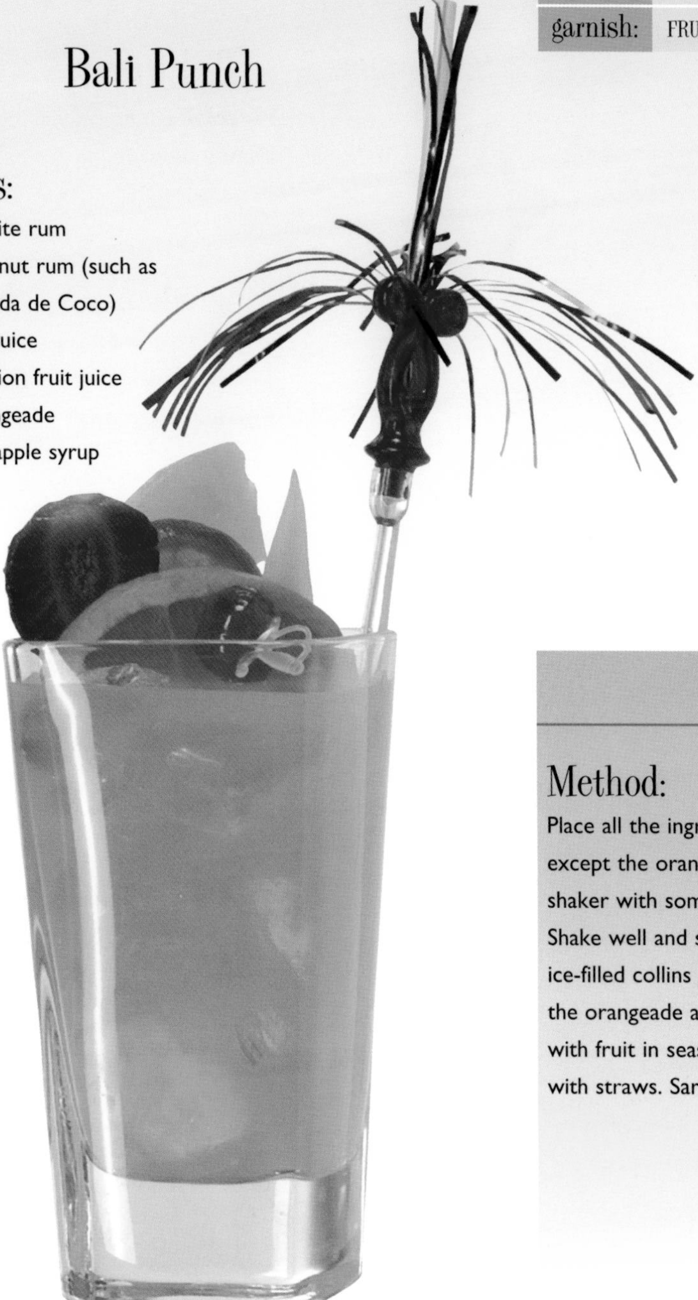

# Rum

## Method:

Place all the ingredients
except the orangeade into a
shaker with some ice cubes.
Shake well and strain into an
ice-filled collins glass. Add
the orangeade and garnish
with fruit in season. Serve
with straws. Sarong optional!

| method: | BUILD |
|---|---|
| glass: | OLD-FASHIONED |

# Ti Punch

*This lime-flavoured drink is a traditional aperitif on the
French-speaking islands of the Caribbean.*

## Ingredients:

1 whole lime
2 measures white rum
1 measure sugar syrup

# Rum

## Method:

Wash the lime, top and tail
and slice thinly. Put the lime
slices into the old-fashioned
glass and, with the flat end of
a bar spoon, crush them to
release the juice. Pour in the
rum and sugar syrup and top
up with broken ice. Muddle
together, add short straws
and serve. *A vôtre santé, cher!*

# Mulata

*This lime-flavoured cocktail was created in the 1940s by*
*Cuban barman extraordinaire, Jose Maria Vazquez.*

## Ingredients:

1¾ measures golden rum
¼ measure dark creme de
cacao
juice of ½ lime

## Rum

## Method:

Put a glass of crushed ice in
the shaker and squeeze in
the lime juice. Add the
golden rum and dark creme
de cacao and shake briefly.
Pour, unstrained, into a large
cocktail glass.

| method: | SHAKER |
|---|---|
| glass: | WINE GLASS |

# Mustique Whammy

*From the hideaway of the rich and famous, the Mustique Whammy features Champagne – naturally, darling!*

## Ingredients:

1 measure golden rum
1 measure orange juice
½ measure lemon juice
¼ measure grenadine
3½ measures well-chilled
  champagne

# Rum

## Method:

Place all the ingredients, except the champagne, into a shaker with some ice cubes and shake until a froth forms. Strain into a wine glass and pour in the chilled champagne.

# Pisang Garuda

*The mythical Garuda – part human, part bird – from ancient Hindu Sanskrit tales is the national emblem of Indonesia, from which comes the green banana liqueur pisang ambon used in this recipe. Because it uses green bananas, pisang ambon has a somewhat different taste to other creme de bananes.*

*But if you don't have any of the Indonesian variety, one of the less sweet creme liqueurs is equally delicious. Mandarine Napoleon is another type of Curaçao, this time made with the skins of Sicilian tangerines as opposed to the bitter Caribbean oranges, and is coloured with carotene to create the vivid yellow colour. Again, at a pinch, if you don't have any of this liquid gold to hand, you can substitute it with Grand Marnier.*

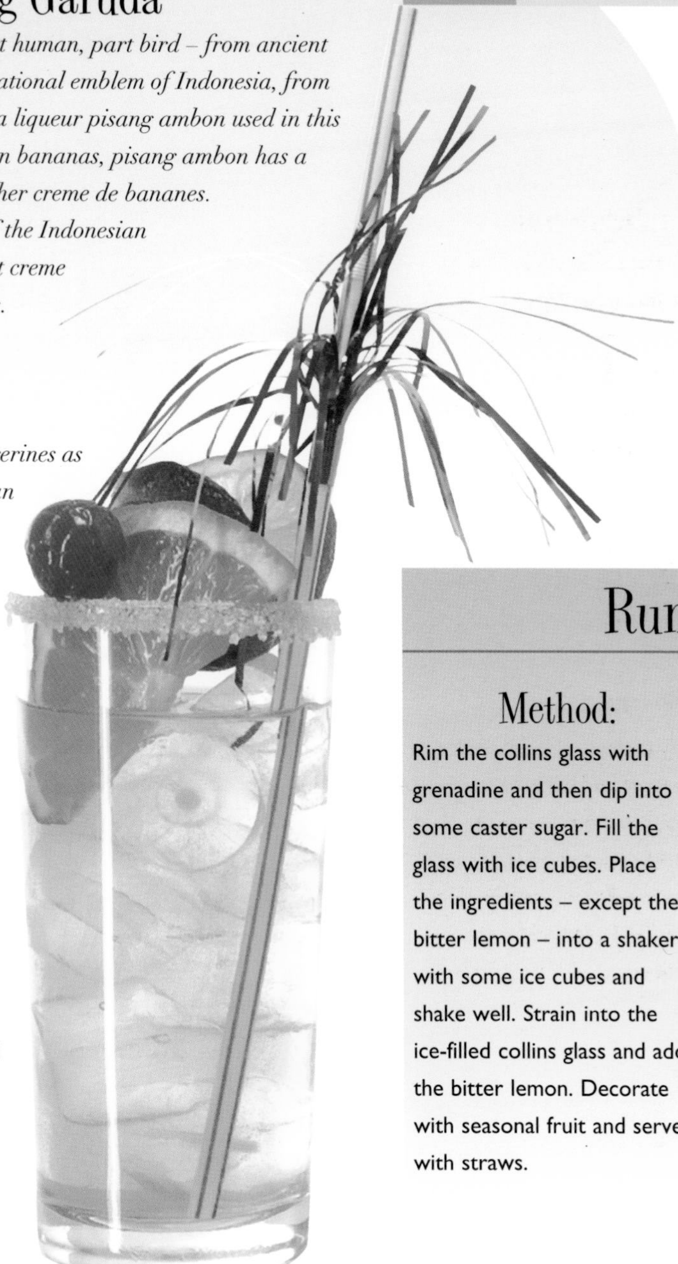

## Ingredients:

1½ measures pisang ambon
  (Substitute: creme de
  banane)
1 measure white rum
½ measure Mandarine
  Napoleon (substitute: Grand
  Marnier)
4 measures sparkling
  bitter lemon

# Rum

## Method:

Rim the collins glass with grenadine and then dip into some caster sugar. Fill the glass with ice cubes. Place the ingredients – except the bitter lemon – into a shaker with some ice cubes and shake well. Strain into the ice-filled collins glass and add the bitter lemon. Decorate with seasonal fruit and serve with straws.

| method: | BUILD |
|---|---|
| glass: | GOBLET OR OVERSIZED WINE GLASS |
| garnish: | SLICE OF LEMON AND A CHERRY |

# Stratocaster

*A delightful, refreshing fruit-flavoured rum-based drink
that's out of this world.*

## Ingredients:

1 measure dark rum

1 measure creme de cassis

1 teaspoon lemon juice

1 measure lemonade

1 measure soda water

# Rum

## Method:

Fill a goblet or oversized
wine glass with broken ice.
Pour in the rum, cassis,
lemon juice, lemonade and
soda water. Garnish with a
slice of lemon and a cherry,
and serve with short straws.

# Coconut Grove

*One recipe to remember when you're cast away on a topical island!*

## Ingredients:

1½ measures coconut rum
  (Malibu or Batida de Coco)
1 measure creme de banane
1 measure white rum
4 measures pineapple juice
1 teaspoon lemon juice

# Rum

## Method:

Place all the ingredients in a shaker with some ice cubes and shake well. Strain into an ice-filled collins glass. Decorate with the cherry and slices of lemon and pineapple. Wait patiently for rescue!

| method: | SHAKER |
| glass: | CHAMPAGNE SAUCER |

# Cafe Trinidad

*The perfect way to end a perfect day.*

## Ingredients:

1 measure dark rum –
   preferably Trinidad rum
¾ measure amaretto
¾ measure Tia Maria
1 measure double cream

# Rum

## Method:

Place all the ingredients in a
shaker with some ice cubes
and shake well. Strain into a
champagne saucer.

# Tree House

*An opportunity to use rum tree, the white-rum-based citrus-flavoured liqueur.*

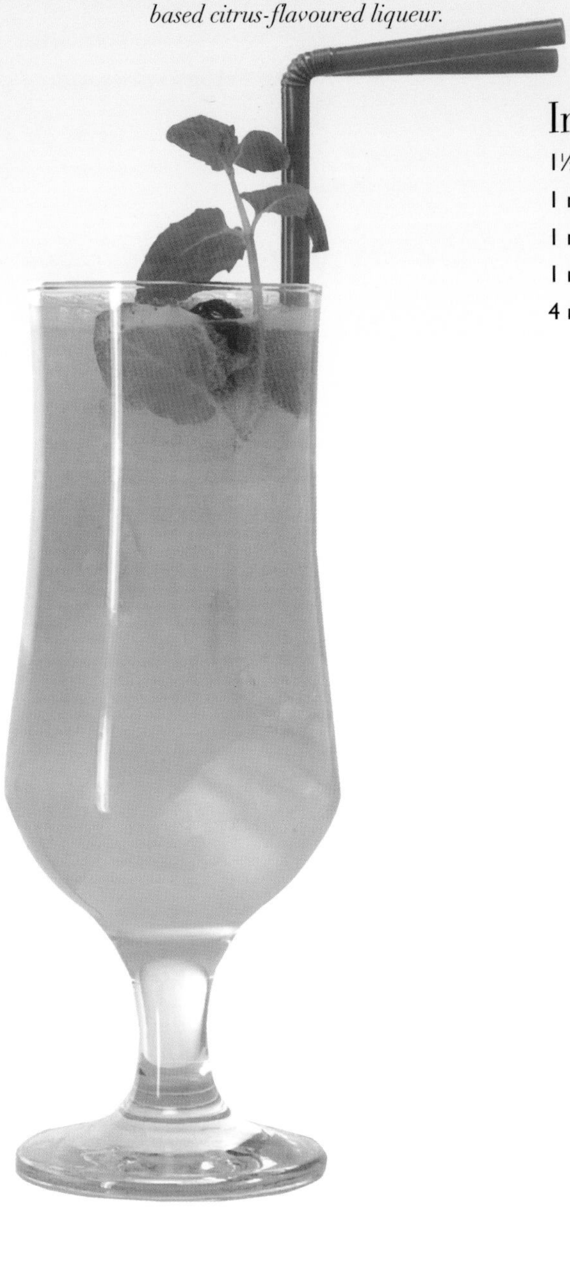

## Ingredients:

1½ measures rum tree

1 measure gold tequila

1 measure grapefruit juice

1 measure pineapple juice

4 measures sparkling bitter lemon

# Rum

## Method:

Fill a piña colada, hurricane or oversized wine glass two-thirds full with ice. Pour in the ingredients, finishing with the sparkling bitter lemon. Garnish with the sprig of mint and the cherry and serve with straws.

# Caribbean Harvest

*A medley of tropical fruit flavours in one glass.*

## Ingredients:

1 measure white rum
1 measure coconut rum
  (Malibu or Batida de Coco)
½ measure creme de banane
1 measure passion fruit juice
1 measure mango juice
1 teaspoon grenadine

# Rum

## Method:

Place all the ingredients in a
shaker with some ice cubes
and shake vigourously. Strain
into a chilled cocktail glass.

# Black Widow

*Always remember: the female of the species is more deadly than the male!*

## Ingredients:

1 measure white rum

1 measure kahlua

# Rum

## Method:

Fill an old-fashioned glass two-thirds full with broken ice. Pour in the light rum and the kahlua. Serve with a stirrer and a very seductive smile.

# Marrakech Express

*Conjure up memories of the casbah with this luxurious long drink.*

## Ingredients:

I measure white rum

I measure dry vermouth

I measure white creme de cacao

2 measures grapefruit juice

I measure mandarin juice

½ measure lime juice

I level teaspoon caster sugar

# Rum

## Method:

Place all the ingredients in a shaker with a glassful of broken ice and shake well. Pour, unstrained, into a collins glass.

# Heat Wave

*One to be enjoyed anywhere in the world*
*when the sun comes out.*

## Ingredients:

1¼ measures coconut rum
    (Malibu or Batido de Coco)
½ measure peach schnapps
3 measures pineapple juice
3 measures orange juice
½ measure grenadine

# Rum

## Method:

Half-fill the flute with finely
broken ice and pour in all the
ingredients – except the
grenadine. Top with the
grenadine and garnish with
the slice of fresh peach.

| method: | MIXING GLASS |
|---|---|
| glass: | HIGHBALL |
| garnish: | SLICE OF LEMON AND A MINT SPRIG |

# Zombie Christopher

*The king of exotic cocktails, Don Beach, created the original Zombie (see page 54) in 1934. Since then a number of equally wonderful variations have appeared including the Zombie Prince and this wonderfully coloured Zombie Christophe.*

## Ingredients:

juice of 1 lime
juice of ½ orange
250 ml/8 fl oz pineapple juice
1 measure blue Curaçao
1 measure white rum
1 measure golden rum
½ measure dark rum

# Rum

## Method:

Put some ice cubes in a mixing glass and squeeze on the lime juice, pressing hard to release the oil from the skin. Pour on the other juices and liquors – except the dark rum – and stir vigourously. Pour, without straining, into a highball glass. Top with the dark rum and stir gently. Garnish with the mint sprig and lemon slice and serve with a stirrer.

# Lost Bikini

*Loose all inhibitions and 'go native'!*

## Ingredients:

¾ measure Galliano

¾ measure amaretto

½ measure white rum

½ measure lime juice

2 measures mandarin juice

# Rum

## Method:

Place all the ingredients in a shaker with some ice cubes and shake vigourously. Strain into a cocktail glass and garnish with the two cherries.

| method: | SHAKER |
|---------|--------|
| glass: | HIGHBALL |
| garnish: | SLICE OF LEMON |

# Green Caribbean

## Ingredients:

1½ measures Midori melon
  liqueur
1½ measures white rum
soda water

## Rum

### Method:

Place all the ingredients
except the soda water into a
shaker with some ice cubes
and shake well. Strain into an
ice-filled highball glass,
garnish with a lemon slice
and top with soda water.

# Worried Monk

*Perhaps the Carthusian monks never envisaged
their health-inducing elixir being mixed with
other spirits for pure pleasure!*

## Ingredients:

1 measure white rum

½ measure coconut rum
(Malibu or Batida de
Coco)

¼ measure triple
sec/Cointreau

¼ measure yellow
Chartreuse

¾ measure lime juice

¼ measure orgeat (almond
syrup)

# Rum

## Method:

Place all the ingredients in a
shaker with some ice cubes
and shake well. Strain into an
old-fashioned glass three-
quarters filled with broken
ice.

| method: | SHAKER |
| glass: | COLLINS |
| garnish: | SEEDLESS GRAPES |

# Bacchanalian Cocktail

*In honour of Bacchus, the Roman god of wine.*

## Ingredients:

1 measure white rum
½ measure brandy
½ measure yellow Chartreuse
2 measures red grape juice
1 measure orange juice
½ measure lime juice
3 measures lemonade

# Rum

## Method:

Place all the ingredients except the lemonade in a shaker with some ice cubes. Shake well and strain into an ice-filled collins glass and garnish with the grapes.

# Five Hundred Proof

*A mixed drink for the connoisseur: the proof rating of the five spirits used in this drink should total over 500!*

## Ingredients:

½ measure over-proof white rum

½ measure 100-proof bourbon

½ measure green Chartreuse

½ measure 100-proof vodka

½ measure Southern Comfort

1 measure lemon juice

1 measure orange juice

½ measure sugar syrup

½ measure grenadine

# Rum

## Method:

Place all the ingredients in a shaker with some ice cubes and shake well. Strain into an ice-filled pilsner glass and garnish with a cherry on a stick.

| method: | BUILD |
|---|---|
| glass: | FLUTE |
| garnish: | TWIST OF ORANGE |

# Tomorrow We Sail

*A name that conjures up the luxurious ocean liners, but one to enjoy at any port of call!*

## Ingredients:

1 teaspoon triple sec/Cointreau
½ measure dark rum
½ measure LBV port
chilled champagne

# Rum

## Method:

Pour the triple sec/Cointreau, rum and port into the Champagne flute and add the chilled champagne and garnish with a twist of orange.

# Arrowhead

*A delightful fruit-rum flavour, hints of peach, bananas and citrus fruits. Traditionally served on the rock, it's also very nice long, with more lemonade!*

## Ingredients:

1 measure dark rum

½ measure Southern Comfort

½ measure creme de banane

¼ measure lime juice

2½ measures (or more) lemonade

# Rum

## Method:

Add the ingredients to an old-fashioned glass, three-quarters full of broken ice. If you prefer a longer drink, use a collins glass, and top with more lemonade.

| method: | BUILD |
| glass: | HIGHBALL |
| garnish: | MINT SPRIG (OPTIONAL) |

## Ingredients:

I measure golden rum
I measure Punt e Mes
½ measure creme de fraise
4 measures lemonade

# Escape Route

*This refreshing strawberry-flavoured drink traditionally used Punt e Mes, one of the world's most popular vermouths. In 1786 Antonio Carpano opened the Carpano Bar behind the Turin Stock Exchange, Italy, where he offered variations of the basic Carpano vermouth – some sweet, some bitter. Stockbrokers who regularly frequented the bar began to grade the relative bitterness of the vermouths in 'points'. In 1876, Punt e Mes (point and a half) was launched commercially.*

# Rum

## Method:

Simply add the ingredients to an ice-filled highball glass and garnish with a sprig of mint and escape into pure bliss.

# Hurricane

*One to enjoy when you've got to ride out a storm!*

## Ingredients:

1½ measures dark rum

1 measure light rum

1 measure lime juice

2 measures passion fruit juice

1 measure pineapple juice

1 measure orange juice

½ measure blackcurrant syrup

# Rum

## Method:

Place the ingredients in a shaker with two or three ice cubes and shake well. Strain into an ice-filled piña colada or oversized wine glass, filled with broken ice. Garnish with a sprig of mint and slice of lemon.

| method: | BUILD |
| --- | --- |
| glass: | OLD-FASHIONED |
| garnish: | FRUIT IN SEASON, TWIST OF LEMON |

# Santa Cruz Fix

*The original recipe for this cherry-rum drink calls for Santa Cruz rum, but you can use a good, dark rum if you wish.*

## Rum

### Method:
Add to old-fashioned glass filled with crushed ice and garnish with fruit in season and a twist of lemon. Serve with straws.

## Ingredients:
2 measures dark rum
1 measure cherry brandy
1 measure lemon juice
¾ measure sugar syrup

| method: | SHAKER |
| glass: | PINA COLADA OR OVERSIZED WINE GLASS |
| garnish: | SPENT SHELL OF LIME |

## Sun City

*A great fruity flavour that's perfect for a hot sunny afternoon.*

### Ingredients:

1 measure light rum
½ measure dark rum
½ measure Galliano
½ measure apricot brandy
2 measures pineapple juice
juice of ¼ lime
4 measures lemonade

# Rum

### Method:

Place all the ingredients except the lemonade into a shaker with two or three ice cubes. Shake well and strain into ice filled piña colada or oversized wine glass. Drop in the spent shell of the lime and top up with lemonade. Serve with straws.

| method: | SHAKER |
| --- | --- |
| glass: | COCKTAIL |
| garnish: | SLICE OF LIME AND A CHERRY |

# Hen Night Zipper-ripper

*What more can we say?*

# Rum

## Method:

Place all the ingredients in a shaker with some ice cubes and shake vigourously. Strain into a cocktail glass and garnish with the slice of lime and the cherry.

## Ingredients:

1½ measures white rum

1 measure advocaat

¾ measure mandarin juice

¾ measure lime juice

¼ measure grenadine

# Pan-galactic Gargle Blaster

*You've heard of it, so now's your chance to try it!*

## Ingredients:

1½ measures Midori melon liqueur

½ measure white rum (over-proof rum if available)

½ measure lime juice

¼ measure pineapple syrup

1½ measures lemonade

# Rum

## Method:

Place all the ingredients except the lemonade in a shaker with some ice cubes and shake well. Strain into a flute and add the lemonade.

(with grateful acknowledgement to the late, great Douglas Adams!)

| method: | SHAKER |
|---|---|
| glass: | COLLINS |
| garnish: | SLICE OF LIME AND A CHERRY |

# Zulu

*Raise your glass and give the traditional Zulu toast of 'Ooogy Wawa'.*

## Ingredients:

1 measure dark rum

1 measure dark creme de cacao

½ measure creme de banane

1 measure lime juice

1 teaspoon grenadine

1 teaspoon Pernod or Ricard

4 measures cold cola

# Rum

## Method:

Place all the ingredients except the cola in a shaker with ice cubes and shake well. Strain into an ice-filled collins glass and add the cola. Garnish with the lime slice and cherry.

# Angel's Treat

*This cocktail is definitely one for the chocoholics!*

## Ingredients:

1½ measures dark rum

1 measure amaretto

1½ measures whipping cream

½ teaspoon sifted cocoa powder

# Rum

## Method:

Place all the ingredients into a shaker with two or three ice cubes and shake well. Strain and pour into a cocktail glass and decorate with chocolate flakes.

| method: | SHAKER |
|---------|--------|
| glass: | COCKTAIL |
| garnish: | TWO SLICES OF BANANA SPEARED EITHER SIDE OF A CHERRY |

# Banana Bliss

*A creamy banana confection that always satisfies.*

# Rum

## Method:

Put all the ingredients except the grenadine into a shaker with two or three ice cubes and shake well. Strain and pour into cocktail glass. Carefully pour the grenadine inside the rim of the glass so it runs down the inside leaving a red smear as it sinks to the bottom. Garnish with two slices of banana speared either side of a maraschino cherry.

## Ingredients:

1¼ measures creme de banane

1¼ measures white rum

¾ measure orange juice

1¼ measures double cream

2 teaspoons grenadine

2 drops bitters

# Fluffy Duck

*This drink gives you the opportunity to use the Dutch speciality, Advocaat. Essentially it is a 'custom-made' egg nogg with a velvet texture and somewhat bland taste. In the Netherlands it is drunk as an aperitif and as a digestif, but it does mix well – and you can add it to a mug of hot chocolate at bedtime too!*

## Ingredients:

1 measure white rum
1 measure Advocaat
⅓ measure fresh cream
lemonade

# Rum

## Method:

Pour the rum and Advocaat into a highball glass, add the lemonade and mix well. Pour the cream carefully over the back of a spoon so it floats on top. Decorate with the strawberry and mint spring and serve with straws and a stirrer.

| method: | BLENDER |
|---|---|
| glass: | PINA COLADA, GOBLET OR HURRICANE |

# Love in the Afternoon

*If you like strawberries, you'll love this – and you don't just have to reserve it for afternoons!*

## Rum

### Method:

Keep a lovely strawberry aside for the garnish and place the other ingredients in the blender and blend until smooth. Add half a glass of crushed ice and blend briefly once more. Pour into a piña colada, goblet or hurricane glass and garnish with the strawberry. Serve with straws.

### Ingredients:

2 measures dark rum

½ measure creme de fraise

1 measure orange juice

¾ measure coconut cream

½ measure sugar syrup

½ measure whipping cream

3 to 4 strawberries, plus one for garnish

# Devil's Tail

*Just a little wicked!*

## Rum

## Ingredients:

1½ measure light rum

1 measure vodka

1 tablespoon lime juice

1½ tablespoon grenadine

1½ tablespoons apricot brandy

## Method:

Combine all the ingredients with half a glass of crushed ice in a blender and blend at low speed. Pour into the champagne flute and add the lime peel twist.

| method: | BLENDER |
| --- | --- |
| glass: | FLUTE |
| garnish: | SPRIG OF MINT |

# Frozen Mint Daiquiri

## Ingredients:

2 measures light rum
1 tablespoon lime juice
6 mint leaves,
1 teaspoon sugar

# Rum

## Method:

Combine all the ingredients
in a blender with a glass of
crushed ice and blend at low
speed. Pour into the flute
and decorate with a sprig of
mint.

# Hummer

*A coffee-rum flavour that can be enjoyed at any time.*

## Ingredients:

1 measure Tia Maria or kahlua
   coffee liqueur
1 measure light rum
2 large scoops vanilla ice cream

## Rum

### Method:

Combine all the ingredients
in a blender and blend briefly.
Pour into a highball glass and
serve with a straw.

178

| method: | BLENDER |
| glass: | PARFAIT OR WHITE WINE GLASS |
| garnish: | WHIPPED CREAM AND A CHERRY |

# Maraschino Cherry

## Ingredients:

1 measure light rum
½ measure amaretto
½ measure peach schnapps
1 measure cranberry juice
1 measure pineapple juice
1 dash grenadine

# Rum

## Method:

Place all the ingredients in a blender with two to three glasses of ice and blend until smooth. Pour into parfait or white wine glass and top with whipped cream and a maraschino cherry.

| method: | BLENDER |
| glass: | PILSNER |
| garnish: | PINEAPPLE WEDGE AND A CHERRY |

# The Big Chill

*Chill out with one of these.*

## Ingredients:

1½ measures rum

1 measure pineapple juice

1 measure orange juice

1 measure cranberry juice

1 measure cream of coconut

# Rum

## Method:

Combine the ingredients with a glass of ice in a blender and blend until smooth. Pour into a pilsner glass and decorate with the pineapple wedge and the maraschino cherry.

| method: | BLENDER |
| --- | --- |
| glass: | GOBLET |
| garnish: | SLICE OF LIME AND A CHERRY |

# Frozen Key Lime

*A wonderfully sharp and tangy lime flavour.*

## Rum

### Method:

Blend all the ingredients with half a glass of ice in a blender until smooth. Pour into a goblet and decorate with the lime slice and the cherry.

### Ingredients:

2 measures rum (light or dark, or try half and half)

1½ measures lime juice

3 tablespoons vanilla ice cream

# Frozen Miami

## Ingredients:

2½ measures light rum

½ measure white creme de menthe

½ measure lime juice

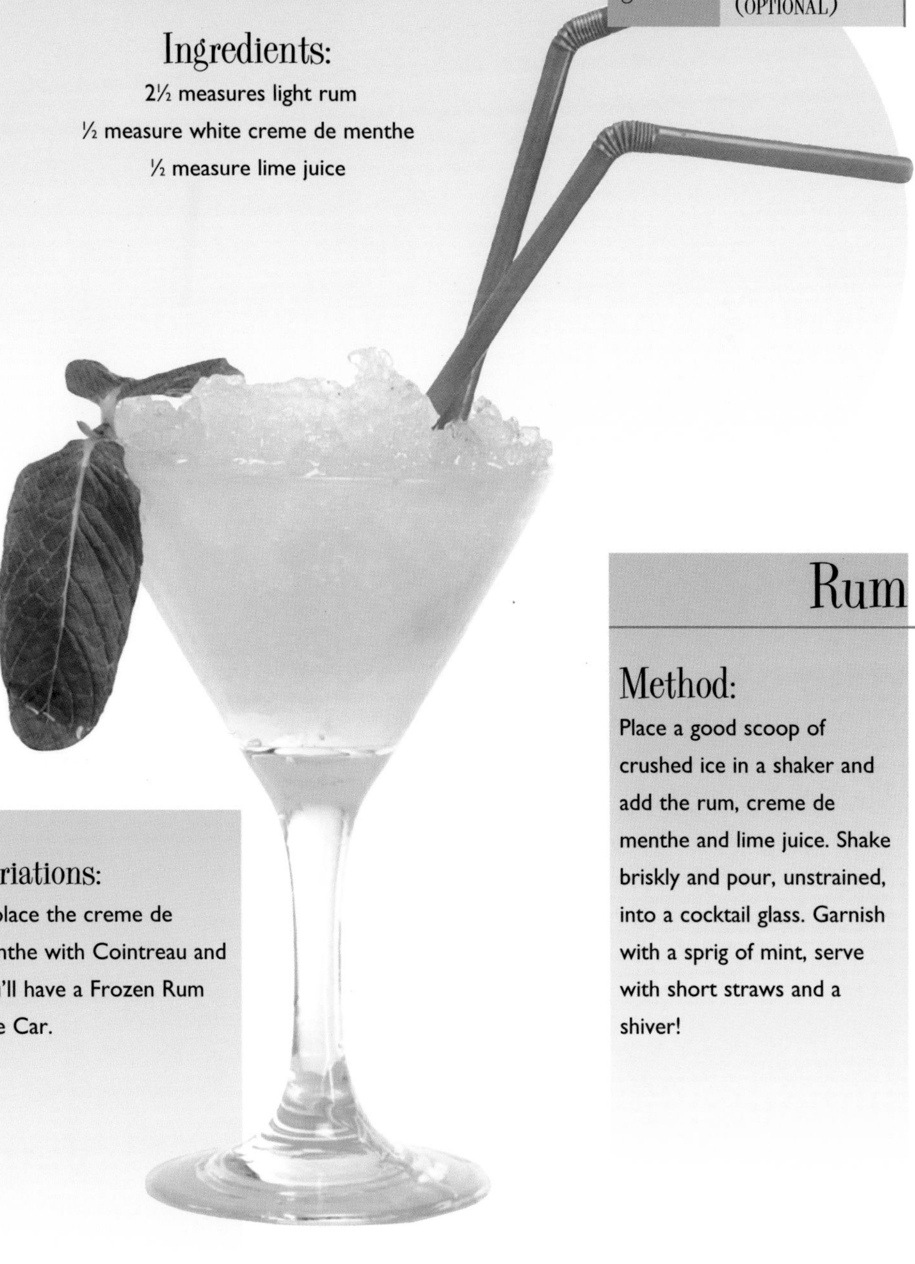

# Rum

## Method:

Place a good scoop of crushed ice in a shaker and add the rum, creme de menthe and lime juice. Shake briskly and pour, unstrained, into a cocktail glass. Garnish with a sprig of mint, serve with short straws and a shiver!

## Variations:

Replace the creme de menthe with Cointreau and you'll have a Frozen Rum Side Car.

| method: | MIXING GLASS |
|---|---|
| glass: | SHOT |

# Blue Marlin

*The smoothness of the rum combined with the sweet orange flavour of the Curaçao and balanced by the sharpness of the fresh lime juice is a delight. Curaçao comes in a range of 'novelty' colours in addition to the clear, colourless version, but the flavour is always orange. The bright blue Curaçao used here goes someway in explaining an old Arabic saying in Tunisia, North Africa, which goes 'The land is blue like an orange'!*

## Ingredients:

1 measure light rum
½ measure blue Curaçao
1 measure lime juice

# Rum

## Method:

Stir the light rum, blue Curaçao and lime juice in a mixing glass with two or three ice cubes. Strain into a shot glass.

# Ship's Cat

*In the UK, this shooter is often made with Vimto – an odd, though popular, purple-coloured fruit cordial that is diluted with water. If you don't have a bottle of Vimto handy, substitute with creme de cassis. In both cases you'll have a delightfully fruity-rum flavoured drink.*

## Ingredients:

1 measure over-proof dark rum
1 teaspoon Vimto or creme de cassis

# Rum

## Method:

Put one ice cube in a shot glass, add the Vimto or creme de cassis and the rum.

**method:** MIXING GLASS

**glass:** SHOT

# Silver Spider

## Ingredients:
½ measure light rum
½ measure vodka
½ measure triple sec or Cointreau
½ measure white creme de menthe

# Rum

## Method:
Place all the ingredients in a mixing glass with two or three ice cubes and stir. Strain into a shot glass.

# Vodka cocktails

Golden Russian
see page 197.

Vodka is a paradox among spirits, for it has no taste, no aroma and no colour. It is nothing more (and nothing less) than pure, high-proof grain alcohol (usually wheat, corn or rye with a little added malt) and water. Nevertheless, vodka can, in fact, be made from any manner of ingredients: in the Czech Republic, potatoes are used; in Turkey they use beets, in Britain, molasses, while in the United States, vodka is made from grains. It is the starch in these ingredients that produces the ethyl alcohol in the distillation process.

The word vodka is a diminutive of the Russian *voda*, meaning 'water'; vodka is literally 'little water', but this 'little water' can pack a very strong punch! Vodkas are available from 35 to the 80 per cent proof of pure Polish spirit. Vodka was mentioned as early as the 12th century in Russian literature, but at the time it referred to any spirit, regardless of how it was distilled or flavoured. By the 17th century, vodka

played an important part in both civil and religious
ceremonies. It was served at all imperial banquets
and was drunk ceremonially at religious festivals
and as part of church ritual.

Poland and Russia continue to produce a wide
variety of spiced and fruit versions and in a range of
colours. The most celebrated is the delicately flavoured
'Zubrowka', with a blade of grass in each bottle – which also
gives it a yellow-green colour. The grass is that found most
appetising to the wild European bison which graze on the
borders of Poland and Russia. Pertsovka and Okhotchinaya
are fiery 'pepper' vodkas, the former infused with cayenne and
capsicum, the latter with additional herbs, and are said to have
been 'invented' by Tsar Peter the Great, who added pepper to
his drink. One governor of Moscow apparently trained a large
bear to serve pepper vodka to his guests. If they declined, the
bear removed the unfortunate guest's clothes one item at a
time. You can make your own pepper vodka by steeping a hot
Mexican or Italian pepper in a bottle of neutral vodka and
leaving it there for as long as possible.

Jarzebiak is flavoured with rowan berries (the fruit of the
mountain ash) and is a delicate pink colour. Lemon vodka,

Harvey Wallbanger
see page 198.

Cosmopolitan
see page 192.

with a yellow colour, can also be easily made at home by grating a small quantity of lemon peel, letting it dry for two or three days and then adding it to the bottle. Allow it to stand for around ten days, shaking it occasionally, and then decant the liquid.

The aim of producing unflavoured vodka was not simply for the neutral spirit to make a wonderful base for mixed drinks. The original purpose was, in fact, to produce a strong spirit that would not freeze in the extreme cold of the Eastern European winters! Filtering the spirit through charcoal or fine quartz sand removes the aroma and taste. Vodka is not aged, but bottled straightaway. There is, however, a spirit called Starka (which means 'old') vodka, which has been aged in wine casks for ten years.

| method: | BUILD (OR CAN BE SHAKEN) |
|---|---|
| glass: | HIGHBALL |
| garnish: | CELERY STICK WITH LEAVES (OPTIONAL), WEDGE OF LIME |

# Bloody Mary

*Harry's New York Bar in Paris in 1921 was the birthplace of this classic drink. In 1921 barman Fernand 'Pete' Petiot mixed tomato juice, vodka, salt, pepper and Worcestershire sauce. While there was nothing new about the combination of vodka and tomato, the name was. According to many accounts, Petiot named his mix in honour of Hollywood actress Mary Pickford.*

*The celery-stick garnish originated in the 1960s: when a drinker at the Pump Room in the Ambassador Hotel in Chicago received his Bloody Mary without the usual swizzle stick, he picked up a celery stick from a tray of crudites and used it to stir his drink and the garnish was born. Eat your garnish if you want to!*

# Vodka

## Method:

In a highball glass two-thirds filled with ice cubes, pour the tomato juice, lemon (or lemon and lime) juice and the vodka.

Add the spices and stir.

Garnish with the lime wedge and celery stick.

Add a stirrer.

Play around with the quantities of spices and sauces: some people like it 'mild', some, as they say, like it 'hot'!

## Ingredients:

ice cubes

2 measures vodka

5 measures tomato juice

½ teaspoon lemon juice
(or a less sharp mix using lemon and lime juice if preferred)

2–3 dashes Worcestershire sauce

1–2 dashes Tabasco sauce
(or more if you like it spicy)

1 pinch salt
(celery salt if possible)

1 pinch black pepper

1 celery stalk with leaves
(optional)

# Brazen hussy

*The name conjures up images of 'jazz babies' and platinum-blonde Hollywood starlets.*

## Ingredients:

ice cubes

1 measure vodka

1 measure triple sec or
Cointreau

1½ measures lemon juice

## Vodka

## Method:

Hall-fill the shaker with ice
cubes.

Add all the ingredients and
shake well.

Strain into a cocktail glass.

| method: | BUILD |
| --- | --- |
| glass: | HIGHBALL |
| garnish: | LEMON WEDGE |

# Bullfrog

*A lovely, long drink for a hot summer's evening.*

## Ingredients:

ice cubes
2 measures vodka
1 teaspoon triple sec or
Cointreau
4 measures lemonade
1 lemon wedge

# Vodka

## Method:

Almost fill the highball glass
with ice cubes.
Add the vodka, triple sec or
Cointreau and lemonade.
Stir well and garnish with the
lemon wedge.

# Cape Codder

*If you like the dryness of cranberry juice, try this
out. Simple and delicious, it's a
refreshing alternative to the usual
'vodka-tonic' combination.*

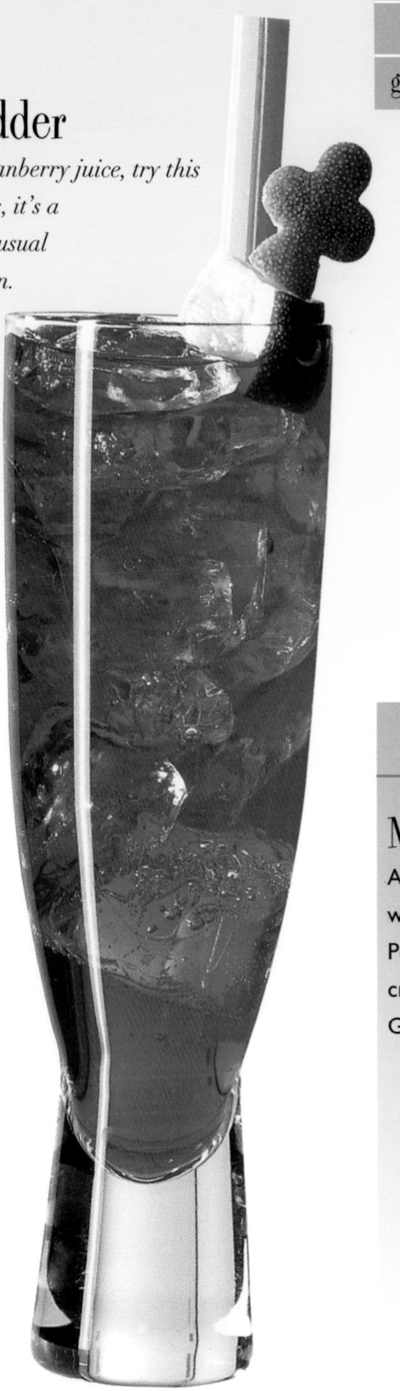

## Ingredients:

ice cubes

2 measures vodka

5 measures cranberry juice

1 lime wedge

# Vodka

## Method:

Almost fill the highball glass
with ice cubes.
Pour in the vodka and
cranberry juice and stir well.
Garnish with the lime wedge.

| Method: | SHAKER |
|---|---|
| glass: | COCKTAIL |
| garnish: | TWIST OF LIME |

# Cosmopolitan

*A relatively new drink from America, the cosmopolitan
is a Martini-style aperitif that's growing in popularity.*

## Ingredients:

ice cubes
1½ measures vodka
1 measure triple sec
or Cointreau
1 dash cranberry juice
(or to taste)
1 lime twist

# Vodka

## Method:

Half-fill the shaker with
ice cubes.
Add the vodka, triple sec or
Cointreau and cranberry
juice.
Shake sharply and strain into
well-chilled cocktail glass.
Garnish with the lime
twist and discard.

## Variations:

Adjust the measures of
cranberry juice to suit your
taste. You could even add
some more lime juice if you
want your cosmopolitan a
little more sour.

# Cooch Behar

*This drink was devised by the Maharajah of Cooch Behar,
and it's a great drink to have with a curry.
Although an Indian recipe, the vodka used originally was a
Russian pepper vodka, such as Okhotnichaya.
You can make your own pepper vodka quite easily:
simply steep a hot Mexican or Italian pepper in regular
vodka for a few weeks.*

## Ingredients:

ice cubes
2 measures pepper vodka
4 measures tomato juice

## Vodka

## Method:

Half-fill the shaker with ice
cubes.
Add the vodka and tomato
juice and shake thoroughly.
Strain and serve on the rocks
in an old-fashioned glass.

| method: | SHAKER |
|---|---|
| glass: | COLLINS OR HIGHBALL |

# Down-under fizz

*This attractive-looking drink pays homage to the Antipodes. The clear top of soda water floats on the vodka, grenadine and orange juice 'sun' at the bottom of the glass to be sucked up through a straw!*

## Ingredients:

ice cubes

3 measures vodka

½ measure lemon juice

1 measure orange juice

½ teaspoon grenadine

soda water

# Vodka

## Method:

Half-fill the shaker with ice cubes.

Add the lemon and orange juice, grenadine and vodka.

Shake well and pour unstrained into a Collins/highball glass.

Top with soda water and serve with a straw.

# Fire and ice

*Use some more of the pepper vodka you've made*
*(see page 87) in this neat little cocktail.*

## Ingredients:

ice cubes

2 measures pepper vodka

1½ teaspoons dry vermouth

# Vodka

## Method:

Half-fill the mixing glass with
ice cubes.
Add the pepper vodka and
dry vermouth and stir well.
Strain into a cocktail glass.
As with the Martini, try
different proportions of the
vermouth until you find the
one you like best.

method: BUILD

glass: HIGHBALL

# Firefly

*Not only is this an attractive drink, it's the best way to drink grapefruit juice! The grenadine is just enough to cut through the sour of the juice.*

## Ingredients:

ice cubes

2 measures vodka

4 measures grapefruit juice

I teaspoon grenadine

# Vodka

## Method:

Almost fill a highball glass with ice cubes.
Pour the vodka and grapefruit juice into the glass.
Drop the grenadine carefully into the centre of the drink.
If you really like the sharpness of the juice, leave out the grenadine and you'll have made yourself a greyhound.

# Golden Russian

*Many vodka-based drinks inevitably have names associated with Russia, such as the Soviet (page 103) and the Moscow mule (page 99). Try a golden Russian on a cold, snowy night!*

## Ingredients:

broken ice

1½ measures vodka

1 measure Galliano

1 teaspoon lime juice

1 lime slice

## Vodka

## Method:

To a highball glass, three-quarters full of broken ice, add the vodka, Galliano and lime juice and mix gently. Garnish with the slice of lime.

## Variations:

If you use the Italian liqueur Strega (a sweet and spicy mix made from more than 70 herbs, said to have been created by beautiful maidens who, for some unknown reason, disguised themselves as witches), you'll make a warlock.

| method: | SHAKER |
|---|---|
| glass: | HIGHBALL |
| garnish: | ORANGE SLICE |

# Harvey Wallbanger

*Harvey, according to the legend, was a California surfer. After losing an important contest, he consoled himself with a screwdriver, but added a dash of Galliano. After several drinks, he tried to leave the bar, but unfortunately kept bumping into furniture and the wall. Harvey 'the Wallbanger' became his nickname and the famous drink was born.*

## Ingredients:

ice cubes
2 measures vodka
¾ measure Galliano
5 measures orange
juice

# Vodka

## Method:

Half-fill the shaker with ice cubes.
Add the vodka and orange juice and shake well.
Strain into an ice-filled highball glass.
Gently float the Galliano on top and garnish with the orange slice.

# Hawaiian vodka

*The tropical sunshine of Hawaii melts the icy heart of the
Russian steppes in this delicious and refreshing mix.*

## Ingredients:

ice cubes

3 measures vodka

I measure pineapple juice

I measure orange juice

I measure lemon juice

I teaspoon grenadine

I lemon slice

# Vodka

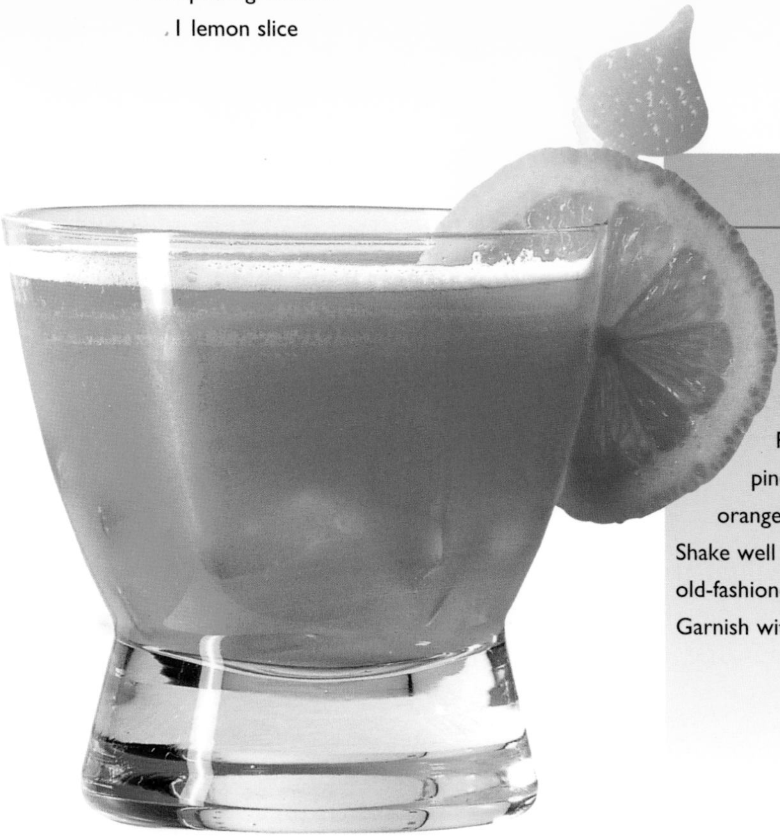

## Method:

Half-fill the
shaker with ice
cubes.
Pour in the
pineapple, lemon and
orange juice and vodka.
Shake well and strain into an
old-fashioned glass.
Garnish with the lemon slice.

| method: | MIXING GLASS |
|---|---|
| glass: | COCKTAIL |

# Kamikaze

*Kamikaze is the Japanese for 'divine wind'.*
*The original drink, made with Stolichnaya vodka and a teaspoon*
*of Rose's Lime Juice, was drunk in one go – as fast as the wind –*
*and was designed to get a person drunk quickly.*

## Ingredients:

ice cubes

2 measures vodka

1 teaspoon Rose's Lime Juice

# Vodka

## Method:

Half-fill the mixing glass with ice cubes.

Add the vodka and lime juice.

Stir well and strain into a cocktail glass.

Drink in one go.

| method: | MIXING GLASS |
| glass: | COCKTAIL (OR ON THE ROCKS IN AN OLD-FASHIONED GLASS IF YOU PREFER) |
| garnish: | GREEN OLIVE OR A TWIST OF LEMON (AS PREFERRED) |

# Kangaroo

*This is what some people might call a 'vodkatini'. The original Martini (page 48) was gin-based, but this vodka version is increasingly popular and, like the original, is stirred.*

## Ingredients:

ice cubes

2 measures vodka

1 measure dry vermouth

1 green olive or 1 lemon twist

# Vodka

## Method:

Half-fill the mixing glass with ice cubes.

Add the vodka and the dry vermouth and stir.

Strain into a chilled cocktail glass (or strain over ice cubes in an old-fashioned glass).

Garnish with the green olive or twist of lemon if preferred.

| method: | MIXING GLASS |
|---|---|
| glass: | COCKTAIL |
| garnish: | LEMON TWIST |

# Laughing at the waves

*You probably will be after one of these!*

## Ingredients:

ice cubes

1½ measures vodka

½ measures dry vermouth

½ measure Campari

1 lemon twist

## Vodka

### Method:

Half-fill the mixing glass with ice cubes.

Add the vodka, dry vermouth and Campari.

Stir well and strain into a cocktail glass.

Garnish with the lemon twist.

# Long Island iced tea

*This drink could actually be placed in several sections of
this book since it contains equal measures of vodka, gin, rum,
tequila and triple sec. In early versions, however,
the tequila and triple sec were omitted.*

## Ingredients:

ice cubes
broken ice
½ measure vodka
½ measure gin
½ measure tequila
½ measure white rum
½ measure triple sec
or Cointreau
1 measure lemon juice
½ measure gomme
syrup
3–4 measures cold cola
1 lemon wedge

## Vodka

## Method:

Half-fill the shaker with
ice cubes.
Add the vodka, gin, rum,
tequila, triple sec or
Cointreau, lemon juice and
gomme syrup.
Shake well and strain into a
Collins glass half-full of
broken ice.
Add the cola and garnish
with the lemon wedge.

## Variations:

Leave out the triple sec or
Cointreau for Texas tea. Use
lemonade instead of cola, and
you have Long Island
lemonade. For Long Beach
iced tea, use cranberry juice
in place of the cola.

# Madras

*The colour of this drink is similar to the famous bright
cottons and silks of Madras in southern India.*

## Ingredients:

ice cubes

1½ measures vodka

2 measures cranberry juice

2 measures orange juice

# Vodka

## Method:

Fill a highball glass two-thirds
full with ice cubes.
Pour in the orange juice,
cranberry juice and vodka
and stir.

# Moscow mule

*Despite its name, the Moscow mule is an American invention. In 1947, John Martin, of Heublin & Co, USA, who had acquired the rights to Smirnoff vodka, was trying to find ways to encourage sales. A chance conversation with Jack Morgan, of the Cock 'n' Bull Saloon in Los Angeles, revealed that Morgan was overstocked with ginger ale. They added the two, with a dash of lime juice, and created the Moscow mule, which they originally served in a copper mug. Adjust the amount of vodka to vary the mule's kick.*

## Ingredients:

broken ice cubes
2 measures vodka
1 measure lime juice
4 measures ginger ale
1 lemon and 1 orange slice

### Variations:

Try a Moscow mule with ginger beer in place of ginger ale.

# Vodka

## Method:

Almost fill the highball (or Collins) glass with broken ice.
Pour in the vodka and lime juice.
Add the ginger ale and stir well.
Garnish with the lemon and orange slices, or, for a change, try a slice of cucumber.

| method: | SHAKER |
|---------|--------|
| glass: | HIGHBALL |

# Purple passion
*The purple comes from the addition of red grape juice.*

## Ingredients:
ice cubes
2 measures vodka
2 measures grape juice
2 measures grapefruit juice
1–2 teaspoons castor sugar
(according to taste)

# Vodka

## Method:
Half-fill the shaker with ice cubes.
Add the grape juice and the grapefruit juice.
Add the sugar and then the vodka.
Shake well and strain into a highball glass two-thirds full of ice cubes.

# Salty dog

*This is basically a drink known as a greyhound,
but the difference is that the rim of the highball glass is
'frosted' with salt. Try it and see.*

## Ingredients:

ice cubes

2 teaspoons salt

2 measures vodka

5 measures grapefruit juice

1 lime wedge

## Vodka

## Method:

Place the salt in a saucer.
Rub the rim of the highball
glass with the wedge of lime.
Dip the glass into the salt to
coat the rim thoroughly.
Discard the lime.
Fill the glass two-thirds full
with ice cubes.
Half-fill the shaker with ice
cubes.
Add the vodka and grapefruit
juice and shake well.
Strain into the glass.

## Variations:

For added decoration, why not add a spiral of grapefruit peel? Cut a
thin (as thin as possible) continuous spiral of peel and drape it over
the rim of the glass. Spirals can be cut from any citrus fruit and are the
'traditional' garnish of drinks called 'coolers' (see page 162).

BUILD

HIGHBALL

LIME WEDGE

# Sea breeze

*This drink has undergone some changes since it was first invented. In the 1930s, it was made with gin and grenadine. The more modern version uses vodka, cranberry and grapefruit juice to create a long, fruity drink.*

## Ingredients:

ice cubes

1½ measures vodka

2 measures grapefruit juice

3 measures cranberry juice

1 lime wedge

# Vodka

## Method:

Almost fill the highball glass with ice cubes.

Add the vodka, cranberry and grapefruit juices.

Stir well.

Garnish with the lime wedge.

## Variations:

Still not happy with grapefruit juice? Try pineapple juice instead for a bay breeze!

# Soviet

*A toast to* Glasnost! *One for the James Bonds of the new millennium, perhaps?*

## Ingredients:

ice cubes

3 measures vodka

½ measure dry vermouth

½ measure dry sherry

## Vodka

## Method:

Place the ice cubes in the old-fashioned glass. Add the vodka, vermouth and sherry and stir. *Prosit!*

| method: | SHAKER |
|---|---|
| glass: | ACOLLINS/ HIGHBALL |
| garnish: | CHERRY |

# Slow, comfortable screw against the wall

*One of those incredibly named drinks that everyone's heard about. It's 'slow' because it should properly use sloe gin (basically gin which has had sloe berries macerated in it); 'comfortable' because it uses Southern Comfort (a well-known proprietary blend of bourbon and peach liqueur); 'screw' from the screwdriver, but with the Galliano of the Harvey Wallbanger, hence 'against the wall'. You may wish to try one!*

## Vodka

### Method:

Half-fill the shaker with ice cubes.
Add the vodka, Southern Comfort, gin and orange juice.
Shake and strain into the highball or Collins glass filled with broken ice.
Float the Galliano on the top and garnish with the cherry.
Add straws and a muddler (or use a screwdriver if you prefer).

## Ingredients:

ice cubes
broken ice
1 measure vodka
¾ measure Southern Comfort
¾ measure gin – preferably sloe gin
½ measure Galliano
5 measures orange juice
1 cherry

# Volga

## Ingredients:

ice cubes
broken ice
2 measures vodka
½ measure lime juice
½ measure orange juice
1 dash grenadine
1 dash bitters

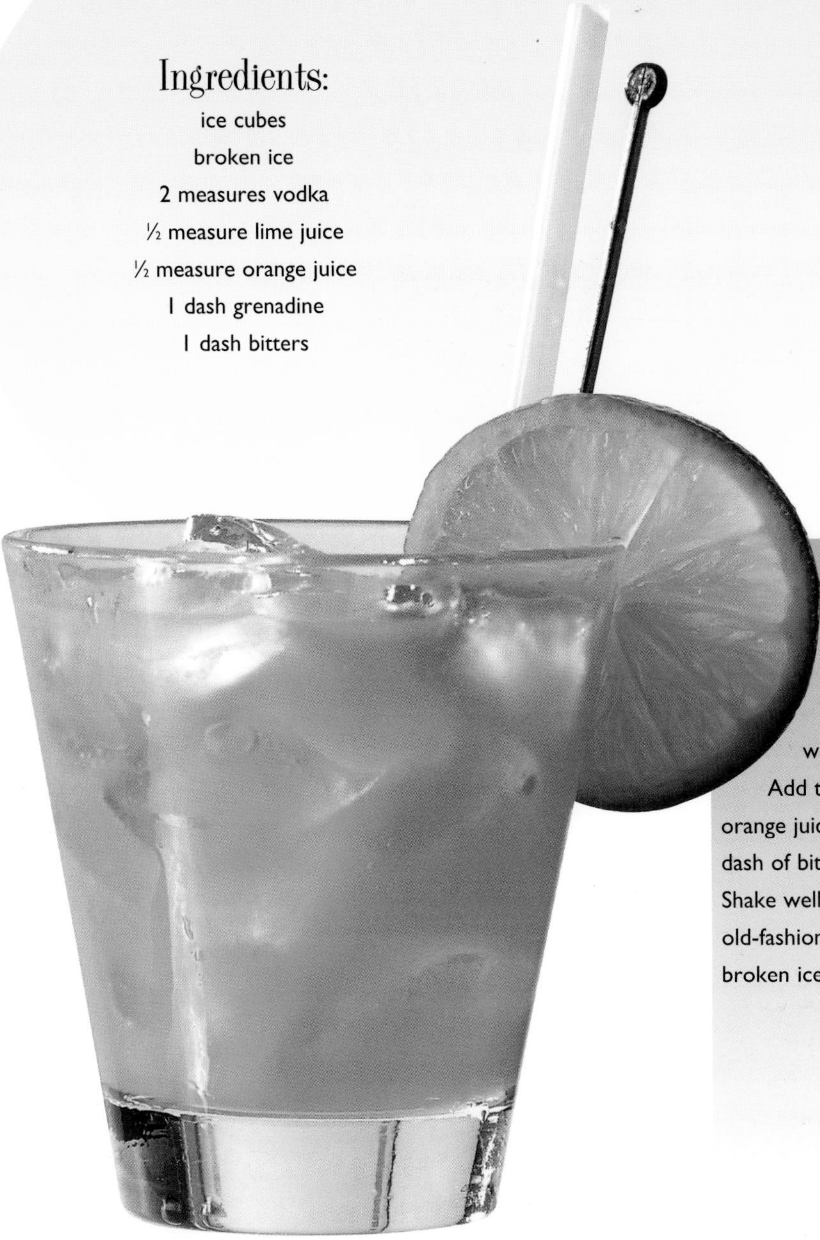

## Vodka

## Method:

Half-fill the shaker
with ice cubes.

Add the vodka, lime and
orange juice, grenadine and
dash of bitters.

Shake well and strain into an
old-fashioned glass filled with
broken ice.

| method: | BUILD OR SHAKE |
| --- | --- |
| glass: | COCKTAIL, OLD-FASHIONED OR HIGHBALL |

# Black Russian

*Originally, this drink was served as a short drink – either on the rocks or shaken and strained. In the 1950s, cola was added to make a long drink and a more popular version. Try one either way.*

## Ingredients:

1½ measures vodka
1 measure Tia Maria
(cold cola if long version is desired)

# Vodka

## Method:

Shaker: place ingredients in shaker with two or three ice cubes. Shake and strain into cocktail glass.

Build (short): Fill an old-fashioned glass two-thirds full with ice cubes, pour in vodka, then the Tia Maria and stir.

Build (long): Fill a highball glass with ice cubes and pour in the vodka, the Tia Maria and top with cold cola. Serve with straws.

# Japanese Slipper
*'Kampai!' – the traditional Japanese toast.*

Vodka

## Ingredients:

1⅓ measures vodka
1⅓ measures Midori melon
  liqueur
¾ measure lemon juice

## Method:

Place all the ingredients in a
shaker with some ice cubes
and shake well. Strain into a
champagne saucer and
garnish with a slice of lemon.

| method: | SHAKER |
| --- | --- |
| glass: | HIGHBALL |
| garnish: | MINT SPRIG |

# Gremlin Fixer

*Another very good excuse to use pisang ambon.*

## Ingredients:

⅔ measure vodka

⅔ measure pisang ambon

(substitute: creme de banane)

⅔ measure dry vermouth

⅓ measure apricot brandy

3 measures pineapple juice

# Vodka

## Method:

Place all the ingredients in a shaker with some ice cubes. Shake well and strain into a highball glass filled with crushed ice. Garnish with the mint sprig and serve with straws.

# Wiki Waki Woo

*Whacky name, wicked taste!*

## Vodka

## Ingredients:

½ measure vodka

½ measure white rum

½ measure dark rum
(over proof if possible –
to provide the 'Woo'
bit no doubt!)

½ measure tequila

½ measure triple
sec/Cointreau

I measure amaretto

I measure orange juice

I measure pineapple juice

I measure cranberry juice

## Method:

Place all the ingredients in a mixing glass with some ice cubes and stir. Strain into a goblet or oversized wine glass filled two-thirds with broken ice. Garnish with the cherry and the orange slice and serve with straws – and a deck chair.

| method: | SHAKER |
|---|---|
| glass: | HIGHBALL OR COLLINS |
| garnish: | PINEAPPLE SLICE |

# Caribbean Cruise

*Why limit yourself to one island when you can have them all!*

## Ingredients:

2 measures vodka

½ measure white rum

½ measure coconut rum
   (Malibu or Batida de Coco)

2 dashes grenadine

4 measures pineapple juice

# Vodka

## Method:

Put some ice cubes into a shaker and pour in the ingredients. Shake well and strain into a highball or Collins glass half-filled with broken ice. Garnish with the pineapple slice and serve with straws.

# Polynesian Cocktail

*The Pacific Ocean islands are divided into three groups:
Micronesia (the islands lying north of the equator and east of the
Philippines), Melanesia (the islands
in the South Pacific, northeast
of Australia), and Polynesia (the
islands from the Hawaiian
Islands south to New Zealand.) One
drink alone could not possibly sum
up the richness of the culture of these
islands – but it's worth trying!*

## Ingredients:

juice of 1 lime
1½ measures vodka
¾ measure cherry brandy

# Vodka

## Method:

Moisten the rim of the
cocktail glass with a little lime
juice and dip into caster
sugar. Put some ice cubes in
the shaker and squeeze in
the lime juice. Pour in the
vodka and cherry brandy and
shake well. Strain into the
prepared cocktail glass.

218

| method: | SHAKER |
| glass: | COCKTAIL |
| garnish: | LEMON TWIST |

# Bikini

*The essential item of clothing for the castaway.*

## Ingredients:

2 measures vodka

1 measure white rum

½ measure milk

1 teaspoon caster sugar

½ measure lemon juice

# Vodka

## Method:

Place all the ingredients in a shaker with ice cubes and shake well. Strain into a chilled cocktail glass.

# Hong Kong Fizz

*This magnificent concoction is credited to one Maude Jones, the Madame of a Hong Kong brothel in the 19th century. It is said that Ms. Jones consumed several of these drinks every day – before lunch!*

## Ingredients:

½ measure vodka

½ measure gin

½ measure Benedictine

½ measure yellow Chartreuse

½ measure green Chartreuse

½ measure lemon juice

4 measures soda water

½ teaspoon caster sugar

# Vodka

## Method:

Place some ice cubes into a shaker and pour in the ingredients – except the soda water. Shake vigourously so the caster sugar is dissolved. Strain into a highball glass half-filled with ice and top with soda water. Serve with straws and a muddler.

method: SHAKER

glass: COCKTAIL

## Tovarich

*A welcome opportunity
to use kümmel, a
caraway-flavoured
liqueur, that was a
favourite of Peter the Great
of Russia. If you wanted an
ultra-elegant version of this
cocktail, try using goldwasser,
flecked with real gold!*

## Ingredients:

1½ measures vodka
1 measure kümmel
juice of ½ lime

# Vodka

## Method:

Place some ice cubes into a
shaker and squeeze in the
juice of ½ lime. Pour in the
kümmel and vodka and
shake. Strain into a cocktail
glass.

# Bennet cocktail  Brandy Champarelle

*The original recipe for this Champarelle – or Shamparelle – dates from the late 19th century when it was made as a poussecafé and used twice the volume of spirits and liqueurs as shown here!*

## Vodka

## Ingredients:

¾ measure triple sec/Cointreau

¾ measure cognac

½ measure anis (substitute: Pernod or Ricard)

½ measure green Chartreuse

## Method:

Place the ingredients in a mixing glass with some ice cubes and stir. Strain into a cordial or liqueur glass.

| method: | MIXING GLASS |
|---|---|
| glass: | BRANDY SNIFTER |

# Brandy Fino

*This very smooth drink is an opportunity to use one of Scotland's famous contributions to the world of liqueurs, glayva, created just after the Second World War, although the original formula for this whisky-based liqueur is much older and makes use of the finest Scottish heather, honey, herbs, and orange peel in its recipe.*

## Ingredients:

1½ measures cognac
½ measure dry sherry
¼ measure glayva

# Vodka

## Method:

Place the ingredients in a mixing glass along with some ice cubes and stir. Strain into a brandy snifter.

# Viking's Helmet

*A gorgeous lime-flavoured long drink that uses aquavit and, if possible, Swedish vodka.*

## Ingredients:

1½ measures aquavit

¾ measure vodka – Swedish if possible!

¾ measure lime juice

⅓ measure pineapple syrup

3 measures ginger ale

## Vodka

## Method:

To a highball glass half-filled with ice cubes, add the ingredients and top with the ginger ale and add the twist of lime. *Skol!*

| method: | BUILD |
|---|---|
| glass: | HIGHBALL |
| garnish: | CHERRY AND SLICE OF LEMON |

# Blue Lagoon

*Blue Curaçao hit the bar scene in 1960 and this fabulous orange-lemon flavoured drink was created at Harry's Bar in Paris by Andy MacElhone, the famous son of the famous Harry MacElhone. Originally, Andy served this drink short, with one measure of lemon juice in place of the lemonade. Both ways are equally fine.*

## Ingredients:

1 measure vodka

1 measure blue Curaçao

4 measures lemonade

## Vodka

## Method:

Add the ingredients to highball glass filled with ice and garnish with cherry and slice of lemon.

# Kiss and Tell

*One to console yourself with while you discuss matters with tabloid journalists!*

## Ingredients:

1 measure vodka
½ measure Galliano
¼ measure dry vermouth
1 teaspoon blue Curaçao
2 measures orange juice
1 measure passion fruit juice

# Vodka

## Method:

Place the ingredients in a shaker with a glass full of broken ice and shake well. Pour, unstrained, into an old-fashioned glass. Garnish with the slice of orange and the cherry.

| method: | SHAKER |
| --- | --- |
| glass: | COCKTAIL |
| garnish: | SLICE OF LIME |

# Liberator

*Feel free with this mango-flavoured cocktail.*

# Vodka

## Method:

Place all the ingredients in a shaker with ice cubes and shake well. Strain into a cocktail glass and garnish with a slice of lime.

## Ingredients:

1½ measures vodka
½ measure Midori melon liqueur
2 measures mango juice
½ measure lime juice

# Woo Woo

*Once this was a Teeny-Weeny Woo-Woo and was famous for about 15 minutes in the 1980s when peach schnapps became the flavour 'du jour'. It's a shame it went out of fashion because it really is a lovely cranberry-peach flavour.*

## Ingredients:

1½ measures peach schnapps
1 measure vodka
4 measures cranberry juice

# Vodka

## Method:

Place the ingredients in a shaker with some ice cubes and shake well. Strain into an ice-filled highball glass.

| method: | SHAKER |
|---|---|
| glass: | CHAMPAGNE SAUCER OR COCKTAIL |

# Black Dublinski

*Ireland meets Russia over coffee and a sherry!*

## Ingredients:

1 measure Baileys (Irish cream liqueur)
1 measure kahlua
1 measure vodka
½ measure dry sherry

# Vodka

## Method:

Place all the ingredients in a shaker with two or three ice cubes and shake well. Strain into a cocktail glass or champagne saucer.

# French Kiss

*A subtle raspberry flavour.*

## Ingredients:

1 measure vodka
1 measure creme de framboise
½ measure Grand Marnier
1 measure whipping cream

# Vodka

## Method:

Place all the ingredients into a shaker with two or three ice cubes and shake well. Strain and pour into a champagne flute and garnish with a fresh raspberry or a cherry on a stick.

| method: | SHAKER |
| --- | --- |
| glass: | HIGHBALL |
| garnish: | CHERRY AND A SPRIG OF MINT |

# Lazy Days

*This long, smooth, slow sipper is the perfect recipe for a relaxing summer evening.*

## Vodka

### Method:

Place all the ingredients except the cream and the lemonade, in a shaker with two or three ice cubes and shake vigourously. Strain into ice-filled highball glass. Float whipped cream on top and garnish with the cherry and mint sprig.

### Ingredients:

1 measure vodka
1 measure Tia Maria or Kahlua
1 measure Midori
⅓ measure green creme de menthe
1 ¼ measure whipping cream
2 measures lemonade

# Blushin' Russian

*The Russian is the vodka, the blush is the strawberry!*

## Ingredients:

1 measure coffee liqueur such as
   Tia Maria or kahlua

¾ measure vodka

1 scoop vanilla ice cream

5 large fresh strawberries
   (including one for the garnish)

# Vodka

## Method:

Put one strawberry aside for garnish. Combine all the ingredients in a blender and blend until smooth. Pour into a parfait or white wine glass and garnish with the strawberry – covered in chocolate if you wish!

| method: | BLENDER |
|---|---|
| glass: | RED WINE GLASS |
| garnish: | SLICE OF PINEAPPLE AND A CHERRY |

# Chi-chi

*A very popular iced drink after a long day at the beach.*

## Ingredients:

1½ measures vodka

1 measure cream of coconut

4 measures pineapple juice

# Vodka

## Method:

Blend all the ingredients with the glass of crushed ice at high speed in the blender. Pour into red wine glass and garnish with slice of pineapple and a cherry.

# Frozen Steppes

## Ingredients:

- I measure vodka
- I measure dark creme de cacao
- I scoop vanilla ice cream

## Vodka

## Method:

Place all the ingredients in a blender and blend until smooth. Pour into a large wine glass and garnish with a maraschino cherry.

| method: | BUILD |
| --- | --- |
| glass: | SHOT |
| garnish: | SMALL LIME WEDGE |

# Bloody Caesar Shooter

*Not only delicious, but there's the added bonus of a surprise tasty treat at the bottom of the glass. If you feel like pushing the boat out, put an oyster in instead of the clam – but you may need to use a larger glass!*

## Ingredients:

1 clam (or oyster)
1 measure vodka
1½ measures tomato juice
2 drops Worcestershire sauce
2 drops Tabasco sauce
1 dash horseradish
Celery salt

# Vodka

## Method:

Put the clam (or oyster) in the bottom of the glass. Add the Worcestershire sauce, Tabasco and horseradish. Add the vodka and tomato juice, sprinkle with celery salt and garnish with a small wedge of lime.

# 4th of July Tooter

*You can have this on Independence Day, 4th July, and then 10 days later on Bastille Day to celebrate the French national day. Numerous countries have national flag colours of red, white and blue, so you could raise a glass to them as well!*

## Ingredients:

1 measure grenadine
1 measure blue Curaçao
1 measure vodka

## Variations:

How about an Italia: First level: mix ¾ measure of grenadine and 1 teaspoon of cherry brandy. Second level: mix ¾ measure of anisette and 1 teaspoon white creme de menthe. Third level: 1 measure yellow Chartreuse with a few dashes of blue Curaçao, to make the green part of the flag. Mix the three 'colours' first then pour each carefully into the glass: red first, then white, then green. *Salute!*

## Vodka

## Method:

Into a shot, pousse-café or cordial glass, carefully add the ingredients in the order stated above, so that they float one on top of the other.

| method: | SHAKER |
|---------|--------|
| glass: | SHOT |

# Galactic Ale

*This fruity recipe will serve two: one for you and one for you, in a parallel universe.*

## Ingredients:

1¼ measures vodka

1¼ measure blue Curaçao

1 measure lime juice

½ measure creme de framboise (raspberry liqueur)

# Vodka

## Method:

In a shaker with two to three ice cubes, shake all the ingredients vigourously. Then strain into two shot glasses. Live long and prosper.

# Green Demon

*A chance to use one of the most idiosyncratic liqueurs, the melon-flavoured Midori, which, in Japanese, means 'green'.*

## Ingredients:

½ measure vodka
½ measure light rum
½ measure Midori (melon liqueur)
½ measure lemonade

# Vodka

## Method:

In a shaker with two or three ice cubes, shake the vodka, rum and Midori. Add the lemonade to the shaker – do not shake but stir twice. Strain into shot glass.

# Hay Fever Remedy

*I find I feel better instantly!*

## Ingredients:

½ measure vodka

¼ measure Southern Comfort

¼ measure amaretto

½ measure pineapple juice

I teaspoon grenadine

## Vodka

## Method:

Shake all the ingredients with two or three ice cubes in a shaker. Strain into a shot glass.

# Johnny on the Beach

*This recipe will serve two beach bums and keep them
happy until surf's up.*

## Ingredients:

1½ measures vodka

1 measure Midori (melon liqueur)

1 measure creme de framboise (raspberry liqueur)

½ measure pineapple juice

½ measure orange juice

½ measure grapefruit juice

½ measure cranberry juice

# Vodka

## Method:

In a mixing glass with two or three ice cubes,
add the ingredients and stir. Strain into two
shot glasses.

# Purple Hooter

*Gorgeous colour and great taste too.*

## Ingredients:

1½ measures vodka (try a citrus
vodka if you want!)
½ measure triple sec or Cointreau
¼ measure creme de framboise
(raspberry liqueur)

# Vodka

## Method:

Shake the ingredients with two to three ice cubes in a shaker and strain into a chilled shot glass.

# Teeny Weeny Woo Woo

## Ingredients:

½ measure vodka

½ measure peach schnapps

I measure cranberry juice

## Vodka

## Method:

Shake with two or three ice cubes in a shaker then strain into a shot glass.

# Whisky cocktails

Manhattan
see page 253.

The word whisky is a corruption of the Gaelic *usige beatha*, or *uisgebaugh*, which mean ' water of life'. There is whisky and there is whiskey: in Scotland and Canada, there is no 'e', while in America and Ireland, it's whiskey. Each of the whisk(e)y-producing countries has its own style and there are many different varieties of whiskies.

Scotch is whisky from Scotland and nowhere else. It cannot be made in England or America, although it can be imported for blending and bottling in different countries. Most Scotch whiskies are blended, often from the products of several distilleries. At least 60 per cent of a blend will be made of grain whiskies, with the rest from malts (barley that has been germinated to release fermentable sugars and then heated to stop the germination process) in order to achieve the balance of taste that each brand is known for. An unblended malt whisky is commonly described as being a single malt. The individual flavours of Scotch whiskies are derived from several influencing factors:

the water from which they are made; the peat over which the water flows; the air surrounding the cask during maturation; the shape of the pot still; and the oak casks in which the whisky is aged.

The Irish were probably the first people to make whiskey, and their secrets of distillation were exported with monks to Scotland in the early Middle Ages. Where the Scots use a peat fire to dry their barley (and which influences the flavour), the Irish dry theirs in a kiln using coal. Furthermore, the Irish are unique in that they use uncooked cereal (usually unmalted barley) and triple distillation in pot stills (Scotch is twice-distilled).

The main ingredient of bourbon is corn. It was in Bourbon County, Kentucky, that America's first corn whiskey was made. Today, half the bourbon distilleries in the US are in Kentucky. Some say it was distiller John Ritchie who made it at Lin's Fort, near Bardstown, in 1777, others credit the Reverend Elijah Craig of Georgetown in 1789. Bourbon is made in a continuous still from a fermented cereal mash – by law bourbon must be a minimum of 51 per cent corn, but in practice it is more likely to be 60 to 80 per cent and matured in new, charred, white-oak barrels for a minimum of two years, but generally for between six and eight years. Under US laws, the casks can only be used a single time. Once used, the casks are

## Rebel raider
see page 258.

sought after by the distillers of Caribbean rums for their produce. Sour mash is a style of bourbon: a proportion of the mash already used in a previous distillation (hence 'sour') is added to the fresh mash about to be used. One of the most famous sour-mash whiskies is Jack Daniel's from Lynchburg, Tennessee. A Tennessee whiskey must be made in that state and must be made from at least 51 per cent of any one grain.

Rye whiskey was probably the first whiskey ever to be produced in the United States, made by Irish and Scottish immigrants to the New World in the 17th century. Rye must be made with a minimum of 51 per cent of the grain that gives it its name, and, like bourbon, is distilled in a continuous still and aged in charred, new oak barrels for not less than one year.

The smooth-bodied whiskies manufactured in Canada are made from cereal grains such as barley, corn, wheat and rye (both malted and rye grain) in varying proportions according to individual makers. Both old and new casks are used for ageing, which must be for a minimum of three years, although six years is more common.

Highball
see page 252.

# Affinity

*A classic cocktail from Harry Craddock's* The Savoy Cocktail
Book, *the affinity was one of the most fashionable aperitifs of the
1920s.*

## Ingredients:

ice cubes

1 measure Scotch whisky

1 measure rosso vermouth

1 measure dry vermouth

1 dash bitters

1 lemon twist

## Whisky

## Method:

Half-fill the mixing glass with
ice cubes and pour in the
two vermouths.

Add the Scotch and the dash
of bitters and stir.

Strain into a cocktail glass
and squeeze the lemon twist
over the glass and then
discard it.

# Artist's special

*This fruity Scotch-flavoured cocktail was invented at the Artists'*
*Club in the Rue Pigalle, Paris, in the 1920s. It was typically avant-*
*garde of artists to disregard the sanctity and tradition associated*
*with Scotch whisky.*

## Ingredients:

ice cubes

I measure Scotch

I measure sherry

½ measure grenadine

½ measure lemon juice

# Whisky

## Method:

Half-fill the shaker with ice
cubes and pour in the lemon
juice and grenadine.
Add the sherry and the
Scotch and shake well.
Strain into a cocktail glass.

# Algonquin

*From the famous hotel of the same name, this drink
makes use of rye, the first whiskey
of the United States.*

## Ingredients:

ice cubes

broken ice

2 measures rye

I measure dry vermouth

I measure pineapple juice

# Whisky

## Method:

Half-fill the shaker with ice
cubes.

Pour in the pineapple juice,
vermouth and rye.

Shake and strain into an old-
fashioned glass three-
quarters filled with broken
ice.

method: BUILD

glass: OLD-FASHIONED

# The bairn

*In Scotland and the north-east of England,*
*a 'bairn' is a child. There is, however,*
*nothing juvenile about this drink.*

## Ingredients:

broken ice

2 measures Scotch

¾ measure Cointreau

1 teaspoon Campari

# Whisky

## Method:

Fill an old-fashioned glass
three-quarters full with
broken ice.
Pour in the Cointreau and
Scotch and add the Campari.
Serve with a stirrer.

# Cablegram

*Perhaps someone will devise an 'e-mail cocktail'!*
*Traditionally, this drink uses Canadian whisky;*
*a blended whisky works just as well.*

## Ingredients:

ice cubes
1½ measures Canadian
whisky/blended whisky
½ measure lemon juice
½ teaspoon castor sugar
4 measures ginger ale
1 lemon slice

# Whisky

## Method:

Half-fill the shaker with ice
cubes.
Add the lemon juice, sugar
and whisky and shake well.
Strain into a highball glass
almost filled with ice cubes
and garnish with the slice of
lemon.

| method: | SHAKER |
|---|---|
| glass: | OLD-FASHIONED |
| garnish: | TWIST OF LEMON |

# Fancy bourbon

*It is said that a little of what you fancy does you good. In fact, you can make fancies with gin, Scotch or brandy, as well as bourbon.*

## Ingredients:

ice cubes

Broken ice

2 measures bourbon

½ teaspoon triple sec or
Cointreau

½ teaspoon castor sugar

2 dashes bitters

1 lemon twist

# Whisky

## Method:

Half-fill the shaker with ice cubes.
Pour in the triple sec or Cointreau and bourbon. Add the sugar and the bitters and shake well. Strain into an old-fashioned glass three-quarters filled with broken ice.

# Golden daisy

*We've already met the daisy in the section on gin (page 41),
but there is a growing consensus that bourbon makes one
of the finest drinks. While the original daisies included
a fruit syrup (such as grenadine), this
golden daisy includes Cointreau.
Try this version and see what you think.*

## Ingredients:

ice cubes

broken ice

½ measure bourbon

½ measure Cointreau

1 measure lemon juice

1 lime wedge

# Whisky

## Method:

Half-fill the shaker with ice
cubes.
Pour in the lemon juice,
Cointreau and bourbon and
shake vigorously.
Strain into an old-fashioned
glass half-filled with broken
ice and garnish with the lime
wedge.

| method: | BUILD |
|---|---|
| glass: | HIGHBALL (naturally!) |
| garnish: | TWIST OF LEMON (OPTIONAL) |

# The highball

*So popular was this drink, that in the 1920s*
The New York Times *set out to discover the truth about its origins. Investigations proved that some time around 1895, New York barman Patrick Duffy created the highball, a drink which took its name from the 19th-century American railroad practice of raising a ball on a high pole as a signal to train drivers to increase their speed. Since a 'highball' meant 'hurry', Duffy devised a drink that could also be made quickly by simply pouring the ingredients over ice in a tall glass.*

## Ingredients:

ice cubes
½ measure bourbon
5 measures soda
(or ginger ale)

# Whisky

## Method:

Drop 3 or 4 ice cubes into the highball glass.
Pour in the bourbon and top with soda or ginger ale.
Add the lemon twist (optional).
Stir lightly.

## Variations:

Add 2 dashes of bitters, and you've got horse feathers.

# Manhattan

*You've been to the Bronx (page 30), now visit Manhattan!
One of the basic, classic cocktails, the Manhattan is reputed to
have been invented in around 1874 at the Manhattan Club in New
York for Winston Churchill's mother, Lady Randolph Churchill.
Originally, a Manhattan was made with 1 measure whiskey and 2
measures vermouth and served straight up. Today, they are more
often served on the rocks and with a lot less vermouth. Rye
whiskey was used, but many prefer bourbon.*

## Ingredients:

ice cubes

broken ice

2 measures rye or bourbon

1 measure rosso vermouth

1 dash bitters

1 maraschino cherry

# Whisky

## Method:

Put a glass full of broken ice
into the shaker.
Pour in the whiskey and
vermouth and add a dash of
bitters.
Shake briefly and pour
unstrained into an old-
fashioned glass.
Add the cherry.

As with the Martini (page 48), experiment with the proportions
of whisky and vermouth to suit your taste.

| method: | BUILD |
| --- | --- |
| glass: | COLLINS |
| garnish: | SPRIGS OF MINT |

## Mint julep

*Traditionally served on Kentucky Derby Day – the first Saturday in May – no other tall drink is so delicious – and no other is likely to cause as much debate as how to make it. Do you crush the mint or not? Do you leave it in the glass or take it out? Should you drink it through a straw? An early record of the mint julep was written by an English teacher, John Davis, in 1803, while he was working in Virginia. He described the julep as a 'dram of spirituous liquor that has mint in it' and also noted that the Virginians drank it in the mornings as an 'eye-opener'. The 'spirituous liquor' Davis mentioned was most likely brandy. After the Civil War, bourbon became more widely available and this has continued to be the most popular base spirit for mint juleps.*

# Whisky

## Method:

Pre-chill the Collins glass. Pour in the gomme syrup and add the sprigs of mint. Gently crush the mint with a muddler. How much juice you crush out of the mint leaves is up to you. (Some flatly refuse to crush them at all.) Add the bourbon and stir gently while filling the glass with crushed ice. Clip off the end of each sprig of mint so that the juice flows into the julep and arrange the sprigs of mint on top. Serve with straws and a stirrer.

## Ingredients:

crushed ice – crushed as fine as possible – the more like snow the better!
3 measures bourbon – Kentucky bourbon is best
1 measure gomme syrup
4 sprigs mint – use small, tender leaves. Use more if you like more mint!
mint sprigs for garnish

# New York

*A toast to the Big Apple!*

## Ingredients:

ice cubes

broken ice

2 measures whisky –

traditionally, Canadian whisky

¾ measure lime juice

½ measure gomme syrup

1 teaspoon grenadine

# Whisky

## Method:

Half-fill the shaker with ice cubes.

Pour in the lime juice, gomme syrup, grenadine and whisky.

Shake well and strain into an old-fashioned glass three-quarters filled with broken ice.

Add the twist of orange.

## Variations:

Replace the Canadian whisky with bourbon, and leave out the gomme syrup, and you have a New Yorker.

| method: | BUILD |
|---|---|
| glass: | OLD-FASHIONED |
| garnish: | SLICE OF LEMON AND CHERRY (some prefer a slice or twist of orange) |

# Old fashioned

*This classic whiskey cocktail – made with American whiskey, but some will argue specifically for rye – first appeared at the Pendennis Club in Louisville, Kentucky, in 1900. It was made especially at the request of bourbon distiller Colonel James E Pepper. It's simply bourbon added to a glass containing a bitters-soaked sugar cube and then filled with ice – but some advocate sugar muddled in a little water.*

## Ingredients:

broken ice

2 measures bourbon

1 sugar cube

1 dash bitters

1 dash soda water (optional)

## Variations:

Old fashioneds don't have to be bourbon: replace the whiskey with the base spirit of your choice.

# Whisky

## Method:

Place the sugar cube in the old-fashioned glass. Add the dash of bitters. When the sugar cube has soaked up all of the bitters, three-quarters fill the glass with broken ice. Pour in the whiskey.

Add the garnish and dash of soda water (optional) and serve with a muddler.

# Opening

*A classic cocktail and a perfect, pre-theatre or interval drink.*

## Ingredients:

ice cubes

1 measure whisky

2 teaspoons rosso vermouth

2 teaspoons grenadine

# Whisky

## Method:

Half-fill the shaker with ice cubes.

Pour in the whisky, vermouth and grenadine and shake vigorously.

Strain into an old-fashioned glass two-thirds filled with ice cubes.

# Rebel raider

*A number of mixed drinks have 'rebel' in their names: rebel rouser, rebel yell and this, the rebel raider. Rebs (short for rebels) was the name given to Confederate soldiers during the American Civil War, but these cocktails are named because, traditionally, the bourbon used in their making is a brand known as Rebel Yell.*

# Whisky

## Method:

Half-fill the shaker with ice cubes.
Pour in the Campari, sherry, bourbon and mandarin juice. Shake well, strain into an ice-filled Collins glass and top with lemonade.

## Ingredients:

ice cubes

1½ measures bourbon (Rebel Yell if available)

½ measure sherry

1 teaspoon Campari

3 measures mandarin juice

3 measures lemonade

# Scots guard

*As the name suggests, this cocktail should be made with
Scotch whisky.*

## Ingredients:

ice cubes

2 measures Scotch whisky

I measure lemon juice

I measure orange juice

½ teaspoon grenadine

## Whisky

### Method:

Half-fill the shaker with ice cubes.

Pour in the lemon and orange juice.

Add the grenadine and the whisky and shake well.

Strain and pour into a cocktail glass.

**method:** SHAKER

**glass:** OLD-FASHIONED

# Southern delta

*Southern Comfort lends its distinctive peach flavour
to this delight.*

## Ingredients:

broken ice

1½ measures bourbon

½ measure Southern Comfort

⅓ measure lime juice

⅓ measure pineapple juice

# Whisky

## Method:

Put a glassful of broken ice in
the shaker.

Pour in the pineapple juice,
lime juice, Southern Comfort
and the bourbon.

Shake well and pour
unstrained into an old-
fashioned glass.

# Suburban

*Leave the city behind and head for the 'burbs'.*

## Ingredients:

ice cubes

broken ice

3 measures Scotch or bourbon

1 measure port

1 measure dark rum

3 drops bitters

# Whisky

## Method:

Half-fill the mixing glass with ice cubes.

Pour in the rum, port, whisky and add the bitters.

Stir well and strain into an old-fashioned glass half-filled with broken ice.

| method: | SHAKER |
|---|---|
| glass: | SOUR (or white-wine glass) |

# The sour

*The original sour of the 1850s was the brandy sour, but since then sours have been made with practically every base spirit available and the whisky sour is now one of the most popular. It's called a sour because very little sweetener and a relatively large amount of lemon juice is used. It's traditionally served in a stemmed sour glass, although it can also be served in an old-fashioned glass when the optional soda water is added. While a sour should never taste sweet, do adjust the amount of sugar to suit. If you ask for a whisky sour in a bar, don't forget to specify which whisky or whiskey you want. You can also have gin sour, vodka sour, tequila sour, rum sour and brandy sour.*

## Ingredients:

ice cubes

2 measures whisky of choice

1 measure lemon juice

½ measure gomme syrup

# Whisky

## Method:

Half-fill the shaker with ice cubes.

Pour in the lemon juice and gomme syrup and add the whisky.

Shake well and strain into a sour glass.

If you want to add a dash of soda water, serve on the rocks in an old-fashioned glass.

# Strongarm

*Oddly named, since this drink is oh-so very easy to lift to one's lips.*

## Ingredients:

ice cubes
2 measures Scotch
½ measure triple sec or
Cointreau
½ measure lemon juice

# Whisky

## Method:

Half-fill the shaker with ice cubes.
Pour in the triple sec or Cointreau and the Scotch and shake well.
Strain into a cocktail glass.

# Thunderclap

*Too many of these, and that's what a pin dropping
will sound like!*

## Ingredients:

ice cubes
1½ measures whisky of choice
1 measure gin
1 measure brandy

## Whisky

## Method:

Half-fill the mixing glass with
ice cubes.
Pour in the brandy, gin and
whisky and stir well.
Strain into a cocktail glass.

# Tiger juice

## Ingredients:

ice cubes
1½ measures whisky
1 measure orange juice
½ measure lemon juice

# Whisky

## Method:

Half-fill the mixing glass with ice cubes.
Pour in the lemon and orange juice and add the whisky.
Shake well and strain into a cocktail glass.

| method: | SHAKER |
| --- | --- |
| glass: | HIGHBALL/ COCKTAIL |

# Ward Eight

*A slight variation on the whisky sour will result in this classic. You can serve it either as a cocktail in such a glass, or in a tall glass with broken ice and a dash of soda water, some fruit to garnish and with straws. Try it both ways – the ingredients are the same.*

# Whisky

## Method:

Put a glassful of broken ice into the shaker.

Pour in the orange and lemon juices, grenadine and whisky.

Shake well and strain into a cocktail glass or, as illustrated, into a highball glass two-thirds filled with broken ice and top with soda water. Garnish with citrus fruit.

## Ingredients:

broken ice

2 measures whisky

¼ measure orange juice

½ measure lemon juice

¼ measure grenadine

sodawater

citrus fruit

# Whisky squirt

*Squirts are sweet drinks made with a base spirit or wine in combination with fresh fruit.*

## Ingredients:

crushed ice
ice cubes
2 measures whisk(e)y
1 teaspoon triple sec or Cointreau
½ measure gomme syrup
½ crushed fresh peach (without skin)
2 measures soda water

## Whisky

## Method:

Crush the peach half in a bowl or in a mixing glass.
Put a glassful of crushed ice into the shaker.
Add the crushed peach, the gomme syrup, triple sec or Cointreau and whisky.
Shake well and then strain over 3–4 ice cubes in a highball glass.
Top up with soda water.
Serve with a straw.

# Scoff Law Cocktail

*This cocktail was devised in 1924 by Jock, the bartender at Harry's Bar in Paris, and was named in honour of all those Americans who were intent on dodging Prohibition.*

## Ingredients:

1 measure Canadian whisky
1 measure dry vermouth
½ measure lemon juice
½ measure grenadine

# Whisky

## Method:

Place all the ingredients in a shaker with some ice cubes. Shake well and strain into a chilled cocktail glass while turning a blind eye!

# Bobby Burns

*Staying 'north of the border', here's one drink that's perfect to celebrate Burn's Night for it is named after Scotland's most famous poet and song writer Robert Burns (1759–96), the composer of 'Auld Lang Syne'.*

## Ingredients:

1½ measures scotch

1½ measures sweet red (rosso) vermouth

1 teaspoon Benedictine

## Variations:

Replace the Benedictine with a teaspoon of sugar syrup and a dash of angostura bitters to make a Flying Scotsman.

Replace the Benedictine with a teaspoon of sugar syrup alone and you have a Harry Lauder, another famous son of Scotland.

# Whisky

## Method:

To an old-fashioned glass, filled two-thirds with broken ice, add the liquid ingredients and the twist of lemon.

| method: | MIXING GLASS |
|---|---|
| glass: | COCKTAIL |

# St. Patrick's Day

*A very pleasant change from stout on March 17th.*

## Ingredients:

1 measure green creme de menthe

1 measure green Chartreuse

1 measure Irish whiskey – of course!

1 dash angostura bitters

# Whisky

## Method:

Place the ingredients in a mixing glass with some ice cubes and stir. Strain into a cocktail glass and say Slainte!

# Duck Soup

*Homage to the Marx brothers perhaps? Break out that apricot brandy for a real treat.*

## Ingredients:

2 measures bourbon

½ measure apricot brandy

¾ measure lemon juice

¾ measure pineapple juice

½ teaspoon caster sugar

# Whisky

## Method:

Dissolve the sugar in the lemon juice and add, along with other ingredients, to a shaker with two or three ice cubes. Shake well and strain into old fashioned glass three-quarters filled with broken ice.

# Sunbeam

*A play on the producers names: Midori melon liqueur by Suntory and bourbon by Jim Beam.*

## Ingredients:

1 measure Midori melon
liqueur
1 measure Jim Beam bourbon
½ measure creme de banane
2 measure mandarin juice
2 measures pineapple juice
¼ measure grenadine

# Whisky

## Method:

Place all the ingredients
except the grenadine into a
shaker with two or three ice
cubes and shake well. Strain
into an ice-filled highball
glass, then add the grenadine
– but do not stir.

# Trouser Rouser

*If the Hen Night Zipper-ripper is for the girls, then this must be for the 'stags'!*

## Ingredients:

1½ measures scotch

½ measure creme de banane

2 measures mango juice

1 measure pineapple juice

½ measure lime juice

1 teaspoon egg white

# Whisky

## Method:

Place all the ingredients in a shaker with some ice cubes and shake well. Strain into a Collins glass three-quarters filled with broken ice and garnish with the mint sprig and cherry.

| method: | BLENDER |
|---------|---------|
| glass: | PARFAIT OR WHITE WINE GLASS |

# Cranberry Cooler

*Kentucky Derby Day isn't the only time to enjoy bourbon: try it in September as well, to celebrate National Bourbon Week!*

## Whisky

### Method:

Combine all the ingredients in a blender with a glass of crushed ice and blend until smooth. Pour into parfait or white wine glass and wait while your horse comes home.

### Ingredients:

1½ measure bourbon
1½ measure cranberry juice
½ measure lime juice
1 teaspoon sugar

# Tequila cocktails

Margarita
see page 287.

The spirit of Mexico is made from the sap of the mezcal, also known as the century or argarth plant. It is not a cactus, but a type of aloe (related to the lily) of the genus *Agave*, specifically the blue-coloured *Agave tequilana weber*. There are over 120 types of agave, but only the blue agave, which grows in abundance around the town of Tequila in Jalisco state in Mexico, 65km (40 miles) west of Guadalajara, is used in tequila production. The manufacture of tequila is governed by strict quality standards. Mezcal, a much inferior form of tequila not subject to the same rigours, is produced in a number of regions from different varieties of agave.

Before the Conquistadors arrived in Mexico, the Aztecs had been happily drinking a low-alcohol wine made from the agave plant called pulque. This is still drunk in Mexico today. In the 16th century, the Spaniards imported the arts of distillation and tequila was born. It take between eight and ten years for an agave plant to grow to maturity, when it resembles a pineapple and is called a *pina* (the Spanish word for pineapple). The base of a mature agave plant is steamed to

Tequila sunrise
see page 299.

release the sap. The sap is then fermented for around ten days to make the 'mother pulque'. This is then added to fresh sap and allowed to ferment to produce the pulque wine. To make tequila, the pulque is double-distilled in pot stills.

It took a long time for tequila to cross the border into the United States, however. The first recorded shipment of just three barrels was in 1873. More Americans discovered the taste when US troops pursued Pancho Villa along the Mexican–American border in 1916, and by the time Prohibition kicked in, tequila had established a following. One of the mixed drinks that become popular in the 1930s was the tequila sunrise. In 1944 a 'gin famine' struck the United States and considerable amounts of tequila were imported to use as the base for cocktails. Tequila gained in popularity in the 1950s and by the 1960s had something of a cult status, particularly with students in California, who erroneously believed that tequila contained the hallucinogenic drug mescaline.

Nevertheless, tequila is a relative newcomer to the cocktail circuit, and is still the subject of experimentation among bartenders and adventurous drinkers. It certainly quickly acquired a number of drinking rituals and many a party-goer has lived to regret that final tequila slammer pressed upon them by enthusiastic friends. Stories about worms in tequila bottles are greatly exaggerated.

Despite Mexican government rules regarding the production of tequila, there are no laws governing how it is aged. Tequila Añejo simply means 'aged tequila', and it must be aged for one year in white-oak casks. Most producers claim that gold tequila has been aged in white-oak casks for between two and four years (rarely more than five years, as there is no improvement in flavour). silver tequila is aged in wax-lined vats and is more mellow than ordinary, 'white' tequila, although it, too, has no colour.

You either love it or hate it, but there is no mistaking the hydrogen sulphide odour (or rotten-egg smell) of neat tequila. Get past that and wait as the warm glow grows out from your stomach and travels south, right down to your toes!

## Viva Mexico!

**Pepper eater**
see page 291.

| method: | MIXING GLASS |
|---|---|
| glass: | OLD FASHIONED OR COLLINS |
| garnish: | SLICE OF ORANGE |

# Ambassador

*A very simple drink to make, and a very refreshing one too!*

## Ingredients:

ice cubes

2 measures tequila

2–4 measures (or more) orange juice

dash of gomme syrup

I orange slice

## Tequila

## Method:

Put some ice cubes in the mixing glass.

Add the orange juice, gomme syrup and tequila.

Stir and pour over ice cubes in an old-fashioned glass.

Decorate with the orange slice.

## Variation:

If you prefer a longer drink, add more orange juice and serve in a Collins glass.

## Chimayo cocktail

*Try this combination of tequila and apple juice.*

### Ingredients:

ice cubes

1½ measures tequila

½ measure lime juice

½ measure apple juice

apple wedge

## Tequila

### Method:

Place some ice cubes in the shaker.

Add the lime juice, apple juice and tequila and shake well.

Strain into an ice-filled old-fashioned glass and garnish with the apple wedge.

| method: | BUILD |
| glass: | HIGHBALL |
| garnish: | LIME WEDGE |

# Border crossing

*Mexico meets America in this tequila-cola blend.*

## Ingredients:

ice cubes
1½ measures tequila
2 teaspoons lime juice
1 teaspoon lemon juice
4 measures cola
1 lime wedge

# Tequila

## Method:

Almost fill a highball glass
with ice cubes.
Pour over the lime juice,
lemon juice and tequila and
top with cola.
Stir well and garnish with the
lime wedge.

# California dream

## Ingredients:

ice cubes

2 measures tequila

1 measure rosso vermouth

½ measure dry vermouth

1 maraschino cherry

## Tequila

## Method:

Half-fill the mixing glass with ice cubes.

Pour on the rosso vermouth, dry vermouth and tequila.

Stir well, strain into a cocktail glass and garnish with the maraschino cherry.

| method: | SHAKER |
|---|---|
| glass: | HIGHBALL |
| garnish: | LIME SLICE |

## Doralto

### Ingredients:

ice cubes
1½ measures tequila
½ measure lemon juice
½ teaspoon castor sugar
1 dash bitters
4 measures tonic water
1 lime slice

# Tequila

### Method:

Put some ice cubes in the shaker and pour in the lemon juice, sugar, dash of bitters and the tequila.
Shake well and strain into a highball glass two-thirds filled with ice cubes.
Top with the tonic water and garnish with the lime slice.

# Fruits of the desert

*A delicious grapefruit flavour, softened by the addition of the orange-flavoured triple sec. Try it with 'gold' tequila – aged for between two and four years.*

## Ingredients:

ice cubes
broken ice
1 ½ measures tequila
(gold tequila if preferred)
½ measure triple sec or
Cointreau
2 measures grapefruit juice
1 teaspoon castor
sugar
1 maraschino cherry

# Tequila

## Method:

Half-fill the shaker with
ice cubes.
Pour in the grapefruit
juice, triple sec or
Cointreau, tequila and add
the sugar.
Shake well and strain into an
old-fashioned glass half filled
with broken ice. Garnish
with the maraschino cherry.

| method: | SHAKER |
| --- | --- |
| glass: | COLLINS |
| garnish: | ORANGE SLICE |

# El Dorado

*The legendary city of gold sought*
*by the Spanish explorers*
*in South America gives its name to*
*this drink. It's also a great honey*
*and vitamin C 'health drink'.*
*But if you believe that,*
*then you really do believe in fairy*
*tales!*

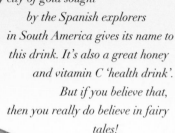

## Ingredients:

ice cubes
2 measures tequila
1½ measures lemon juice
1 tablespoon clear honey
(about ½ measure)
1 orange slice

## Tequila

## Method:

Half-fill the shaker with ice
cubes.
Pour in the lemon juice,
honey and tequila and shake
vigorously. (That's the
aerobic-exercise part!)
Strain into a Collins glass
filled with ice cubes and
garnish with the orange slice.

# Gentle Ben

*Don't be fooled by the name: tequila, vodka
and gin pack a real punch. Best drunk through
a straw while lying in a hammock.*

## Ingredients:

ice cubes

1½ measures tequila

½ measure vodka

½ measure gin

4 measures orange juice

## Tequila

## Method:

Fill a highball glass two-thirds
full of ice cubes.
Pour over the orange juice,
gin, vodka and tequila and
stir well.

| method: | BLENDER |
| --- | --- |
| glass: | SOUR |
| | (OR WHITE-WINE GLASS) |

# Icebreaker

*A relative of the Daiquiri, you can make this tequila drink in a blender or food processor.*

## Ingredients:

crushed ice
2 measures tequila
2 measures grapefruit juice
½ measure grenadine
2 teaspoons triple sec or
Cointreau

# Tequila

## Method:

Put about a glassful of
crushed ice in the blender.
Pour on the tequila,
grapefruit juice, grenadine and
triple sec or Cointreau.
Blend at low speed for about
12 to 15 seconds.
Strain into the sour glass and
serve straight up.

meth

glass

garnish:

method:

glass

288

# Margarita

*This is one of the best-known tequila-based drinks and also one of
the most popular. Many young women called Margarita have
claimed to be the inspiration for the drink, but most now accept
that the muse was not, in fact, a Mexican señorita, but the
American actress Marjorie King. Marjorie was a guest at Danny
Herrera's Rancho La Gloria in Tijuana in 1948, when he
discovered that the actress was allergic to every spirit except
tequila. Herrera mixed this drink for her and named it Margarita,
the Spanish for Marjorie. Since then, the Margarita has evolved
from the original classic recipe into frozen versions and frozen
fruit Margaritas which use fruit liqueurs.*

## Ingredients:

ice cubes
2 measures tequila
1¼ measures triple sec
or Cointreau
¾ measure lime juice
(or lemon if preferred)
limewedge

# Tequila

## Method:

Rub the rim of the glass with
a wedge of lime and dip the
rim into a saucer of salt.
Half-fill the shaker with ice
cubes.
Pour in the lime juice, triple
sec or Cointreau and tequila.
Shake well and strain into the
champagne saucer.
Garnish with a wedge of lime
on the edge of the glass.

# Massacre

*Ginger ale is a popular mixer with tequila and is the mixer for the infamous tequila slammer – known in France as tequila rapido and in Germany as tequila boom-boom. The slammer is not so much a drink as a 'method' of drinking: 1 measure of tequila and 1 measure ginger ale in a shot glass covered with one hand or a beer mat, banged twice on the table and downed in one. Someone even had the nerve to use champagne instead of ginger ale and created the slammer royale!*
*Why have a slammer when you can have a massacre instead?*

## Tequila

### Method:
Almost fill a highball glass with ice cubes, add the tequila and Campari.
Top with ginger ale and stir well.

### Ingredients:
ice cubes
2 measures tequila
1 teaspoon Campari
4 measures ginger ale

# Mexicano

*The pineapple juice makes tequila go down nice and smoothly.*

## Ingredients:

ice cubes

2 measures tequila

1 measure pineapple juice

1 teaspoon grenadine

½ measure lemon juice

## Tequila

## Method:

Half-fill the shaker with ice cubes.

Pour in the lemon juice, pineapple juice, grenadine, and tequila and shake well.

Strain into a cocktail glass.

# Mexican itch

*If you've got an itch, you just have to scratch it.
This is tequila the Mexican way. Again, it's not really a cocktail or
even a mixed drink, but a way of coming to terms with the often
ripe odour of neat tequila prior to swallowing it. It's sometimes
called a tequila cruda or a tequila shot.*

## Ingredients:

1 measure tequila
1 small pinch of salt
1 wedge of lime

## Tequila

## Method:

Rub the lime wedge on your
hand where your thumb and
index finger meet.
Sprinkle the salt on this now
wet part of your anatomy.
Hold the lime wedge
between your thumb and
index finger.
Hold the shot glass with the
tequila in your other hand.
Take a deep breath and lick
the salt off your hand.
Down the tequila in one
swallow.
Bite on the lime wedge.

# Pepper-eater

*The trouble with tequila is that it brings out the
dare-devil in quite the most innocent of people.
Will you dare eat the red-pepper garnish?*

## Ingredients:

ice cubes
broken ice
I measure tequila
I measure triple sec
or Cointreau
I teaspoon pepper vodka
(see page 87 for how to
make your own)
I measure orange juice
I measure cranberry juice
I hot red pepper

## Tequila

## Method:

Half-fill the shaker with
ice cubes.
Pour in the tequila,
triple sec or Cointreau,
pepper vodka, orange
juice and cranberry juice.
Shake well and strain into
an old-fashioned glass
three-quarters filled with
broken ice.
Garnish with the red pepper.
Take bets on who will eat
their garnish.

# Poker face

*A nice, long drink that does allow you to keep a straight face –
even if it's only for a short while!*

## Ingredients:

ice cubes
1 measure tequila
½ measure triple sec or
Cointreau
4 measures pineapple juice
1 lime wedge

# Tequila

## Method:

Almost fill a highball glass
with ice cubes.
Pour on the pineapple juice,
triple sec or Cointreau and
tequila.
Stir well and garnish with the
lime wedge.

| method: | SHAKER |
| glass: | OLD FASHIONED |
| garnish: | MARASCHINO CHERRY ON A STICK |

# Purple cactus

*This drink uses passionfruit juice – a pleasant change and a lovely flavour.*

## Variations:

Replace the tequila with koniak (Greek brandy) for a purple lizard or with Wild Turkey (straight bourbon) for a purple turkey.

## Ingredients:

ice cubes
broken ice
1½ measures tequila
1½ measures passionfruit juice
½ measure sherry
1 teaspoon grenadine
1 maraschino cherry on a stick

# Tequila

## Method:

Half-fill the shaker with ice cubes.
Add the tequila, passionfruit juice, sherry and grenadine.
Shake well and strain into an old-fashioned glass three-quarters filled with broken ice.
Garnish with the cherry on a stick.

| method: | SHAKER |
|---|---|
| glass: | CHAMPAGNE SAUCER |
| garnish: | ORANGE SLICE AND MARASCHINO CHERRY |

# Ridley

*This drink was invented in London at the Duke's Hotel in around 1960. The addition of Galliano gives a subtle aniseed flavour to the drink.*

## Ingredients:

ice cubes

crushed ice

I measure tequila

I measure gin

I teaspoon Galliano

I orange slice

I maraschino cherry

# Tequila

## Method:

Half-fill the shaker with ice cubes.

Pour in the tequila and gin and shake well.

Strain into the champagne saucer filled with crushed ice.

Sprinkle the Galliano on top and garnish with an orange slice and a cherry.

# Rosita

*The Campari and sweet vermouth make
the pink colour of this 'little rose'.*

## Ingredients:

crushed ice

1½ measures tequila

1 measure Campari

½ measure rosso vermouth

½ measure dry vermouth

1 dash bitters

1 lemon twist

# Tequila

## Method:

Almost fill a highball glass
with crushed ice.
Pour in the tequila, Campari,
rosso and dry vermouths and
add the dash of bitters.
Stir well and add the twist of
lemon.

| method: | MIXING GLASS |
|---------|--------------|
| glass:  | COCKTAIL     |

# Scottie was beamed up

*Star Trek fans will no doubt understand the significance of the name!*

## Ingredients:

ice cubes
2 measures tequila
½ measure Galliano

# Tequila

## Method:

Half-fill the mixing glass with ice cubes.
Pour in the tequila and Galliano and stir.
Strain into a cocktail glass.

# Spanish fly

*This almond-flavoured drink should not be confused with
the infamous 'Spanish fly' (Lytta vascatoria), found in
abundance in Spain and powdered to make the dubious
aphrodisiac of the same name.*

## Ingredients:

broken ice
1½ measures tequila (gold
tequila if possible)
½ measure sherry

## Tequila

### Method:

Fill an old-fashioned glass
with broken ice. Add the
tequila and the sherry and
serve with a stirrer.

| method: | BUILD |
|---|---|
| glass: | HIGHBALL OR PILSNER |

# Submarino

*This is a must for anyone who likes beer! Try the tequila moonrise (page 155) as well. No tequila and no Mexican beer? Then make a dog's nose: pour 1 measure of gin into the beer of your choice.*

## Ingredients:

I measure tequila

I glass Mexican beer

# Tequila

## Method:

Pour the beer into the glass and add the tequila!

# Tequila sunrise

*Created in Mexico in the 1930s, this long, beautifully coloured drink has remained incredibly popular – and even inspired a couple of songs! The ingredients are poured straight into the glass and the grenadine is allowed to sink to the bottom.*

## Ingredients:

ice cubes (if desired)
2 measures tequila
½ measure grenadine
4 measures orange juice
1 orange slice
1 maraschino cherry

# Tequila

## Method:

Pour the orange juice and tequila into the highball glass almost filled with ice cubes. Stir well and let it come to a rest.
Drop the grenadine into the centre of the drink and allow it to settle to the bottom.
Garnish with the orange slice and cherry.

## Variation:

Use 2 measures pineapple and 2 measures orange juice, and you'll enjoy a Florida sunrise.

method: SHAKER

glass: COLLINS

# Tequila moonrise

*After the sun goes down, up comes the moon!*

## Ingredients:

ice cubes

3 measures tequila

1 measure light rum

1 measure dark rum

2 measures beer

½ measure Rose's Lime Juice

½ measure lemon juice

1 teaspoon castor sugar

# Tequila

## Method:

Half-fill the shaker with ice cubes.

Pour in the tequila, light and dark rums, lime juice, lemon juice and the sugar.

Shake well and strain into a Collins glass half-filled with ice cubes.

Top up with the beer.

# Viva Villa

*Francisco Doroteo Arango Villa, better known as the Mexican revolutionary general Pancho Villa (1877–1923) was, in fact, a well-known teetotaller. Perhaps then it's for fans of Aston Villa – although it's not in their club's colours!*

## Ingredients:

ice cubes

2 measures tequila

1 measure lime juice

1 teaspoon lemon juice

2 teaspoons castor sugar

1 lime wedge

## Tequila

## Method:

Place the sugar in a saucer. Rub the rim of the cocktail glass with the lime wedge and dip the rim into the sugar.

Discard the lime.

Half-fill the shaker with ice cubes and pour in the lemon juice, lime juice and tequila. Shake well and strain into the sugar-frosted cocktail glass.

| method: | SHAKER |
| glass: | COCKTAIL |
| garnish: | CHERRY AND A SLICE OF ORANGE |

# Acapulco

*Tequila and kahlua from Mexico blended with rum and coconut from the Caribbean in a drink to make you bold enough to make the famous high dive into the Pacific Ocean!*

## Ingredients:

1 measure gold tequila
1 measure kahlua
⅔ measure dark rum
½ measure coconut cream

# Tequila

## Method:

Shake all the ingredients together in a shaker with some ice cubes. Shake well and strain into a cocktail glass and garnish with the orange slice and the cherry.

# Tequila Exotica

## Ingredients:

1½ measures gold tequila
¼ measure white creme de cacao
1 teaspoon triple sec/Cointreau
1 measure mango juice
1 measure white grape juice
½ measure lime juice

## Tequila

## Method:

Place all the ingredients,
except the garnish, into a
cocktail shaker with some ice
cubes. Shake and strain into
an old-fashioned glass filled
two-thirds with broken ice.
Garnish with seasonal fruit
and serve with straws.

| method: | SHAKER |
|---|---|
| glass: | OLD-FASHIONED AND A SHOT GLASS |
| garnish: | LIME WEDGE |

# Tequila

## Method:

Rub one of the lime wedges around the rim of an old-fashioned glass, then dip the rim into some sea salt. Fill the glass two-thirds full with ice cubes. Into the cocktail shaker with some ice cubes, squeeze the juice from 2 lime wedges. Press the lime rind to release the oil and then drop the spent shells into the shaker. Pour the tequila, Cointreau, lime juice and cranberry juice into the shaker and shake vigourously. Strain into the ice-filled old-fashion glass and garnish with the remaining lime wedge. Pour the Grand Marnier into a shot glass and serve along side: just before drinking, the Grand Marnier is poured on top of the cocktail.

## Pink Cadillac Convertible

*A wonderful name for a fun drink.*

### Ingredients:

4 lime wedges

sea salt

1¼ measures gold tequila

½ measure Cointreau

¾ measure lime juice

¾ measure cranberry juice

¾ measure Grand Marnier

# Mezcarita

*If you do happen to have some mescal, here's a way to enjoy it without having to eat the worm! If not, gold tequila makes a very palatable substitute.*

## Ingredients:

1½ measures mescal (or gold tequila)
¾ measure Cointreau
1¼ measures lemon juice
salt (chilli salt makes a
    spicy change!)

# Tequila

## Method:

Dampen the rim of the cocktail glass with a little lemon juice and dip into the salt. Add the mescal, Cointreau and lemon juice to a shaker with some ice cubes and shake well. Strain into the cocktail class and decorate with a spiral of lemon peel.

| method: | SHAKER |
| glass: | COCKTAIL |
| garnish: | LIME SLICE |

# Tequila Mockingbird
*Raise a glass to Harper Lee.*

# Tequila

## Method:

Place all the ingredients in a shaker with some ice cubes and shake well. Strain into a cocktail glass and garnish with lime slices.

## Ingredients:

1½ measures silver tequila
¾ measure green creme de menthe
½ measure lime juice

# Buttock Clencher

*The 'fun and funky' name betrays the modern origins of this drink – as does the inclusion of tequila which, although it has been made for centuries in its native Mexico, is a relative newcomer to the cocktail scene. Try this pineapple-flavoured delight.*

## Ingredients:

1 measure silver tequila
1 measure gin
¼ measure Midori melon liqueur
2 measures pineapple juice
2 measures lemonade

## Tequila

### Method:

Place all the ingredients, except the lemonade, in a shaker with two to three ice cubes. Shake and strain into an ice-filled highball glass and add the lemonade. Garnish with the cherry and pineapple cube.

# Cactus Juice

*Here's another way to enjoy the juice of the Agave tequiliana and an opportunity to use Scotland's fine contribution to the world's classic liqueurs, Drambuie. A unique blend of whisky (of course), heather (naturally), honey and herbs based on a recipe said to have been given as a reward to Captain Mackinon in 1745 following the defeat of Bonnie Prince Charlie at the Battle of Culloden. Mackinon was the protector of the 'Pretender' after the prince was ferried 'over the sea to Skye' and on to safety in France. While the story may be a little invented, the Mackinon family are still making Drambuie in Edinburgh, Scotland.*

## Ingredients:

2 measures gold tequila

1 teaspoon Drambuie

1 measure lemon juice

1 teaspoon caster sugar

## Tequila

## Method:

Dissolve the sugar in the lemon juice and pour into a shaker with a glass full of broken ice cubes. Add the tequila and Drambuie and shake well. Pour, unstrained, into an old-fashioned glass.

# Firebird

*In the ballet of the same name, a high golden fence protects the garden of golden fruits grown of the sinister Katschei, who has imprisoned the lovely princess. The firebird tries to steal the golden fruit but is captured by Prince Ivan, who lets her go in exchange for one of her magical feathers: armed with this, Ivan is assured of the firebird's help should he need it. Prince Ivan then discovers the beautiful captive princess who warns him that Katschei will turn him to stone if discovered. When this happens, Ivan waves the firebird's feather in Katschei's face and the firebird appears, forcing the evil monsters who attend the magician to dance until they collapse. The firebird shows Ivan a great golden egg, which holds the soul of the magician. Ivan throws the egg into the air, and when it falls, it breaks and Katschei dies. Ivan marries his princess and the firebird flies away forever. This has absolutely nothing to do with the cocktail, but it's a great ballet, choreographed by George Balanchine to magnificent score by Igor Stravinsky!*

## Tequila

## Ingredients:

1½ measures silver
   tequila
½ measure creme de
   banane
½ measure lime juice
2 measures lemonade

## Method:

Add the ingredients to an old fashioned glass three-quarters filled with broken ice. Dream of a handsome prince/beautiful princess/big bird.

| method: | BLENDER |
|---|---|
| glass: | PINA COLADA OR HURRICANE GLASS |
| garnish: | PINEAPPLE SLICE |

# Las Vegas

*Like the town, it's over the top – but completely addictive!*

## Tequila

## Method:

Place half a glass of crushed ice in the blender and add the ingredients. Blend briefl and pour into a piña colada or hurricane glass. Garnish with the slice of pineapple and serve with straws.

If you replace the tequila with vodka, you'll have a Vodka Las Vegas.

## Ingredients:

1 ½ measures tequila (gold, preferably)
2 measures coconut cream
2 measures orange juice
2 measures pineapple juice
1 measure whipping cream

# Cavalier

*This has a delightful madarin-herb flavour.*

## Ingredients:

1 measure gold tequila
½ measure Galliano
2 measures mandarin juice
1 measure whipping cream

# Tequila

## Method:

Place all the ingredients into a shaker with two or three ice cubes and shake well. Strain into a cocktail glass.

| method: | SHAKER |
|---|---|
| glass: | LARGE CHAMPAGNE SAUCER |
| garnish: | LEMON SLICE |

# Frozen Blue Margarita

*This is the frozen version of the famous tequila classic. Why not whizz a few up for Cinco de Mayo (5th May) to celebrate Mexico's national holiday.*

# Tequila

## Method:

Rim the glass with a little lemon juice and 'frost' the rim with salt. Place the ingredients in a shaker with two or three ice cubes. Shake and strain into a large champagne saucer filled with crushed ice and garnish with a slice of lemon.

## Ingredients:

1¾ measures silver tequila
¾ measure blue Curaçao
¾ measure lemon juice
lemon juice
salt

# Frozen Matador

## Ingredients:

1½ measures tequila
2 measures pineapple juice
1 tablespoon lime juice

# Tequila

## Method:

Combine the ingredients in a
blender with a glass of
crushed ice and blend at low
speed. Pour into an old-
fashioned glass and garnish
with a stick of pineapple.

# C.C. Kazi

## Ingredients:

1½ measures tequila

2 measures cranberry juice

1 teaspoon lime juice

# Tequila

## Method:

Into a shaker with some ice cubes, add the lime juice, cranberry juice and tequila. Shake and strain into a cordial glass.

# Brandy cocktails

Any spirit distilled from fruit, rather than grain, is a brandy. The French term *eau-de-vie de vin* ('water of life from wine') is the generic term for all brandies. Good brandies come from France, Spain, Greece, Australia, South Africa, Portugal, the United States of America – wherever grapes are grown, brandy is made. Peru also produces a recently popular brandy called Pisco.

Only the spirit that is distilled in the registered district of France, however, has a right to be called cognac. The area is located north of Bordeaux and south of La Rochelle on the west coast of France and stretches inland to Angoulême. The river Charente runs through the region and gives its name to the two *départements* in which most of the vineyards are planted, the Charente and Charente-Maritime.

The boundaries of the area were set down in 1909, and because of the variations in the soil and consequently the quality of spirit produced, it was further subdivided into five

## Horse's neck with a kick
see page 330.

'divisions'. In the centre, around the town of Cognac itself, are the two finest areas of production, which account for around 21 per cent of cognac production: Grande Champagne and Petite Champagne. Next in quality is the cognac from Les Borderies, from the areas surrounding the Fine Champagne area, followed by that from Fins Bois and Bons Bois. Finally, production from the two outermost areas, Bois Ordinaires and Bois Cummuns, cannot be blended to make Grande or Fine Champagne, or, indeed, be added to the other three AOC (*Appellation d'Origine Contrôlé*) regions.

All cognac is made from wine that is fermented from whole grapes and then double-distilled in pot stills. It is then aged in new oak casks for one year and transferred to aged oak casks to stop the cognac from taking on too much tannin from the new oak. The labels on cognac bottles are designed to denote the quality of the spirit: V (Very), S (Special), O (Old), P (Pale), F (Fine), X (Extra), C (Cognac) and E (Especial). VO and VSOP mean that the cognac has been aged for at least 4½ years. The words Extra, Napoleon and Vieille Reserve are a government guarantee that the cognac has been aged at least 5½ years. The stars found on labels are also related to age: three-star cognac is the youngest, aged for a minimum of 18 months.

The second great *eau-de vie de vin*, also from France, is arma-

Mate
see page 332.

Sidecar
see page 337.

gnac, which is produced in Gascony, south of Bordeaux. While cognac is double-distilled in pot stills, armagnac is single-distilled in its own type of still and takes much of its flavour and colour from casks made of local oak, in which it matures.

Calvados is a brandy made from apples. A speciality of the Normandy region of northern France, Calvados is distilled from apple cider fermented for one month and then aged, sometimes for as long as 40 years. Calvados is known as *eau-de-vie de cidre* ('water of life from cider'). America also produces fine apple brandies known as applejack.

Other fruits are used to make *eau-de-vie* or brandy. The spirits are almost always colourless since they are bottled immediately after distillation to retain the fruit flavours and high alcohol content. The best known are Kirsch (made from cherries), Poire William (from pears), Mirabelle, Quetsch and Slivovitz (from different varieties of plums), Framboise (from raspberries), Prunelle (from sloe berries) and Fraises (from strawberries).

| method: | MIXING GLASS |
|---|---|
| glass: | OLD FASHIONED |

# Betsy Ross

*Named after Betsy Griscom Ross (1752–1836),*
*who made the very first United States flag*

## Ingredients:

ice cubes
2 measures brandy
1 measure port
½ teaspoon triple sec or
Cointreau
1 dash bitters

# Brandy

## Method:

Put some ice cubes in the
mixing glass and pour in the
brandy, port, triple sec or
Cointreau and bitters.
Stir well and strain into an
old-fashioned glass filled with
ice cubes.

# Between the sheets

*A perfect (and seductively named) after-dinner drink, this classic cocktail was created in the 1930s.*

## Ingredients:

ice cubes

1½ measures brandy

1 measure white rum

1 measure Cointreau

½ measure lemon juice

1 twist lemon (optional)

# Brandy

## Method:

Half-fill the shaker with ice cubes.

Pour in the brandy, rum, Cointreau and lemon juice and shake sharply.

Strain into a cocktail glass and garnish with the lemon twist (optional).

**method:** MIXING GLASS

**glass:** COCKTAIL

# Burnt orange

## Brandy

### Method:

Put some ice cubes into the mixing glass and shake the bitters over the ice.
Pour in the orange juice and brandy and stir vigorously.
Strain into a cocktail glass.

### Ingredients:

ice cubes

3 measures brandy

2 measures orange juice

3 drops bitters

# Brandy cooler

*A cooler is a long drink, similar to a Collins, but which usually contains a spiral of citrus peel trailing over the edge of the glass. It's also a little like a horse's neck (see page 171), but while that is made with ginger ale, the original Remsen cooler of the 1880s was made with soda water. The 19th-century fashion was for sweet coolers, sometimes topped with ice cream. Today, coolers are generally much drier and more thirst-quenching drinks, but you can sweeten yours according to taste.*

## Ingredients:

ice cubes
2 measures brandy
5 measures soda water
long spiral of lemon peel

## Variations:

If you find it too dry, add a little sugar or try substituting a lemon-lime soda (such as 7-Up) for the plain soda water. Any base spirit can be used for a cooler.

# Brandy

## Method:

Decorate the Collins glass with the long spiral of peel so that it hangs over the side of the glass.
Place three or four ice cubes in the glass and pour in the brandy.
Add the soda and stir thoroughly.

322

| method: | BUILD |
| glass: | HIGHBALL |
| garnish: | LIME SLICE |

# Brandy Cuban

*This is a little like the Cuba libre (page 60), but uses brandy in place of rum. A surprisingly good mix!*

## Ingredients:

ice cubes
2 measures brandy
1 measure lime juice
4 measures cold cola
1 slice lime

# Brandy

## Method:

Half-fill the highball glass with ice cubes.
Pour in the lime juice and brandy and top up with the cola.
Stir lightly and decorate with the lime slice.

# Brandy perfect

*Who are we to disagree?*

## Ingredients:

ice cubes
3 measures brandy
½ measure dry vermouth
½ measure rosso vermouth
1 lemon twist

# Brandy

## Method:

Place some ice cubes in the mixing glass and pour in the dry vermouth, rosso vermouth and the brandy. Stir vigorously and strain into the cocktail glass.
Add the twist of lemon and discard, or drop it into the glass if you wish.

| method: | BUILD |
|---|---|
| glass: | HIGHBALL |
| garnish: | NUTMEG |

# Brandy sangaree

*An English corruption of the Spanish word 'sangria', the Iberian red-wine drink, sangarees were originally made of sweetened, fortified wines served in a tumbler and iced. They could also be made with ales and beers, again sweetened with sugar, and often served hot. This was done by heating a poker in a fire until it was red hot and then immersing it in the drink. Modern sangarees use spirits and soda water served in a highball glass with a traditional dusting of nutmeg on the top.*

## Ingredients:

broken ice
2½ measures brandy
½ measure port
½ measure gomme syrup
2½ measures soda water
grated nutmeg

# Brandy

## Method:

Fill a highball glass two-thirds full with broken ice.
Pour in the brandy and the gomme syrup.
Add the soda and float the port on top.
Dust with the nutmeg and add straws.

## Variation:

Sangarees can be made with any spirit: gin, bourbon, whisky or sherry can be used in place of the brandy.

# Brandy smash

*Smashes are drinks flavoured with crushed mint – a short version of the mint julep (see page 117). Smashes first appeared in America in the 1850s, and it is believed they took their name from the fine smashed ice used to make them. Smashes can be made in the same way with any spirit: replace the brandy with two measures of either vodka, gin, rum, Scotch, rye or bourbon.*

## Ingredients:

crushed ice

2 measures brandy

½ measure gomme syrup

2 sprigs mint

1 mint sprig for garnish

## Brandy

## Method:

Drop the two sprigs of mint into the old-fashioned glass. Pour in the gomme syrup and gently crush the mint with a muddler.

Add the brandy and then fill the glass with the crushed ice.

Garnish with the sprig of mint and serve with a muddler and straws.

| method: | MIXING GLASS/ LINE |
|---|---|
| glass: | COCKTAIL |

# Charles cocktail

## Ingredients:

ice cubes
2 measures brandy
½ measure rosso vermouth
2 dashes bitters

## Brandy

## Method:

Put some ice cubes in the mixing glass and pour in the rosso vermouth and brandy. Add the bitters and stir well. Strain into a cocktail glass.

# City slicker

*For when you've closed the big deal!*

## Ingredients:

ice cubes
2 measures brandy
½ measure triple sec or
Cointreau
½ measure lemon juice

# Brandy

## Method:

Half-fill the shaker with ice cubes.
Pour in the brandy, triple sec or Cointreau and lemon juice and shake well.
Strain into a cocktail glass.

| method: | MIXING GLASS |
|---|---|
| glass: | COCKTAIL |
| garnish: | LEMON TWIST |

# Comforting tiger

*Drinks that contain the peach-, orange- and herb-flavoured bourbon, Southern Comfort (one of America's oldest liqueurs from St Louis, Missouri), often have 'comfort' or 'southern' in their names. See the slow comfortable screw (page 104) and the Southern delta (page 123).*

## Ingredients:

crushed ice
2 measures brandy
½ measure Southern
Comfort
I teaspoon rosso vermouth
I lemon twist

# Brandy

## Method:

Half-fill the mixing glass with crushed ice.
Pour in the rosso vermouth, Southern Comfort and brandy and stir well.
Strain into a cocktail glass and garnish with the lemon twist.

# Esquire

*An elegant brandy and gin cocktail.*

## Ingredients:

ice cubes
2 measures brandy
1 measure gin
3 drops bitters

## Brandy

## Method:

Put some ice cubes into the mixing glass.
Shake the bitters over the ice and then pour in the gin and brandy.
Stir vigorously and strain into a chilled cocktail glass.

| | |
|---|---|
| method: | BUILD |
| glass: | HIGHBALL |
| garnish: | SPIRAL OF LEMON PEEL |

# Horse's neck with a kick

*The original horse's neck started life in the 1890s as a non-alcoholic mix of lemon peel, ice and ginger ale. By around 1910 it had become a whisky drink and Scotch, Irish, rye or bourbon was used as requested. This became known as a 'stiff horse's neck'. With Prohibition, the horse's neck reverted to its 'plain' formula – although speakeasies might add some bath-tub gin. Now the horse's neck with a kick is made with either brandy or bourbon and is usually served like a cooler – with a long spiral of citrus peel.*

# Brandy

## Method:

Cut a long spiral of lemon peel and hang it over the highball glass.
Half-fill the glass with ice cubes and pour in the brandy. Add the bitters and top with ginger ale.

## Ingredients:

ice cubes
2 measures brandy
1 dash bitters
4 measures ginger ale
1 lemon-peel spiral

# Lord Chamberlain

## Ingredients:

ice cubes

2 measures brandy

1 measure port

1 measure dry vermouth

3 drops bitters

1 lemon twist

# Brandy

## Method:

Put some ice cubes in the mixing glass and pour the vermouth and port over the ice.

Add the bitters and then pour in the brandy.

Stir well and then strain into a chilled cocktail glass.

Add the twist of lemon.

| method: | MIXING GLASS |
| --- | --- |
| glass: | SOUR (OR WHITE-WINE GLASS) |

Mate

## Ingredients:

ice cubes

3 measures brandy

1 measure dry vermouth

1 measure orange juice

½ teaspoon grenadine

# Brandy

## Method:

Put some ice cubes into the
mixing glass and pour in the
orange juice, grenadine,
vermouth and brandy.
Stir until the mix becomes
frothy and then strain into a
sour or white-wine glass.

# Metropolitan

*For the man – or woman – about town.*

## Ingredients:

crushed ice

2 measures brandy

½ measure rosso vermouth

1 teaspoon castor sugar

1 dash bitters

# Brandy

## Method:

Half-fill the shaker with crushed ice.

Pour in the rosso vermouth, sugar, dash of bitters and the brandy.

Shake well.

Strain into a cocktail glass.

| method: | MIXING GLASS |
| --- | --- |
| glass: | COCKTAIL |

# Montana

*A taste as big as the state, and an interesting presentation.*

## Ingredients:

ice cubes

2 measures brandy

2 teaspoons port

2 teaspoons dry vermouth

# Brandy

## Method:

Put some ice cubes in the mixing glass and pour in the brandy, port and vermouth. Strain into a cocktail glass with a single ice cube in it.

# Monte rosa

*This lime-flavour cocktail was invented in the 1920s. Originally it was served 'straight up' without the sugar. It is also sometimes served in an old-fashioned glass filled with broken ice. Try the variations for yourself.*

## Ingredients:

ice cubes
3 measures brandy
1 measure Cointreau
½ measure lime juice

# Brandy

## Method:

Put some ice cubes in the mixing glass and pour in the lime juice.
Add the Cointreau and brandy and stir well.
Strain into a chilled cocktail glass.

| method: | MIXING GLASS |
|---|---|
| glass: | SOUR (OR WHITE-WINE GLASS) |

# Robinson

*A drink for when you're cast away on a desert island! (With a well-stocked bar, you might not want to be rescued).*

# Brandy

## Method:

Put some ice cubes into the mixing glass and pour in the pineapple juice.
Add the vermouth and brandy and stir until frothy. Strain into a sour or white-wine glass.

## Ingredients:

ice cubes
3 measures brandy
1 measure dry vermouth
1 measure pineapple juice

# Sidecar

*Created shortly after the First World War, at Harry's Bar in Paris, this drink was named in honour of the army captain who arrived at the bar in a chauffeur-driven motorcycle sidecar. Originally served in a champagne saucer, the sidecar is now more often served over broken ice in an old-fashioned glass.*

## Ingredients:

ice cubes
broken ice
2 measures cognac (or armagnac)
1 measure Cointreau
1 measure lemon juice

# Brandy

## Method:

Half-fill the shaker with ice cubes.
Pour in the lemon juice, Cointreau and brandy and shake well.
Strain into an old-fashioned glass nearly filled with broken ice.

## Variations:

You can adjust the amount of lemon juice to suit. Add 1 measure of white rum, and you'll have a Boston sidecar. If Calvados or applejack (apple brandies) are used in place of the cognac, this is an applecart. Replace the brandy with gin, and you have a Chelsea sidecar.

| method: | SHAKER |
|---------|--------|
| glass: | COCKTAIL |

# Star

*This is possibly the best-tasting use of grapefruit juice yet!*

## Ingredients:

ice cubes
3 measures brandy
1 measure gin
1 measure grapefruit juice
½ teaspoon rosso vermouth
½ teaspoon dry vermouth

## Brandy

### Method:

Half-fill the shaker with ice cubes.
Pour in the grapefruit juice, vermouths, gin and brandy and shake well.
Strain into a cocktail glass.

# St Kitts

*Named after the island of St Kitts in the Leeward Islands of the eastern West Indies.*

## Ingredients:

ice cubes

3 measures brandy

1 measure dry vermouth

1½ measures grapefruit juice

1 maraschino cherry

# Brandy

## Method:

Half-fill the shaker with ice cubes.

Pour in the grapefruit juice, vermouth and brandy and shake well.

Strain into a cocktail glass and drop in the maraschino cherry.

| method: | MIXING GLASS |
|---------|--------------|
| glass: | COCKTAIL |

# Tantalus cocktail

*The son of the god Zeus and king of Sipylos in ancient Lydia, Tantalus is remembered for his punishment in Hades for having stolen ambrosia, the food of the gods. For his crime, Tantalus stood in water up to his chin and was 'tantalised' with food and drink, which moved out of his reach whenever he tried to satisfy his hunger and thirst. His name lives on in this equally tantalising cocktail (and in the lockable case for decanters of wines and spirits, a tantalus. The drink can be seen, but not enjoyed, except by the owner of the key).*

## Ingredients:

ice cubes

3 measures brandy

I measure Cointreau

I measure lemon juice

# Brandy

## Method:

Put some ice cubes in the mixing glass and pour in the lemon juice, Cointreau and brandy.

Stir vigorously and then strain into a cocktail glass.

# Beauty Cocktail

*Devised originally by Harry MacElhone of Harry's
New York Bar at 5 rue Daunou, Paris.*

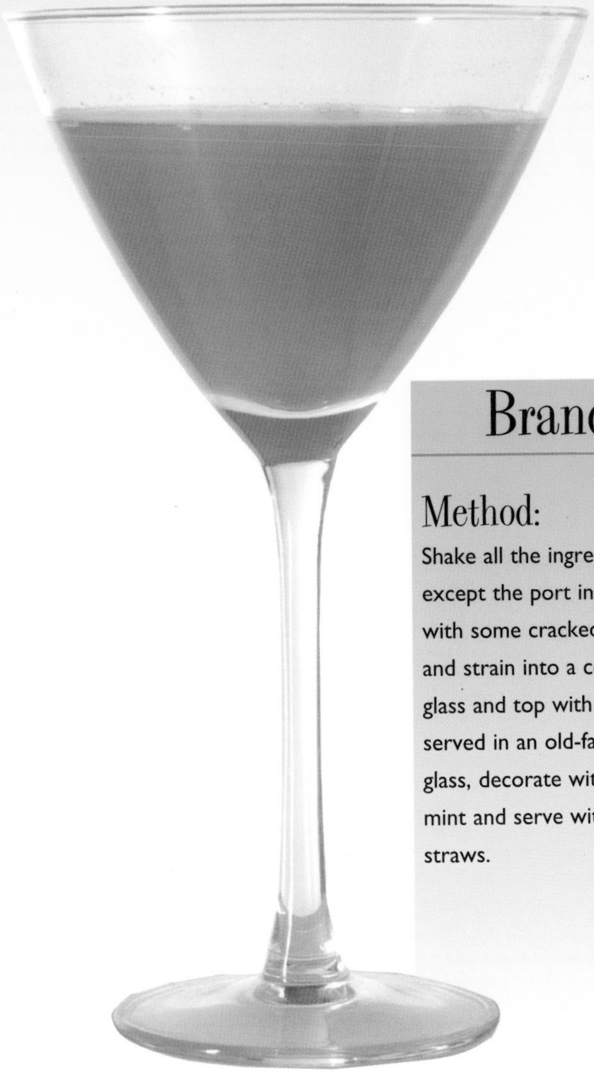

## Brandy

## Ingredients:

¾ measure brandy

¾ measure dry vermouth

¾ measure orange juice

¼ measure white creme de
    menthe

1 dash grenadine

1 dash – or more – port

## Method:

Shake all the ingredients
except the port in a shaker
with some cracked ice. Shake
and strain into a cocktail
glass and top with the port. If
served in an old-fashioned
glass, decorate with a sprig of
mint and serve with short
straws.

| method: | SHAKER |
|---|---|
| glass: | COCKTAIL |

# Block and Fall Cocktail

*This recipe was devised in 1924 at Deauville, France – famous*
*for its casino and horse races – by T. Van Dycke from Ciro's Club.*

## Ingredients:

1 measure Cognac

1 measure Cointreau

½ measure Calvados

½ measure anis (substitute: Pernod)

## Brandy

## Method:

Place the ingredients in a
shaker with some ice cubes
and shake well. Strain and
pour into a cocktail glass.

# Lady be Good

*But be just a little wicked too!*

## Ingredients:

1½ measures brandy
½ measure white creme de menthe
½ measure sweet vermouth

## Brandy

## Method:

Place all the ingredients in a shaker with some ice cubes. Shake and strain into a cocktail glass.

| method: | BUILD |
| --- | --- |
| glass: | OLD-FASHIONED |

# Brandy Fix

*A sweet but simple cocktail that packs a warm punch!*

## Ingredients:

1 measure brandy
½ measure cherry brandy
1 teaspoon sugar
1 teaspoon water
juice of ½ lemon

## Brandy

## Method:

Dissolve the sugar in the water in a tumbler. Mix with the remaining ingredients and pour over ice. Stir and serve with a lemon slice.

# Corpse Reviver

*The wonderfully inspired Corpse Reviver was created by Frank Meier at the Ritz Bar in Paris in the 1920s. The* Savoy Cocktail Book *stated that it should be drunk "before 11 am, or whenever steam and energy are needed"! Harry Craddock maintained that four Corpse Revivers No. 2., drunk one after the other, would 'un–revive the corpse'. The No. 2 calls for Lillet, a dry, light vermouth from France with a slight orange tinge, while The Corpse Reviver No. 3, the creation of Johnny Johnson of the Savoy in 1948, traditionally uses Fernet-Branca, an Italian bitter often recommended as a hangover cure!*

# Brandy

## Method:

### No. 1:
Pour the ingredients into a mixing glass with ice cubes and stir. Strain into a cocktail glass.

## Ingredients:

### Corpse Reviver No. 1:

1 measure brandy
⅔ measure sweet vermouth
⅔ measure Calvados

### Corpse Reviver No. 2:

½ measure lemon juice
½ measure Lillet
½ measure Cointreau
½ measure gin
1 dash Pernod

### Corpse Reviver No. 3:

1 measure brandy
1 measure white creme
de menthe
1 measure Fernet-Branca

## Brandy

### Method:

### No. 2:

Place all the ingredients in a shaker with some ice cubes and shake sharply. Strain into a cocktail glass.

## Brandy

### Method:

### No. 3:

Pour the ingredients into a mixing glass with ice and stir well. Strain into a cocktail glass.

# Vanderbilt

*This cocktail was devised by 'Guido' of the Kursaal Bar in Ostend, Belgium, in 1912 to mark the visit of American millionaire, Colonel Corneluis Vanderbilt. Shortly afterwards the Colonel drowned when the Lusitania was sunk, and the cocktail became internationally famous.*

## Ingredients:

1½ measures cognac

1 measure cherry brandy

1 teaspoon sugar syrup

1 dash angostura bitters

## Brandy

### Method:

Into an old fashioned glass filled with broken ice, add the ingredients. Add the lemon twist.

| method: | SHAKER |
|---|---|
| glass: | COCKTAIL |

# Stinger

*Simple – yet very effective.*

## Ingredients:

1½ measures brandy
½ measure white creme de
menthe

# Brandy

## Method:

Add some ice to a shaker
and pour in the brandy and
creme de menthe. Shake well
and strain into a cocktail
glass.

# Pisco Sour

*A chance to try out pisco, a colourless brandy from South America.*

## Ingredients:

2 measures pisco
juice of ½ lime
1 teaspoon sugar syrup
½ an egg white
1 dash angostura bitters

# Brandy

## Method:

Fill an old-fashioned glass with broken ice and, by hand, squeeze in the juice of ½ a lime. Place the remaining ingredients in the shaker with some ice cubes and shake well. Strain into the ice-filled glass and garnish with a sprig of mint.

| method: | MIXING GLASS |
|---|---|
| glass: | LIQUEUR OR CORDIAL GLASS |

# B & B Cocktail

*One B is for Benedictine, the other for brandy – or preferably Cognac, which is deserving of such a fine companion.*

## Ingredients:

I measure brandy or Cognac

I measure Benedictine

## Brandy

### Method:

Place the ingredients in a mixing glass with some ice and stir. Strain into a cordial or liqueur glass.

# B2 C2

*This drink was invented in 1945 by none other than the United States 21st Army Corps. When they crossed the Rhine, they 'liberated' a Wehrmacht liquor store and what they found – the 2 Bs (brandy and Benedictine) and 2 Cs (Cointreau and champagne) – were immediately pressed into military service! You can also make this delicious formula in a jug and add chopped fruits in season to serve to your own platoon of guests.*

## Ingredients:

1 measure brandy
1 measure Benedictine
1 measure Cointreau
4 measures champagne

## Brandy

## Method:

Add the ingredients to a large wine glass!

352

| method: | BUILD |
| --- | --- |
| glass: | COLLINS |
| garnish: | CHERRY AND SLICES OF ORANGE AND LEMON |

# B & B Collins

*A wonderful hot-weather drink. The name Collins is thought to have come from one John Collins, a famous head waiter at Limmer's hotel and coffee house which was located in London's Conduit Street from 1790–1817.*

## Ingredients:
1½ measures brandy
½ measure Benedictine
1 measure lemon juice
1 measure sugar syrup
5 measures soda water

# Brandy

## Method:
Chill a collins glass and fill two thirds with ice. Pour in the lemon juice, sugar syrup and brandy and top with soda water. Sprinkle the Benedictine over the top and garnish with the cherry and slices of lemon and orange and serve with straws.

# Chartreuse Cocktail

## Ingredients:

1 measure yellow Chartreuse

1 measure cognac

½ measure dry vermouth

## Brandy

## Method:

Place ingredients in a mixing glass with some ice cubes and stir. Strain into a liqueur or cordial glass and garnish with a cherry.

354

| method: | BUILD |
|---|---|
| glass: | COLLINS |
| garnish: | SLICE OF ORANGE AND A CHERRY |

# Lutter

*Cognac is one of the finest spirits available to mankind and should be enjoyed at every opportunity! Purists might argue that such fine spirits should never be mixed, but the more adventurous maintain that clever combinations only enhance these already fine qualities. Try this delicious long drink and judge for yourself.*

## Brandy

### Method:
Half fill a collins glass with broken ice and pour in the ingredients. Garnish with the orange slice and the cherry and serve with straws.

### Ingredients:
1 measure VSOP Cognac
½ measure vodka
½ measure Mandarine Napoleon
4 measures sparkling bitter lemon

## Whoopee Cocktail

*'Don't forget folks, that's what you get, folks, for making whoopee'. This champagne delight comes from Harry MacElhone's* Harry's ABC of Mixing Cocktails.

### Ingredients:

1 lump of ice
½ measure Curaçao
½ measure Cognac
chilled champagne

## Brandy

### Method:

Place the ice cube into the champagne saucer or flute. Pour in the Curaçao and Cognac and fill the glass with chilled champagne.

| method: | SHAKER |
|---|---|
| glass: | CHAMPAGNE SAUCER OR COCKTAIL GLASSL |
| garnish: | SLICE OF ORANGE SPEARED WITH A CHERRY |

# Cherry Blossom

*Cherry brandy may be one of the very few liqueurs to have been 'invented' in England. Said to be the creation of one Thomas Grant from Kent, the 'garden of England', who made his version with black morello cherries. While fruity, it's got a kick to it: cherry brandy was the ruin of the dissolute Prince Regent, later King George IV.*

## Ingredients:

1½ measures cherry brandy

1 measure brandy

¼ measure triple sec/Cointreau

¼ measure lemon juice

⅓ measure egg white

1 teaspoon grenadine

¼ measure sugar syrup

# Brandy

## Method:

Rim the champagne saucer or cocktail glass with a little grenadine and dip into some caster sugar. Place the ingredients in a shaker with two or three ice cubes and shake well. Strain into the 'frosted' champagne saucer and garnish with the slice of orange and the cherry.

## Connoisseur's Treat

*An orange-brandy flavour with just a hint of anise
(liquorice), almonds and vanilla, courtesy of the
golden-yellow Italian liqueur, Galliano.*

### Ingredients:

1½ measures Cognac
½ measure Galliano
½ Grand Marnier

## Brandy

### Method:

Stir and strain the ingredients
into a brandy snifter.

358

| method: | BUILD |
| --- | --- |
| glass: | PINA COLADA GLASS, OR OVERSIZED WINE GLASS |
| garnish: | SPRIG OF MINT |

# Fly Swatter

*The original recipe calls for raki, the aniseed-tinged drink of Greece and Turkey. You can use Pernod or Ricard, the most familiar pastis on the market today.*

# Brandy

## Method:
Add the ingredients to a piña colada or oversized wine glass filled with broken ice. Add a sprig of mint and serve with straws.

## Ingredients:
1 measure Cognac
1 measure whisky
1 teaspoon Pernod or Ricard
3 measures mandarin juice
2 measures pineapple juice

# Brandy Puff

*Before Prohibition, puffs were enormously popular drinks in the United States. Any spirit can be used: whisky and rum go well with milk, and so does brandy. If you're feeling adventurous, try a Gin Puff.*

## Ingredients:

2 measures brandy

3 measures cold milk

3 measures soda water

## Brandy

## Method:

Place the brandy and milk in a shaker with two or three ice cubes and shake vigourously. Strain into a goblet or brandy snifter and add the soda water.

| method: | SHAKER |
|---|---|
| glass: | GOBLET OR OVERSIZED WINE GLASS |
| garnish: | SPRINKLE OF NUTMEG |

# Egg Nogg

*In the 17th century, Nog was a strong beer brewed in East Anglia in England; a noggin was a small mug of beer or liquor. In both England and the USA, a beaten egg was often added, and this seems to be the origin of Egg Nogg. Traditionally the drink of the holiday season from Christmas Eve to New Year's night, Egg Nogg tastes good any time. Today, there are as many arguments raging over the 'perfect Egg Nogg' as the 'perfect Mint Julep': some say an Egg Nogg should be 'liquid', others 'solid', to be eaten with a spoon; some advocate the whole egg, some just the yolk. Different schools of thought have given rise to numerous recipes, so here are just a couple. If you've never tried Egg Nogg, you're in for a real treat.*

# Brandy

## Method:

Shake all the ingredients well in a shaker with two or three ice cubes or cracked ice. Strain and pour into a goblet and sprinkle with nutmeg.

If you reduce the rum to ½ a measure and add 1 measure of Madeira, you'll have yourself a Baltimore Egg Nogg.

## Ingredients:

1 measure brandy
1 measure dark rum
1½ measures milk
1 measure whipping cream
½ measure sugar syrup
1 small egg, beaten

| method: | SHAKER |
|---------|--------|
| glass: | COCKTAIL OR CHAMPAGNE SAUCER |
| garnish: | GRATED CHOCOLATE OR NUTMEG |

361

# Brandy Alexander

*Originally, the Alexander was a gin-based drink, but the use of brandy has made it into one of the most sophisticated after-dinner drinks in spite of it's very simple construction. There are also a whole range of Alexanders that have been developed like the Coffee Alexander and Alexander's Sister, a treat if you like a mint flavour.*

## Ingredients:

1⅓ measures brandy

1⅓ measures dark creme de cacao

1⅓ measures double cream

## Variations:

### Rum Alexander:

Replace the brandy with 1 measure white rum, and ⅓ measure dark rum.

### Amaretto Alexander:

Replace the brandy with 1⅓ measures amaretto.

### Alexander's Sister:

Two measures gin, ⅔ measure green creme de menthe, 1⅓ measures double cream.

### Gin Alexander:

Two measures gin, 1 measure white creme de cacao, 1 measure double cream.

### Coffee Alexander:

One measure brandy, 1 measure Tia Maria or kahlua, 1 measure double cream.

# Brandy

## Method:

Put two or three ice cubes into the shaker and add the creme de cacao and the cream. Next add the brandy and shake well. Strain into a cocktail glass or champagne saucer and decorate with grated chocolate or nutmeg.

| method: | BUILD |
|---|---|
| glass: | LARGE COCKTAIL GLASS OR CHAMPAGNE SAUCER |
| garnish: | MARASCHINO CHERRY ON A STICK |

# Cafe Royale Frappe

*This is a wonderfully elegant way to end dinner on a summer's evening.*

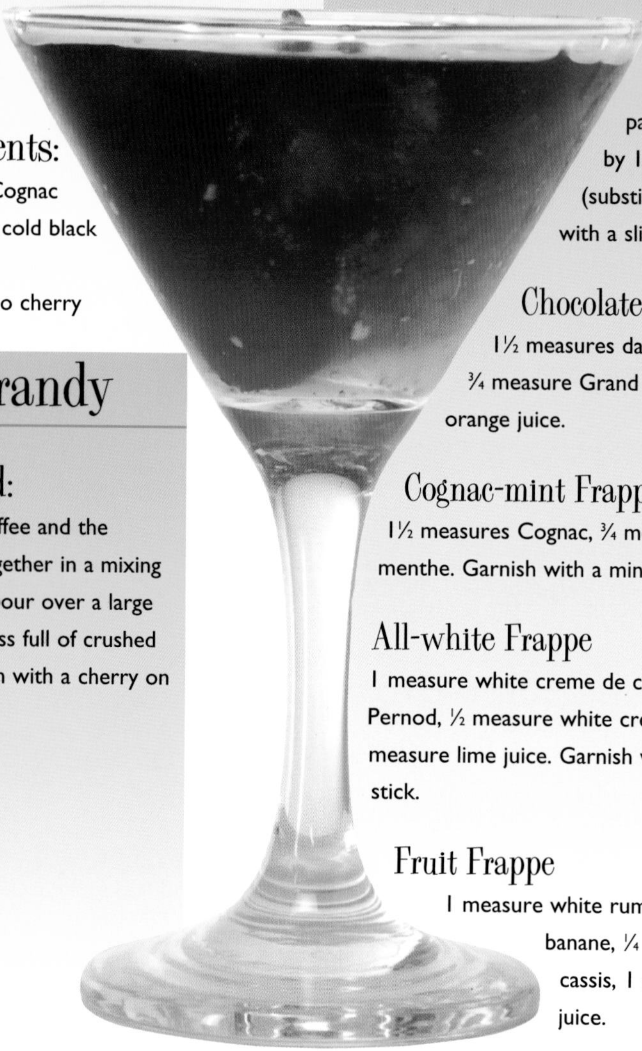

## Ingredients:

1 measure Cognac
3 measures cold black coffee
1 maraschino cherry

# Brandy

## Method:

Mix the coffee and the Cognac together in a mixing glass, and pour over a large cocktail glass full of crushed ice. Garnish with a cherry on a stick.

Try some of these other frappés:

## London Fog

1¾ measures gin (that's the London part!) the fog is supplied by 1¾ measures anisette (substitute Pernod). Garnish with a slice of lemon.

## Chocolate-orange Frappe

1½ measures dark creme de cacao, ¾ measure Grand Marnier, 1 measure orange juice.

## Cognac-mint Frappe

1½ measures Cognac, ¾ measure white creme de menthe. Garnish with a mint sprig.

## All-white Frappe

1 measure white creme de cacao, 1 measure Pernod, ½ measure white creme de menthe, ⅓ measure lime juice. Garnish with a cherry on a stick.

## Fruit Frappe

1 measure white rum, ½ measure creme de banane, ¼ measure creme de cassis, 1 measure mandarin juice.

# Canyon Quake

*This is a delightfully creamy, brandy-almond flavour, and makes a wonderful dessert or after dinner drink.*

## Ingredients:

¾ measure Baileys (Irish cream liqueur)

¾ measure brandy

1 measure amaretto

2 measures fresh, single cream

## Brandy

## Method:

Combine all the ingredients in a blender with two or three cracked ice cubes. Blend until smooth and pour into a large brandy snifter.

| method: | SHAKER WITH CRACKED ICE, OR IN A BLENDER |
|---------|------------------------------------------|
| glass: | CORDIAL |

# Scooter

*You can make this in a blender or shaker: it's a perfect post-dinner drink that you could have in lieu of a dessert!*

## Ingredients:

1 measure brandy

1 measure amaretto

1 measure fresh cream

# Brandy

## Method:

Combine all the ingredients in a blender, or shake with some cracked ice and strain into a cordial glass.

# Wine &
# Champagne
## cocktails

Bellini
see page 372.

Wine can be divided into four categories: still wine; sparkling wine; fortified wine and aromatised wine, and the recipes that follow give you an opportunity to use all of them. There are three types of still wine: red, white and rosé. Each can also be dry, medium dry or sweet. For our purposes, wines will be mixed with other flavourings and liqueurs, so it would be sacrilege to use a very fine wine which is best enjoyed on its own.

The undoubted 'queen' of sparkling wines is, of course, champagne. To truly be called champagne, the wine must come from the designated region in France, 160km (100 miles) north of Paris, around Rheims and Épernay. However, other fine sparkling wines – what the French call *vins mousseux* and the Italians call *spumante* – are made outside the region and outside France. Champagne should be thoroughly chilled, but not icy. Gently ease the cork out – don't pop it! By all means use champagne for those special occasions, but try some of the great sparkling wines from California, Australia, Spain,

# Black velvet
see page 373.

Italy and France as well.

Fortified wines are wines which have had brandy added to them. Port and sherry are the two best-known types of fortified wines. Port comes from the Douro region of Portugal. The brandy added to the wine stops the process of fermentation, leaving some of the sugar behind and resulting in the sweet fortified wine. Vintage port has been declared by the maker as being good enough to be called vintage. It must be bottled within two years and then aged in the bottle for between 8 and 20 years. Tawny port is aged in the barrel and is clarified of sediment by using egg whites. Because it is barrel-aged, the wood takes out some of the colour of the port: the longer it is aged, the paler (tawnier) and drier the port becomes. Ruby port is aged for less time and consequently keeps some of its colour and its full body. White port is drier than the other ports and is made only from white grapes, although it is still barrel-aged. A good tawny port is perfect for making many of the mixed drinks offered here.

Sherry got its name simply because the English had trouble pronouncing the Spanish name Jerez, the town in the Cadiz region of Spain where sherry is made. It is only a true sherry if it is made in the Jerez region, although several other countries (such as South Africa and Cyprus) also produce versions. The wine is placed in casks in order for a yeast scum – called flor – to develop. This is caused by natural airborne yeast and growth is variable. The amount of flor that develops governs the type of sherry produced. At this point, the wine is fortified with brandy. Dry fino sherry makes an excellent mixed drink.

Aromatised wines were originally sour wines sweetened with honey and herbs to make them more palatable. They are generally quite sweet, with a high proportion of mistelle (brandy mixed with grape juice). Some of the most popular aromatised wines are Campari, and the aromatised wines – both dry and sweet – called vermouths.

First avenue
see page 379.

# Adonis

*Named after the beautiful youth of Greek myth, Adonis was also the god of plants and vegetation. In ancient Athens, the midsummer festival the Adonia was celebrated in his honour with pots of bright summer flowers and herbs. This cocktail of sherry and vermouth captures in its flavours the herbs and wine of the island of Aphrodite.*

## Ingredients:

ice cubes

2 measures sherry

1 measure rosso vermouth

2 dashes bitters

# Wine & Champagne

## Method:

Put some ice cubes in the mixing glass and pour in the vermouth, bitters and the sherry. Stir well and strain into a cocktail glass.

# American dream

*This is a fabulous red-wine drink and a refreshing alternative to a 'straight' glass of red wine. Don't be alarmed by the ingredients – it tastes fantastic!*

## Ingredients:

ice cubes
3 measures red wine
(since it's an American dream, try a Californian wine)
⅓ measure bourbon
⅓ measure rosso vermouth
3 measures cold cola
I slice orange
I maraschino cherry

# Wine & Champagne

## Method:

Half-fill a highball glass with ice cubes.
Pour in the wine, vermouth, bourbon and top with cold cola.
Stir gently and garnish with the orange slice and the cherry.
Serve with a stirrer and straws.

| method: | BUILD |
|---|---|
| glass: | HIGHBALL |
| garnish: | LEMON AND ORANGE TWISTS, SLICE OF ORANGE (OPTIONAL) |

# Americano

*One of the classic – and classiest – aperitifs of all time,*
*it is very simple to make well. It's a great drink to have while*
*indulging in that Italian pastime of 'people watching'.*

## Ingredients:

ice cubes
1½ measures Campari
1½ measures rosso vermouth
soda water to taste

# Wine & Champagne

## Method:

Half-fill the highball glass with ice cubes.
Pour the vermouth and then the Campari
into the glass.
Add the twists of lemon and orange.
Stir well.
Decorate with the slice of orange.
Add soda water (optional) to taste – the soda
water gives the drink its freshness.
Sit back and watch the world go by!

# Bamboo

*This cocktail is not only a great aperitif, but tastes wonderful with Chinese or Thai food. The colder the mixing glass and the colder the cocktail glass, the better.*

## Ingredients:

1½ measures sherry
1½ measures dry vermouth
1–2 dashes bitters
1 twist lemon

# Wine & Champagne

## Method:

Make sure the mixing glass is really cold – swill a few ice cubes around first.

Get rid of any melted water by straining the cubes and then return them to the mixing glass.

Pour the sherry and vermouth over the ice and stir well for a few seconds.

Strain and serve in a well-chilled cocktail glass with a twist of lemon.

| method: | BUILD |
|---|---|
| glass: | CHAMPAGNE FLUTE |
| garnish: | SEASONAL FRUIT (OPTIONAL) |

# Bellini

*In 1943, Venice honoured one of its most famous sons, the Renaissance painter Giovanni Bellini (c. 1430–1516) with a major exhibition of his works. At Harry's Bar in Venice, legendary bartender Guiseppe Cipriani marked the occasion by creating this champagne and peach-juice cocktail.*

## Ingredients:

3 measures champagne – thoroughly chilled

1 large peach, skinned and puréed to make 1½ measures peach juice

1 teaspoon gomme syrup

# Wine & Champagne

## Method:

Remove the skin from the peach and purée it in a blender or food processor. You should have enough puree for 1½ measures.

Pour the peach purée/juice into the chilled champagne flute and add the gomme syrup. Pour in the extremely well-chilled champagne. Decorate with garnish if desired.

## variation:

Try a Mango Bellini: use 1½ measures of mango juice instead of the peach juice.

# Black velvet
## (also known as Bismarck)

*This very chic-looking champagne and stout drink was created in 1861 at Brook's Club in London. Prince Albert, husband of Queen Victoria, had died and England was in mourning. At Brook's it was decided that even the champagne should pay its respects and it, too, went into mourning black by being mixed with Guinness. The Black velvet became an immensely popular drink and was the favourite tipple of Prince Otto von Bismarck, Chancellor of Germany, hence its alternative name.*

### Ingredients:
Chilled stout
Chilled champagne

## Wine & Champagne

### Method:
Chill the stout and the champagne.
Half-fill a glass with stout (Guinness, Murphy or Beamish).
Gently fill the glass with the chilled champagne.

### variations:
A lager-champagne is called a Halsted Street Special.

If you don't want to use champagne, try a very dry, sparkling white wine instead.

| method: | SHAKER |
| --- | --- |
| glass: | COLLINS |
| garnish: | SEASONAL FRUIT |

# Camp Grenada

*A clever mix of Campari and grenadine.*

## Ingredients:

ice cubes

1½ measures Campari

½ measure grenadine

2 measures grapefruit juice

1 measure pineapple juice

3 measures cold lemon-lime

soda (e.g., 7-Up)

seasonal fruit

# Wine & Champagne

## Method:

Half-fill the shaker with ice cubes.

Pour in the grapefruit and pineapple juices.

Add the grenadine and Campari and shake

well.

Strain into an ice-filled Collins glass and top

with the lemon-lime soda.

Garnish with the seasonal fruit.

| method: | BUILD |
|---|---|
| glass: | CHAMPAGNE FLUTE |
| garnish: | TWIST OF LEMON |

# Champagne cocktail

*The ultimate cocktail – when absolutely nothing else will do.*
*The champagne cocktail was the result of a cocktail competition*
*held in New York in 1889. The first prize, a gold medal, was*
*awarded to John Dougherty for his recipe – although he had, in*
*fact, discovered it 25 year earlier in the southern states of America.*

## Ingredients:

3 measures well-chilled champagne
⅓ measure cognac (brandy will be OK, but only just!)
1 sugar cube
2 dashes bitters
1 twist lemon
½ orange slice

# Wine & Champagne

## Method:

Drop the sugar cube into the champagne flute.
Add the bitters so that the sugar cubes soaks them up.
Pour in the cognac and then fill the flute with the chilled champagne.
Squeeze the twist of lemon and discard.
Decorate with the half slice of orange.

| method: | MIXING GLASS |
|---|---|
| glass: | COCKTAIL |
| garnish: | 2 MARASCHINO CHERRIES ON A STICK |

# Crimean cocktail

*You'll need a fine sieve for this cocktail.*

## Ingredients:

ice cubes

2 measures dry white wine

⅔ measure Cointreau

grated zest of 1 lemon

1 measure soda water

2 maraschino cherries

# Wine & Champagne

## Method:

Put 3–4 ice cubes into the mixing glass and pour in the white wine and Cointreau.

Add the lemon zest and stir well.

Strain through a fine sieve into a cocktail glass.

Add the soda and garnish with the two cherries.

# Diablo

*We've already 'conjured up' a rum Diabolo (see page 63), and now's the chance to prove that port is not just for old men or to drink with Stilton cheese. The Diablo is also an opportunity to use white port – a drink that is too often overlooked.*

## Ingredients:

ice cubes
2 measures dry white port
1½ measures rosso vermouth
a few drops of lemon juice

# Wine & Champagne

## Method:

Half-fill the shaker with ice cubes.
Pour in the vermouth and the port and
squeeze in a few drops of lemon juice.
Shake well and strain into a cocktail glass.

| method: | BUILD |
|---|---|
| glass: | BALLON OR LARGE WINE GLASS |
| garnish: | SLICE OF ORANGE |

# Diplomatic answer

*This is a great herb- and orange-flavoured long drink based on vermouth and brandy. Vermouth is generally considered an aperitif, while brandy is a digestif. The diplomatic answer – combining the two – means you really can drink this at any time.*

## Ingredients:

broken ice

2 measures rosso vermouth

1 measure brandy

⅓ measure triple sec or Cointreau

4 measures lemonade

slice of orange

## Wine & Champagne

## Method:

Half-fill a large wine glass with broken ice. Pour in the vermouth, brandy and triple sec or Cointreau and top with lemonade. Garnish with the slice of orange.

# First Avenue

*Avenues are short drinks based on sherry and built in a glass which has been chilled enough to have an ice frosting. The First Avenue uses Cointreau, but any fruit liqueur can be used – but only enough so that it makes a subtle contribution to the overall flavour.*

## Ingredients:

broken ice

1½ measures sherry

½ measure Cointreau

¾ measure soda water

1 teaspoon Campari

# Wine & Champagne

## Method:

Fill an old-fashioned glass two-thirds full with broken ice.

Pour in the sherry, Cointreau, Campari and soda.

| method: | BUILD |
|---|---|
| glass: | COLLINS |
| garnish: | ½ SLICE OF LEMON AND A CHERRY |

# French 75

*The original '75 cocktail' was created during the First World War in Paris by Henry at Henry's Bar, and was named in honour of the French 75 light field gun. Post-war, Harry MacElhone, at Harry's Bar in Paris, added champagne and renamed it the French 75. By 1930 it was incredibly popular and spawned a whole number of Frenches – the 25, 45, 65, 95 and the 125.*

Vive la France!

## Ingredients:

ice cubes

5 measures well-chilled champagne

1 measure gin

1 measure lemon juice

1 heaped teaspoon castor sugar

½ lemon slice

1 maraschino cherry

# Wine & Champagne

## Method:

Pour the gin and lemon juice into the Collins glass.

Add the sugar and make sure it dissolves.

Fill the glass two-thirds full with ice and add the champagne.

Garnish with ½ a lemon slice and a maraschino cherry and serve with straws.

## Variations:

Practice your French:

FRENCH 25: 5 measures champagne, 1 measure tequila, 1 measure lemon juice, ½ measure maple syrup.

FRENCH 45: a French 75 with Drambuie instead of gin and only ½ teaspoon sugar.

FRENCH 65: a French 75 with 2 teaspoons brandy floated on top.

FRENCH 95: a French 75 with bourbon instead of gin.

FRENCH 125: a French 75 with cognac instead of gin.

# Hillary Wallbanger

*Meet Harvey's cousin!*

## Ingredients:

ice cubes
4 measures dry white wine
2 measures orange juice
½ measure Galliano

# Wine & Champagne

## Method:

Fill the Collins glass two-thirds full with ice cubes.
Pour in the white wine and orange juice and stir well.
Float the Galliano on top.

| method: | BUILD |
|---|---|
| glass: | CHAMPAGNE FLUTE |

# Mimosa

*There is often a little confusion surrounding the mimosa and its close relative, the buck's fizz. A mimosa is simply a delicious 50:50 mix of champagne and orange juice created in 1925 at the Ritz Hotel in Paris and named after the beautiful tropical flower whose colour it resembles.*

## Ingredients:

3 measures chilled champagne
3 measures orange juice
1 twist orange

# Wine & Champagne

## Method:

Pour the chilled orange juice and champagne into the well-chilled flute. Add the twist of orange.
Add ½ measure Cointreau and you have a grand mimosa.

The buck's fizz is the mimosa's older sister – created in 1921 in London at the Buck's Club. It differs from the mimosa in both the ratio of orange juice to champagne and in the inclusion of grenadine.

# Negroni

*A perfect balance of sweetness and bitterness, the Negroni is named after the Florentine Count Camillo Negroni. The drink was created in 1919 at the Casoni Bar in Florence, where the count usually ordered an Americano. One day, however, he asked for a little gin to be added to his drink and the result was the immensely popular Negroni.*

## Ingredients:

ice cubes
1 measure Campari
1 measure rosso vermouth
1 measure gin
soda water (optional)
slice of orange

# Wine & Champagne

## Method:

Almost fill an old-fashioned glass with ice cubes.
Pour in the gin, vermouth and sherry and stir.
If you want a long drink, add some soda.
Garnish with the slice of orange.
Serve with a stirrer.

| method: | BUILD |
|---|---|
| glass: | BALLON |

# Night and day

*'Night and day, you are the one,*
*Only you beneath the moon and under the sun.'*
*Cole Porter, 'Night and Day' from*
*Gay Divorce (1932).*

## Ingredients:

crushed ice

3 measures champagne

¾ measure cognac

½ measure Cointreau

¼ measure Campari

## Wine & Champagne

## Method:

Half-fill a ballon with crushed ice.

Pour in the cognac, Cointreau and Campari.

Add the chilled champagne.

# Operator

*A great ginger-wine flavour!*

## Ingredients:

2 measures cold, dry white wine

2 measures dry ginger ale

1 teaspoon lime juice

1 slice lime

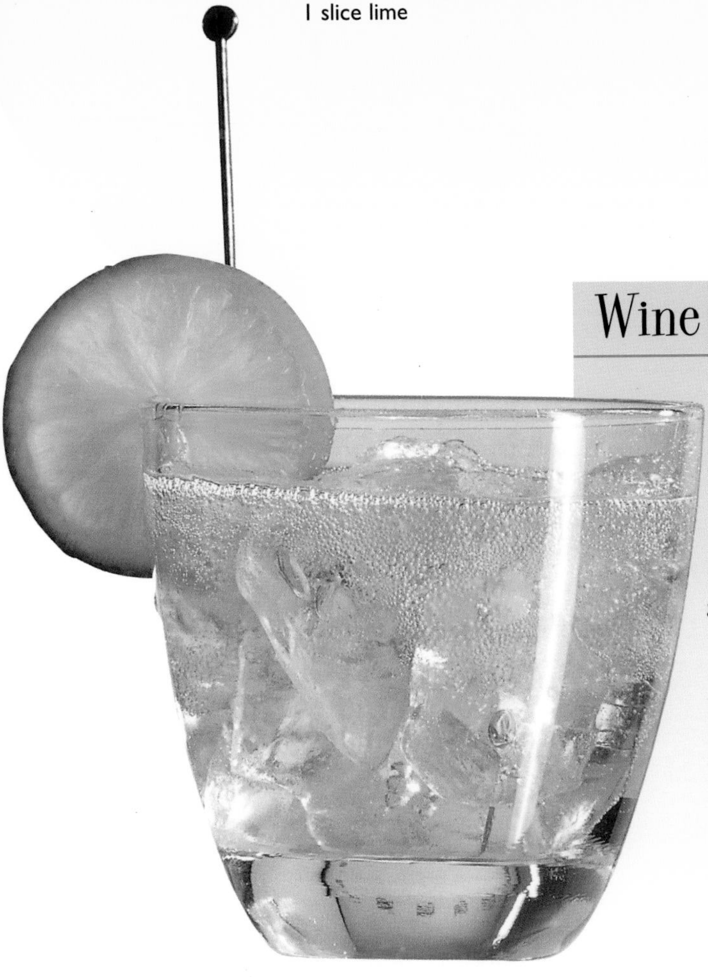

## Wine & Champagne

## Method:

Put 3 or 4 ice cubes in an old-fashioned glass. Pour in the wine.

Add the lime juice and the dry ginger ale.

| method: | SHAKER |
| --- | --- |
| glass: | OLD FASHIONED |

# Ozone

*Sit in the shade or wear a hat with this one!*

## Ingredients:

¾ measure sherry
¾ measure bourbon
1 measure pineapple juice
½ measure lime juice
1 teaspoon Campari
1 teaspoon grenadine

# Wine & Champagne

## Method:

Put a glassful of broken ice into the shaker.
Pour in the sherry, bourbon, lime juice,
pineapple juice, Campari and grenadine. Shake
well and then pour unstrained into an old-
fashioned glass.

## Quick thrill

*If your host asks 'How about a quick thrill?'*
*– don't slap his face!*

### Ingredients:

ice cubes
**3 measures red wine**
⅓ **measure dark rum**
**3 measures cold cola**

# Wine & Champagne

## Method:

Put some ice cubes in the goblet or wine
glass and pour in the wine and rum.
Top with the cold cola and quiver with
delight!

method: BUILD

glass: CHAMPAGNE FLUTE

## Regatta

*A great drink – perfect for Henley or even Cowes Week. Although it has a nautical name, there's not a drop of rum in sight!*

### Ingredients:

3 measures chilled champagne
½ measure Galliano
½ measure triple sec or Cointreau
½ measure lemon juice
1 teaspoon vodka

# Wine & Champagne

### Method:

Pour the Galliano, triple sec or Cointreau, lemon juice and vodka into a chilled champagne flute.
Add the chilled champagne.

# Ritz Bar fizz

*Created at the Ritz Bar of the Ritz-Carlton Hotel in Boston, Massachusetts.*

# Wine & Champagne

## Ingredients:

3 measures chilled champagne

1 measure grapefruit juice

1 measure pineapple juice

1 teaspoon grenadine

1 maraschino cherry

1 sprig of mint

## Method:

Pour the pineapple and grapefruit juices into a chilled champagne saucer.

Pour in the chilled champagne and add the grenadine.

Garnish with the sprig of mint and the cherry.

# Bosom Caresser

*A naughty – but very nice – cocktail from the Prohibition era.*

## Wine & champagne

### Method:
Place all the ingredients in a shaker with some ice cubes and shake vigourously. Strain into a cocktail glass.

### Ingredients:
1 measure Madeira
¾ measure brandy
½ measure triple sec/Cointreau
1 teaspoon grenadine
1 egg yolk

# Alfonso

*This champagne cocktail was created and named in honour of the Spanish King Alfonso XIII (1886–1941) who was deposed in 1931. Alfonso spent much of his exile in France, where he sampled this delight.*

## Ingredients:

1 sugar lump
3 drops angostura bitters
1 measure Dubonnet
4 measures champagne

# Wine & champagne

## Method:

Place the sugar cube into a chilled wine glass or flute, and soak it with the angostura bitters. Add a large ice cube and the Dubonnet. Finish with the champagne and stir. Squeeze a twist of lemon over the top and discard the peel.

| method: | BUILD |
|---|---|
| glass: | GLASS OR FLUTE |
| garnish: | BLACK GRAPE |

# Black Tie

*A chance to use Pineau des Charentes, a ratafia made in the Cognac region of France. Ratafia is not a geographical appellation, but derives from the ancient French practice of concluding a formal agreement, such as a legal transaction, with the Latin words 'rata fiat' (let the deal be settled) and a shared drink – a 'ratifier'.*

# Wine & champagne

## Method:

Place the ingredients in a chilled wine glass or flute and garnish with a black grape. Watch the black grape go up and down!

## Ingredients:

3 measures cold, white Pineau des Charentes

1½ measures champagne

# Pineau-cchio

*A lovely orange-wine flavour, and if you tell
a little lie, your nose won't grow!*

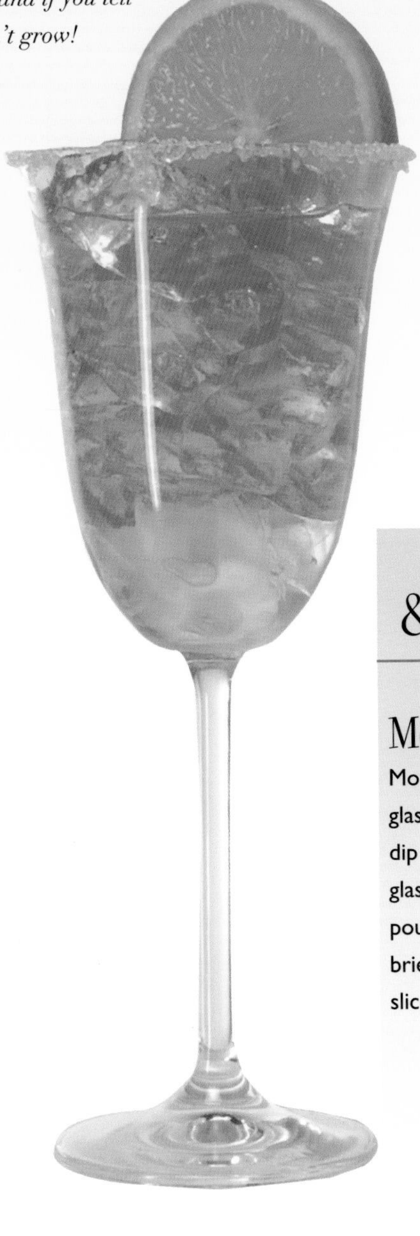

## Ingredients:

1½ measures chilled, white
Pineau des Charentes

½ measure cognac

½ measure triple
sec/Cointreau

# Wine
& champagne

## Method:

Moisten the rim of the wine
glass with a little orange and
dip into caster sugar. Fill the
glass with broken ice and
pour in the ingredients. Stir
briefly and garnish with a
slice of orange.

**method:** SHAKER

**glass:** COCKTAIL

# Urbinos

*A lovely raspberry-flavoured cocktail.*

## Wine & champagne

### Method:

Place all the ingredients in a shaker along with some ice cubes. Shake well and strain into a cocktail glass.

### Ingredients:

3 measures chilled, white Pineau de Charentes
1 measure cognac
½ measure creme de framboise

# Aqua Marina
*Mint-flavoured champagne!*

## Ingredients:

4 measures champagne

1 measure vodka

½ measure green creme de menthe

½ measure lemon juice

# Wine & champagne

## Method:

Into a shaker with some ice cubes place the ingredients – except the champagne – and shake. Strain into a champagne flute and add the champagne.

| method: | BUILD |
| glass: | CHAMPAGNE SAUCER |
| garnish: | 2 CHERRIES ON A STICK |

# Marilyn Monroe

*A classic champagne cocktail which uses Dom Perignon champagne – said to be the Hollywood legend's favourite.*

# Wine & champagne

## Method:

Add the ingredients to a well-chilled champagne saucer and garnish with the two cherries on a stick.

## Ingredients:

1 measure Calvados
1 teaspoon grenadine
4 measures Dom Perignon

# Ritz Fizz

*This delicious and very beautiful champagne cocktail is perfect for a celebration – an engagement, a wedding, an anniversary,, a birthday – or just for dinner à deux perhaps!*

## Ingredients:

1 teaspoon filtered lemon juice

1 teaspoon blue Curaçao

1 teaspoon amaretto

3½ measures champagne

# Wine & champagne

## Method:

Simply add the ingredients to a chilled champagne flute and float a small rose petal on top.

| method: | BUILD |
|---|---|
| glass: | CHAMPAGNE SAUCER |

# Hemingway

*As well as being a daiquiri fan, the great American novelist, Ernest Hemingway, created this champagne and Pernod drink. When he gave the recipe to* Esquire *magazine, Hemingway called his drink Death in the Afternoon and suggested that three – or five – of these sipped slowly would do the trick!*

## Wine & champagne

## Method:

Pour the Pernod into the champagne saucer and add the chilled champagne until the whole mix becomes opalescent.

## Ingredients:

1½ measures Pernod
chilled champagne

# Pernod Fizz

*Another glorious mix of Pernod and champagne, but this time with a little mandarin juice.*

## Ingredients:

¾ measure Pernod

1 measure mandarin juice

chilled champagne

# Wine & champagne

## Method:

Fill a good sized wine glass ¾ full with broken ice. Pour in the Pernod and mandarin juice and top with chilled champagne. Garnish with the slice of orange and the cherry.

| method: | BLENDER |
| --- | --- |
| glass: | FLUTE |
| garnish: | STRAWBERRY |

# Gulf Stream

*One for a special occasion... like a Wednesday!*

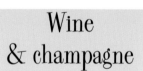

# Wine & champagne

## Method:

Frost the rim of the flute with a little of the lime juice and dip into sugar. Combine the ingredients in a blender with some ice and blend until smooth. Pour into the sugar-rimmed champagne flute and garnish with a strawberry.

## Ingredients:

1 measure blue Curaçao
3 measures champagne
½ measure light rum
½ measure brandy
1 measure lime juice
6 measures lemonade

# Liqueurs
## and other mixers

Travel and tourism over the past one hundred years have opened peoples' eyes to the lands, traditions and cultures of many parts of the world that were once inaccessible to most ordinary people. We also discovered new flavours and new foods that tantalised our taste buds. Exciting new drinks and new ingredients burst on to the scene as travellers ventured to Central and South America, the Pacific, Australasia and Southeast Asia. But even the 'old' cocktail staples like gin, vodka, brandy and rum became more exciting as we discovered the subtle variations in flavours and unique tastes of the same spirits made in other countries.

The invention of rum dates from the establishment of sugar plantations in the West Indies in the early 16th century. The rough spirit that was first produced as a by-product of the sugar industry was described as 'hot, hellish and terrible'! But, as new techniques were developed, the spirit became infinitely more palatable.

Chartreuse Cooler
see page 411.

Today rum is produced all over the West Indies and Eastern South America, in the Indian Ocean – the Philippines and Mauritius – as well as in small quantities in the USA and Australia. In addition to rum, the region also produces a range of flavoured liqueurs: Malibu is perhaps the best known – a blend of white rum and coconut extracts, but Brazil also makes Batida de Coco. Rum tree is a white, rum-based, sweet, but citrus-flavoured, liqueur that is increasingly popular in cocktail recipes.

The tradition of drinking fiery spirits in Central and South America stems from the early Spanish colonists who planted the first vines. In addition to producing wines, fiery brandies were also made. Mexico produces one called Presidente, but an interesting contribution is pisco, a colourless brandy distilled in Peru, Chile and Bolivia.

Other famous products from the new world include kahlua a dark brown, coffee-flavoured liqueur from Mexico. Kahlua is slightly thicker in texture, but a little less sweet than it's famous rival, Tia Maria which, in spite of it's Italian- sounding name, in fact comes from Jamaica.

Snowball
see page 416.

Tropical fruits, either in their 'natural state' as juices or added to a spirit base to make liqueurs, have long been the way to make exotic-flavoured cocktails: orange-flavoured Curaçaos, grenadine ( a sweet, red low or non-alcoholic cordial made from pomegranates) and creme liqueurs are staples of the cocktail bar. Some more recent additions come from Indonesia, Japan and Hawaii: pisang ambon is a green banana and herb flavoured liqueur. Ambon is the name of an Indonesian island, where *pisang* means 'banana'. Sake is Japanese rice beer. Traditionally served warm when neat, it is now appearing in many new cocktails, while okelehao, is a spirit distilled in Hawaii from the mashed and fermented root of the ti plant.

The range of ingredients on offer have inspired bartenders across the world to invent exciting new combinations, and such is their generosity, many of their recipes are freely available for you to recreate. So relive those tropical sunsets at any time of year and share happy moments with friends and loved ones with these magical drinks.

But the mixers in this section are not just from the exotic, tropical countries. All across Europe can be found a variety of liqueurs and creamy mixes that can be used to

## Cool operator
see page 422.

create rich and often fiery cocktails. From France for example come Pernod, Creme de Menthe and anis among others, Denmark brings us aquavit and we have Advocaat from the Netherlands and Schnapps from Germany. Creamy examples include Baileys Irish Cream - perfect for a cold winter's night! ourbon-based, but mixed with orange, Southern Comfort also features in these delicous recipes.

## Flying Grasshopper
see page 434.

# Sazerac

*The Sazerac is a cocktail that made its film debut alongside James Bond in* Live and Let Die. *You can buy ready-mixed Sazerac, but here's how to make it yourself.*

## Ingredients:

4 dashes anis (substitute: Pernod)
1 white sugar cube
4 dashes of angostura bitters
1 small dash soda water
2 measures bourbon

## Liqueurs

## Method:

Coat the inside of an old-fashioned glass with the 4 dashes of anis/Pernod. Place the sugar cube onto a long-handled bar spoon and coat with the angostura bitters. Place the soaked sugar in the bottom of the glass and add a very small dash of soda water. Crush the sugar cube with the back of the bar spoon. Fill the glass two-thirds full with cracked ice and pour in the bourbon. Serve with a stirrer.

| method: | SHAKER |
|---|---|
| glass: | COCKTAIL |
| garnish: | CHERRY |

# Casino

*For the man 'who broke the bank at Monte Carlo'.*

## Liqueurs

### Method:

Place all the ingredients into a shaker with some ice cubes and shake well. Strain into a cocktail glass and add the cherry.

### Ingredients:

2 dashes orange bitters

¼ teaspoon maraschino

¼ teaspoon lemon juice

2 measures gin

# White Lady Cocktail

*This is the original recipe by Harry MacElhone created at Ciro's Club, in London, in 1919. Harry later changed the recipe in 1929 at his own bar in Paris, replacing the white creme de menthe with gin.*

## Ingredients:

1 measure lemon juice
1 measure white creme de menthe
1 measure Cointreau

## Liqueurs

### Method:

Place the ingredients in a shaker with some ice cubes and shake well. Strain into a cocktail glass.

| method: | SHAKER |
| --- | --- |
| glass: | WINE GLASS |
| garnish: | ORANGE SLICE (OPTIONAL) |

# Tropical Cocktail
*Perfect anywhere!*

## Ingredients:

- 1 measure dry vermouth
- 1 measure maraschino
- 1 measure white creme de cacao
- 1 dash angostura bitters

# Liqueurs

## Method:

Place all the ingredients in a shaker with plenty of ice and shake vigourously. Strain into a wine glass.

# Yellow Parrot

*This luxurious cocktail was created around 1935 by Albert Coleman at the famous Stork Club in New York.*

## Ingredients:

1 measure Pernod or Ricard

1 measure yellow Chartreuse

1 measure apricot brandy

## Liqueurs

### Method:

Place the ingredients in a shaker with some ice cubes and shake well. Strain into a cocktail glass filled with crushed ice.

| method: | MIXING GLASS |
|---|---|
| glass: | COCKTAIL |
| garnish: | TWIST OF LEMON |

# Rosalind Russell

*Another great cocktail named after another of Hollywood's great ladies, this time from the 1930s. This subtle caraway-and-herb-flavoured cocktail uses aquavit, 'schnapps' from Denmark. Aquavit is a neutral grain and/or potato spirit, rectified to a very high degree of purity and then aromatised with fragrant spices. Try substituting aquavit for the vodka in a Bloody Mary!*

## Ingredients:

2 measures Danish aquavit
1 measure sweet red
vermouth

## Liqueurs

## Method:

Place the ingredients in a mixing glass with some ice cubes and stir. Strain into a chilled cocktail glass and add a twist of lemon.

# Chartreuse Cooler

*This refreshingly fruity long drink is a wonderful way to indulge in Chartreuse.*

## Ingredients:

1 measure yellow Chartreuse

2 measures orange juice

½ measure lemon juice

3½ measures sparkling bitter lemon

# Liqueurs

## Method:

Add some ice cubes to a collins glass, pour in the ingredients and top with the sparkling bitter lemon. Garnish with a spiral of orange.

| method: | BUILD |
|---|---|
| glass: | FLUTE |
| garnish: | HALF A SLICE OF ORANGE AND CHERRY |

# Horn of Plenty

*In classical mythology, the Horn of Plenty, or cornucopia, is said to have been the horn of the goat belonging to the nymph, Amalthaea, who lost it when she fought in the form of a bull with Hercules. By magic, the horn then contained an abundant and endless supply of of food and drink, while Amalthaea was transformed into the star Capella.*

## Liqueurs

### Method:

Add the first three ingredients to a chilled champagne glass and top with the champagne. Garnish with the half slice of orange and a cherry.

## Ingredients:

⅓ measure Grand Marnier

⅓ measure Campari

¼ measure grenadine

chilled champagne

# Paris Opera

*Try this combination of aniseed and orange flavours.*

## Ingredients:

1 measure Mandarine
   Napoleon
1 measure Pernod
5 measures lemonade

## Liqueurs

### Method:

Add the ingredients to a
pilsner glass filled with
broken ice.

| method: | BUILD |
| glass: | COLLINS |
| garnish: | SPRINKLE OF NUTMEG |

# Brown Cow

*Cows are long drinks made with milk – a bit like a milkshake – but with a kick! Brandy and rum are among the most popular spirits used, but this Brown Cow is coffee flavoured: you can use Tia Maria or kahlua.*

## Ingredients:

1½ measured Tia Maria or kahlua
6 measures cold milk

# Liqueurs

## Method:

Fill a collins glass with ice cubes and pour in the coffee liqueur and milk. Sprinkle grated nutmeg on top. Serve with a stirrer and a straw.

| method: | SHAKER |
|---|---|
| glass: | COLLINS OR HIGHBALL |
| garnish: | CHERRY ON A STICK, SPRINKLE OF NUTMEFG OR CINNAMON |

415

# Comfortable Milk Punch

*Milk punches are a little similar to cows, but with the addition of a little sugar syrup to sweeten them up. Punches are also shaken and poured over rocks in a tall glass. A single spirit, such as brandy, rum, rye, bourbon or Scotch can be used. This recipe adds a touch of peach by using Southern Comfort.*

## Ingredients:

2 measures Southern Comfort

½ measure sugar syrup

5 measures cold, full-cream milk

## Liqueurs

## Method:

Fill a collins or highball glass with ice cubes. Add a few ice cubes to a shaker and pour in the ingredients and shake well. Strain and pour into glass filled with ice cubes. Garnish with a cherry on a stick and a sprinkling of nutmeg or cinnamon. Serve with a straw.

| method: | BUILD |
|---|---|
| glass: | COLLINS OR HIGHBALL |
| garnish: | CHERRY ON A STICK |

# Snowball

*For most people a Snowball is a 'girlie' drink. This is largely because most people are deceived by the taste and think the drink has a low alcohol content. In fact the average alcohol content is about two units. There's nothing girlie about that!*

## Liqueurs

### Method:

Into a collins or highball glass, add some ice cubes. Pour in the Advocaat, add the lime cordial and top up with lemonade. Garnish with a cherry on a stick and serve with straws and a stirrer.

### Ingredients:

2 measures Advocaat
¼ measure Rose's Lime Cordial
5 measures lemonade

| method: | BUILD |
|---|---|
| glass: | GOBLET OR OVERSIZED WINE GLASS |
| garnish: | SLICE OF LEMON AND A CHERRY (TRADITIONALLY A GREEN CHERRY) |

417

# Dizzy Blonde

*A delicious aniseed flavour that's enough to make any head spin!*

## Ingredients:

1¾ measures Advocaat

¾ measure Pernod

1 measure orange juice

2 measures lemonade

# Liqueurs

## Method:

Fill a goblet three-quarters full with broken ice and pour in the Advocaat, Pernod, orange juice and top with lemonade. Garnish with the lemon slice and green cherry – a red one is okay too. Serve with straws and a stirrer and forget everything!

| method: | SHAKER |
| --- | --- |
| glass: | OLD-FASHIONED |

# Climax
*One for the end of the evening perhaps?*

## Ingredients:

1½ measures Southern
Comfort
1 measure kahlua
1 measure whipping cream

## Liqueurs

## Method:

Place all the ingredients in a
shaker with some broken ice
and shake well. Pour,
unstrained, into an old-
fashion glass.

# Golden Dream

*This cocktail was devised in 1960 by the makers of Galliano to promote the use of their golden yellow liqueur, the recipe for which is a very closely guarded secret.*

## Ingredients:

1 measure Galliano
1 measure triple sec/Cointreau
1 measure whipping cream
1 measure orange juice

## Liqueurs

## Method:

Place all the ingredients in a shaker with two or three ice cubes and shake well. Strain into a cocktail glass and watch the sun rise.

420

| method: | SHAKER |
| --- | --- |
| glass: | CHAMPAGNE SAUCER OR COCKTAIL |
| garnish: | CHERRY AND A SPRIG OF MINT |

# Grasshopper

*Sweet, minty, creamy – and delicately green!*
*There's also a Flying Grasshopper too if you're*
*into shooters (see page 233).*

# Liqueurs

## Method:

Place all the ingredients in a shaker with two or three ice cubes and shake well. Strain into a cocktail glass or champagne saucer and garnish with a sprig of mint. Serve with a short straw, if you wish.

## Ingredients:

1⅓ measures white creme de menthe

1 measure green creme de menthe

1⅓ measures whipping cream

# Blue Cloud Cocktail

*This really does look like a blue sky with fluffy white clouds!*
*Think of the cherry as the 'red hot sun'!*

## Ingredients:

1 measure amaretto
½ measure blue Curaçao
2 measures vanilla ice cream

## Liqueurs

## Method:

Combine all the ingredients in a blender and blend until smooth – the consistency of a thick milkshake. Pour into brandy snifter and top with whipped cream and the cherry.

| method: | BLENDER |
| --- | --- |
| glass: | PARFAIT OR WHITE WINE GLASS |
| garnish: | MELON WEDGE AND A CHERRY |

# Cool Operator

## Ingredients:

1 measure Midori melon liqueur

½ measure lime juice

½ measure vodka

½ measure light rum

4 measures grapefruit juice

2 measures orange juice

## Liqueurs

## Method:

Put all the ingredients in the blender and add ice to fill halfway. Blend until thick and pour into a parfait or white wine glass. Garnish with a wedge of melon and a cherry.

| method: | BLENDER |
| --- | --- |
| glass: | PARFAIT OF WHITE WINE GLASS |
| garnish: | WHIPPED CREAM AND CHOCOLATE CURLS OR FLAKES |

# Death by Chocolate

*What a way to go!*

## Ingredients:

1 measure Baileys (Irish cream liqueur)

½ measure dark creme de cacao

½ measure vodka

1 scoop chocolate ice cream

# Liqueurs

## Method:

Combine the ingredients in the blender with a glass of crushed ice and blend until smooth. Pour into parfait or white wine glass. Garnish with whipped cream and sprinkle with grated chocolate curls or flakes of chocolate. Serve with a straw.

| method: | BLENDER |
|---|---|
| glass: | PARFAIT OR WHITE WINE GLASS |
| garnish: | ORANGE SLICE |

# Di Amore Cream

*This is perfect for Valentine's Day – or for sharing with a lover at any time!*

## Ingredients:

1½ measures amaretto

¾ measure white creme de cacao

2 measures orange juice

2 scoops vanilla ice cream

## Liqueurs

## Method:

Combine all the ingredients in a blender and blend until smooth. Pour into parfait or white wine glass and garnish with a slice of orange.

# Italian Dream

## Ingredients:

1½ measure Baileys (Irish
    cream liqueur)
½ measure Amaretto
2 measures fresh single cream

## Liqueurs

### Method:

Combine all the ingredients
in a blender with ice and
blend until smooth. Serve in
a parfait or white wine glass.

| method: | BLENDER |
|---|---|
| glass: | PARFAIT OR WHITE WINE GLASS |
| garnish: | SLICE OF ORANGE AND A CHERRY |

# Surf's Up

*This frothy confection certainly looks like breaking waves.*

## Liqueurs

### Method:

Place the ingredients into a blender and blend until smooth. Pour into a parfait or white wine glass and garnish with the orange slice and the maraschino cherry.

### Ingredients:

½ measure creme de banane

½ measure white creme de cacao

5 measures pineapple juice

1 measure single cream

# Frozen Fuzzy

*Try this Frozen Fuzzy on a hot day.*

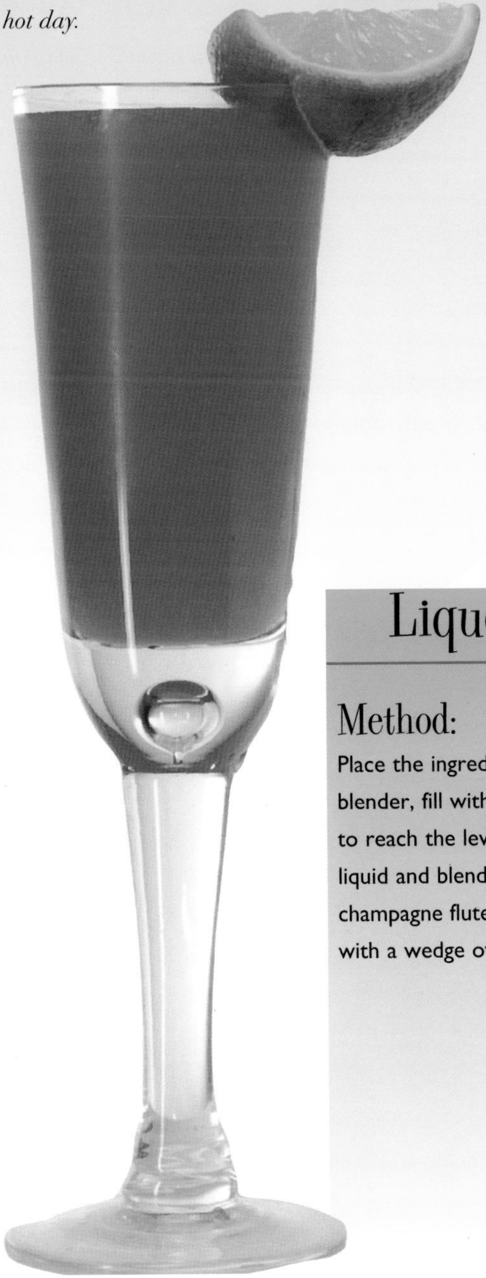

## .Ingredients:

1 measure peach schnapps

½ measure triple sec/Cointreau

½ measure lime juice

½ measure grenadine

1 splash lemon-lime soda

## Liqueurs

## Method:

Place the ingredients in a blender, fill with enough ice to reach the level of the liquid and blend. Pour into a champagne flute and garnish with a wedge of lemon.

428

| method: | SHAKE WITH CRUSHED ICE |
|---|---|
| glass: | COCKTAIL OR CHAMPAGNE SAUCER |

# Scarlett O'Hara

*Naturally, Southern Comfort is used for this pretty pink belle. The peachy flavour of Southern Comfort makes for terrific frozen sour-type drinks.*

## Ingredients:

2 measures Southern Comfort

1 measure grenadine

1 dash lime juice

# Liqueurs

## Method:

Place a good scoop of crushed ice into a shaker and pour in the Southern Comfort, grenadine and the lime juice. Shake and pour, unstrained, into a cocktail or champagne saucer and serve with short straws.

# Rhett Butler

*You can't have Scarlet without Rhett – unless, of course, you frankly don't give a damn!*

## Ingredients:

2 measures Southern Comfort
¼ measure triple sec/Cointreau
¼ measure lime juice
¼ measure lemon juice

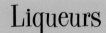

# Liqueurs

## Method:

Put a good scoop of crushed ice into a shaker and add the Southern Comfort, triple sec/Cointreau, lemon and lime juices. Shake and pour, unstrained, into an old-fashioned glass and serve with a short straw.

| method: | MIXING GLASS |
|---------|--------------|
| glass:  | SHOT         |

# Alabama Slammer

## Ingredients:

1 measure amaretto
1 measure Southern Comfort
½ measure sloe gin
1 splash lemon juice

# Liqueurs

## Method:

Stir the amaretto, Southern Comfort and sloe gin with one or two ice cubes in a mixing glass. Strain into a shot glass and add the splash of lemon juice.

# Angel's Tip

*This is a variation of the Prohibition era Angel's Tit, which was made with 1½ measures of maraschino and ⅔ measure fresh cream floated on top, garnished with a maraschino cherry to make a very suggestive cocktail. You can experiment with your favourite flavours.*

## Ingredients:

¾ measure creme de cacao (white)

¼ measure fresh cream

## Liqueurs

## Method:

Pour the white creme de cacao into a cordial glass (no ice) and float the fresh cream carefully on top. Put the cherry on a cocktail stick and arrange so it sits naughtily on the top!

# B-52

*This is one of those 'famous names' in cocktails and, while most people have heard of it, and most know that it was named after the huge B-52 transport planes developed for the US military, few will know that it is a coffee-flavoured drink with just a hint of orange to it.*

## Ingredients:

1 measure kahlua (coffee liqueur)
1 measure Baileys (Irish cream liqueur)
2 teaspoons Grand Marnier

# Liqueurs

## Method:

Into a pousse–café glass, pour in the kahlua. Next, over the back of a spoon, carefully pour in the Baileys so it floats on top of the kahlua. Next, carefully add the Grand Marnier, so this sits on top of the Baileys. If it all goes wrong, don't despair: you can stir and strain all the ingredients into an ice-filled old-fashioned glass and it will taste equally delicious!

# Capri

*This is the adult equivalent of a banana split: the white chocolate flavour of the creme de cacao combined with creme de banane and topped by fresh cream. Instead of a dessert, try one of these instead!*

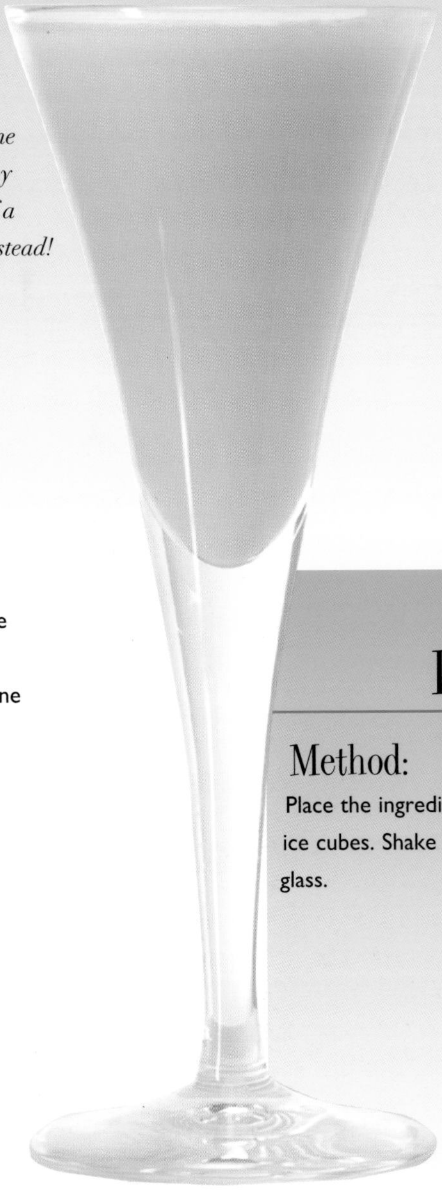

## Ingredients:

¾ measure white creme de cacao

¾ measure creme de banane

¾ measure fresh cream

# Liqueurs

## Method:

Place the ingredients into a shaker with a few ice cubes. Shake well and strain into a cordial glass.

method: MIXING GLASS

glass: CORDIAL

# Flying Grasshopper

*Related to the creamy-minty cocktail called the Grasshopper
this 'high-flying' version is kick started by vodka*

## Ingredients:

¾ measure green creme de
menthe
¾ measure white creme de
cacao
¾ measure vodka

# Liqueurs

## Method:

In a mixing glass with ice, stir together the
creme de menthe, creme de cacao and the
vodka. Strain into a cordial glass.

# Foxy Lady

*Dark and seductive with a chocolate-almond flavour.*

## Ingredients:

I measure amaretto
½ measure dark (brown) creme de cacao
I measure thick fresh cream

## Liqueurs

## Method:

Place all the ingredients in a shaker with two or three ice cubes. Shake well and strain into a cordial glass, or cocktail glass if you prefer.

| method: | MIXING GLASS |
|---|---|
| glass: | CORDIAL |

# Irish Charlie

*Try this on St. Patrick's Day.*

## Ingredients:

1 measure Baileys (Irish cream liqueur)
1 measure white creme de menthe

# Liqueurs

## Method:

Put two or three ice cubes in a mixing glass.
Add the Baileys and creme de menthe and stir.
Strain into a cordial glass.

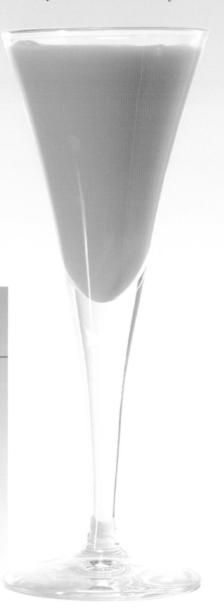

# Melon Ball

*If you like Midori, you'll love this.*

## Ingredients:

1 measure Midori (melon liqueur)
1 measure vodka
1 measure pineapple juice

# Liqueurs

## Method:

Shake all the ingredients with ice then strain into a cordial glass. Garnish, if you wish, with a melon ball.

| method: | MIXING GLASS |
|---------|--------------|
| glass: | SHOT |

# Oh My Gosh

*This is a wonderful wintertime warmer – especially if
you've just come in from the cold.*

## Ingredients:

I measure peach schnapps

I measure amaretto

## Liqueurs

### Method:

Add two to three ice cubes to a mixing glass.
Pour in the peach schnapps and amaretto and
stir. Strain into shot glass.

# Rattlesnake

*Another pousse-café for you to try with your steady hand!*
*This has a lovely whisky-chocolately-coffee flavour,*
*perfect for after dinner.*

## Ingredients:

I measure kahlua

I measure Baileys (Irish cream liqueur)

I measure white creme de cacao

# Liqueurs

## Method:

In a pousse-café or cordial glass, add the kahlua. Next pour the Baileys slowly over the back of a spoon so it floats on top of the kahlua. Finally, carefully pour the white creme de cacao over the back of a spoon so it floats on the Baileys.

| method: | SHAKER |
|---|---|
| glass: | SHOT |

# Rocky Mountain

*Try this subtle combination of peachy-whiskey with almonds.*

## Ingredients:

1 measure Southern Comfort

1 measure amaretto

½ measure lime juice

## Liqueurs

### Method:

Shake all the ingredients in a shaker with two or three ice cubes. Strain into a shot glass.

# Sex on the Beach

*One of those drinks that everyone knows the name of, but few*
*dare to ask for! Now's your chance to try it in the privacy of*
*your own home with 20 or 30 or your very closest friends!*

## Ingredients:

½ measure creme de framboise
  (raspberry liqueur)
½ measure Midori (melon liqueur)
½ measure vodka
1 measure pineapple juice
cranberry juice

## Liqueurs

## Method:

In a mixing glass with two or three ice cubes,
stir all the ingredients except the cranberry
juice. Strain into cordial glass and top with the
cranberry juice.

# Punches, cups & toddies

A punch is a spiced, alcoholic, mixed drink served to a number of people, usually from a bowl. The origins of the word punch are debatable. It may have derived from 'puncheon', a large beer cask that held 72 gallons, or perhaps from the Hindu word *paunch*, which means five. The latter explanation is often believed because a punch usually contains at least five ingredients

In the first half of the 17th century, punches were generally made with ale, brandy or wine. With the colonisation of Jamaica from 1655 onwards, the basis of many punches became rum. The simplest rum punch consists of rum, sugar, water and orange juice.

Party punches are great fun to make and drink. They should be served in a bowl with a large block of ice in it to

Manhattan punch
see page 462.

keep it cool – ice cubes melt quickly and dilute
the punch. You can make a block or brick of ice
quite easily in a clean juice or milk carton.
Alternatively, set the punch bowl on a large salver or
serving dish and surround it with ice cubes.

Cups, such as the stirrup cup, are also made in large
quantities, and were traditionally offered to the mem-
bers of a hunting party before 'the off'. Toddies, which
are hot drinks, may have originated in the East Indies in
the form of 'tarries', the 17th-century word for a drink
made from fermented palm juice. Most toddies
use Scotch whisky as their base, but they can
be made with most spirits with a little
sugar, some spices and a slice of citrus
fruit. They are wonderful on cold
evenings by the fireside, or if you feel a
little under the weather. You will also
find a couple of ideas for hot drinks based

English bishop
see page 453.

Grog
see page 456.

on coffee, cocoa and tea.

For hot drinks, make sure the glasses used are heat-proof and warm them before pouring in the liquids. Heat-proof glasses are available in a range of sizes and styles, from cups to goblets and tall glasses for Irish coffee. If you don't have these, don't worry: these hot drinks look and taste just as good in an attractive china mug or cup.

**Take extra care with hot liquids, especially when igniting spirits!**

# Alhambra (hot)

*This is so simple to make and so delicious: it's really for*
*grown-ups who never really grew up!*

## Ingredients:

5 measures hot cocoa or drinking
chocolate, made how you like it best

I measure cognac

## Punches, cups & toddies

## Method:

Pour the hot cocoa or
drinking chocolate into the
warmed glass and add the
cognac.

| method: | PUNCH BOWL |
| glass: | BALLON/WINE GLASS |
| garnish: | APPLE WEDGES |

# Boston punch (cold)

*This is a wonderfully refreshing*
*apple-wine flavour punch.*
*It will serve around 15 people.*

## Ingredients:

block of ice

750 ml (1 bottle) champagne or sparkling white wine

300 ml (10 fl oz) cider

150 ml (5 fl oz) brandy

2 measures triple sec or Cointreau

3 measures dark rum

4 measures lemon juice

400 ml (14 fl oz) sparkling mineral water

1 tablespoon sugar

apple wedges

# Punches, cups & toddies

## Method:

In the punch bowl, dissolve the sugar in the lemon juice, rum and triple sec or Cointreau.

Add the block of ice to the bowl and pour in the brandy and cider and then the mineral water and champagne or sparkling wine.

Add thin wedges of apple.

To stop cut apple from turning brown, dip the pieces in some lemon juice.

# Brown Betty (hot)

*This is a terrific, hot, beer-based punch. The quantities given will serve around eight people.*

## Variations

Another version of the brown Betty uses the juice of the lemon instead of slices and the whole hot mix is poured over slices of toasted raisin bread that has been dusted with cinnamon and ginger.

## Ingredients:

4 x 12 oz bottles amber ale
(1.3 litres in total)
12 measures brandy
2¼ cups water
½ cup brown sugar
1 lemon, sliced
4 whole cloves
1 cinnamon stick
½ teaspoon grated nutmeg
¼ teaspoon ground ginger

# Punches, cups & toddies

## Method:

In a large saucepan, over a medium heat, add the sugar, lemon slices, cloves, cinnamon, nutmeg, ginger and water. Stir continuously to dissolve the sugar and let the mixture come to the boil. Turn the heat down and let the mixture simmer for around 10 minutes. Add the brandy and the ale, then heat, but do not boil. Serve hot in beer mugs, each garnished with a slice of lemon.

| method: | BUILD |
|---|---|
| glass: | HEAT-PROOF CUP |
| garnish: | DUSTING OF NUTMEG |

# Bumpo (hot)

## Ingredients:

2 measures hot water

2 measures rum

I measure lime juice

I teaspoon sugar

ground nutmeg

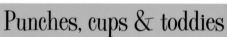

# Punches, cups & toddies

## Method:

Dissolve the sugar in the glass with the lime juice and hot water.

Add the rum and dust lightly with the ground nutmeg.

# Cafe d'Amour (hot)

*This is a coffee made without cream – the perfect way to end an intimate dîner à deux: It is, after all, the 'coffee of love'. Be careful when you heat and ignite the cognac – the only thing that should be inflamed are your passions, not the kitchen.*

## Variation:

For a Café brûlot, add one clove and the zest of half an orange to the saucepan before heating. The cup in this instance is not sugar-rimmed.

## Ingredients:

5 measures hot black coffee

1 ¼ measures cognac

zest of ½ lemon

1 stick cinnamon

sugar (to rim the cup and to sweeten, if desired)

# Punches, cups & toddies

## Method:

Rim the cup with lemon and dip into some sugar. Add the coffee, lemon zest and the cinnamon stick to the saucepan and simmer. Carefully pour the cognac into a large soup ladle and ignite it. Pour the flaming cognac into the coffee and then extinguish the flame by putting the lid on the saucepan. Remove the lid and strain the mixture into the sugar-rimmed cup.

| method: | BUILD |
|---|---|
| glass: | HEAT-PROOF GLASS |

# Colonial boy (hot)

*This is a wonderful, tea-based hot drink that's perfect after a long, winter walk.*

## Ingredients:

5 measures hot black tea
(sweetened to taste)
⅓ measure Irish whiskey
1 dash bitters

### Variation:

For hot-T: omit the bitters and replace the whisky with
1 measure Cointreau. Add a slice of orange to garnish.
Try a fireside tea: combine in a glass 1 measure rum, 5
measures hot black tea, 1 wedge of lemon and 1 stick of
cinnamon.

## Punches, cups & toddies

## Method:

Pour the hot tea into
the glass and add
the whiskey and
bitters.

# Confetti punch (cold)

*A beautiful punch, perfect for a summer wedding.*
*The secret is to chill all the ingredients well in advance.*
*The recipe will serve about 40 people.*

## Ingredients:

700 ml (1¼ pints) white rum
1½ litres (2⅔ pints) champagne
or dry, sparkling wine
1 litre (1¾ pints) lemonade
700 ml (1¼ pints) white
grape juice
500 ml (18 fl oz) orange juice
1 punnet strawberries, halved

# Punches, cups & toddies

## Method:

Chill all the ingredients for at
least two hours – the longer
the better.
Simply pour all the ingredients
into the punch bowl and stir
gently.
Add the halved strawberries.
Serve in chilled ballon or wine
glasses.

| method: | PUNCH BOWL |
|---------|------------|
| glass:  | BALLON OR WINE GLASS |

# Dragoon punch (cold)

*Try this punch when the cavalry arrives! For 12 people.*

## Ingredients:

block of ice

500 ml (1 pint) sherry

500 ml (1 pint) brandy

3 bottles or 1½ pints stout (850 ml)

3 bottles or 1½ pints lager (850 ml)

2 bottles champagne or sparkling white wine

2 lemons, sliced thinly

## Punches, cups & toddies

## Method:

Put the block of ice in the punch bowl and pour the sherry, brandy, lager and stout over the block.

Stir the mixture thoroughly and add the lemon slices.

At the last minute before serving, pour in the champagne or sparkling wine.

Serve in a ballon or wine glass (officers and gentlemen). Other ranks might enjoy it in a beer mug!

# English bishop (hot)

*This is a port-wine drink, made with baked oranges and served hot. Serves six.*

## Variation:

Replace the port with red wine for a cardinal. For a very fancy version called the *Bishop à la Prusse*, let the roasted orange stand in the red wine for a day. Then press out the orange juice and reheat the whole mixture.

## Ingredients:

1 large orange
12 cloves
700 ml (1¼ pints) inexpensive port
1 tablespoon honey
1 teaspoon allspice
2 dashes cognac (optional)

## Punches, cups & toddies

## Method:

Stick the cloves into the whole orange and bake it in the oven on a low heat for 30 minutes. Cut the baked orange into quarters and put it into the saucepan. Pour in the port and add the allspice, honey and cognac if desired. Over a very low flame, simmer gently for 15–20 minutes – do not boil or the flavour of the port will be spoiled. Serve in warmed cups.

| method: | PUNCH BOWL |
| --- | --- |
| glass: | BALLON OR WINE GLASS-COCKTAIL |

# Fruit-juice cup (cold)

*This is a great basic recipe with which to adapt and experiment. Try adding exotic fruit and juices or even adding a little more rum.*

## Ingredients:

700 ml (1 bottle or 1¼ pints)
red Lambrusco (sparkling
red wine)
100 ml (4 fl oz) dark rum
500 ml (1 pint) orange juice
100 ml (4 fl oz) lemon juice
200 ml ( 8 fl oz ) pineapple
juice
100 ml ( 4 fl oz) gomme syrup
1 litre (1¾ pints) ginger ale
slices of orange and lemon

# Punches, cups & toddies

## Method:

Chill all the ingredients first
and then pour them all into
the punch bowl.
Add a block of ice and
garnish with the slices of
fruit.
Serve in chilled ballon or
wine glasses.

# Fresh-fruit punch (cold)

*A festival of fruit flavours. This will serve 12 people and will give them something healthy to nibble on. It's a recipe that needs time, however, as the fruit needs to steep in the rum for at least six hours before the punch is properly prepared.*

## Ingredients:

block of ice

60 cl (15 fl oz) of fresh fruit – either one variety or mixed fruits

500 ml (1 pint) gomme syrup

350 ml (12 fl oz) white rum

700 ml (1¼ pint) gin

2 x 750 ml bottles of dry white wine (2⅔ pints in total)

# Punches, cups & toddies

## Method:

Wash and slice the fresh fruit and place it in a large bowl. Pour the gomme syrup and rum over the fruit and place it in the refrigerator for at least six hours.

Put the block of ice into the punch bowl and pour the 'marinated' fruit and liquid over the ice. Add the gin and the white wine and stir thoroughly.

Let the mix stand for a few minutes before serving in ballons or wine glasses.

| method: | SAUCEPAN |
| glass: | HEAT-PROOF CUP |

# Grog (hot)

*This spiced-rum mix was named after Admiral Sir Edward Vernon, who was nicknamed 'Old Grog' because his cloak was made of the coarse material, grosgrain. Returning from the Caribbean in 1740, in order to save on costs (or perhaps stretch the rum ration), Old Grog diluted the crew's rum with water, a mixture that was immediately named 'Grog'. They soon discovered that it tasted better hot.*

## Ingredients for one cup:

2 measures dark rum

2 measures water

⅔ measure lime juice

I teaspoon brown sugar (or honey)

2 cloves

I small cinnamon stick

## Punches, cups & toddies

## Method:

Add all of the ingredients to a small saucepan and heat gently to dissolve the sugar. When hot, strain into a heat-proof cup.

# Gluhwein (hot)

*In German,* Glühwein *means 'glowing wine' and it is a popular* après ski *drink. In Britain, it is more commonly known as mulled wine and is often served at winter parties. There are 'ready-mixed' mulled-wine spice mixes available, but it is easy (and cheaper) to make your own. You can make* Glühwein *in quantity as a hot punch – multiply the ingredients by the number of people.* Prosit!

## Ingredients:

4 measures red wine

½ measure brandy

1 teaspoon castor sugar

1 slice orange

1 slice lemon

1 cinnamon stick

2 cloves

## Punches, cups & toddies

## Method:

Place all the ingredients into a saucepan and simmer gently – do not boil – for 30 minutes.
Strain into the heat-proof goblet

| method: | SAUCEPAN |
| --- | --- |
| glass: | HEAT-PROOF CUP |

# Hot buttered rum (hot)

*This lime-flavour cocktail was invented in the 1920s.
Originally it was served 'straight up' without the sugar. It is also
sometimes served in an old-fashioned glass filled with broken ice.
Try the variations for yourself.*

## Ingredients:

2 measures dark rum

2½ measures water

1 teaspoon brown sugar
(or honey)

1 pinch ground nutmeg

4 drops vanilla essence

1 small cinnamon stick

1 small knob of butter

## Punches, cups & toddies

## Method:

Place the cinnamon stick, nutmeg and vanilla essence in the heat-proof cup. Heat the rum, water and sugar in the saucepan until almost boiling.

Remove from the heat and pour into the cup over the spices. Put the knob of butter on top and watch it melt into the mixture.

# Hot Scotch toddy (hot)

## Ingredients:

2 measures Scotch

3 measures boiling water

½ measure lemon juice

1 teaspoon brown sugar (or honey)

3 drops bitters

1 slice lemon, studded with cloves

ground nutmeg

## Punches, cups & toddies

### Method:

Put the sugar, bitters, lemon juice and clove-studded lemon slice in the glass.

Add the Scotch and pour in the boiling water. Stir to dissolve the sugar and sprinkle with ground nutmeg.

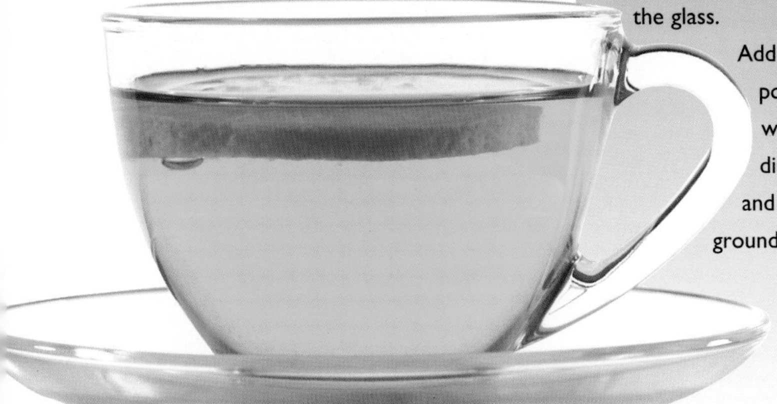

| method: | PUNCH BOWL |
| --- | --- |
| glass: | BALLON OR WINE GLASS |
| garnish: | LEMON SLICES |

## Ingredients:

1 block ice
1 bottle chilled champagne or
sparkling white wine
(750 ml or 1¼ pints)
750 ml (1¼ pints) brandy
2.25 litres ( 3 x 750 ml bottles)
dry red wine
500 ml (1 pint) strong black
tea, chilled
juice of 24 lemons
900 g (2 lb) sugar
lemon slices

## Punches, cups

## Method:

In a large punch bowl, dissolve
the sugar in the lemon juice.
Add the chilled tea and a block
of ice.
Pour in the red wine and the
brandy.
Chill thoroughly.
Immediately before serving, add
the champagne or sparkling
white wine.
Serve in ballons or wine goblets
and garnish with the lemon
slices.

# Independence Day
# punch (cold)

*Just the thing for 4 July. Serves around 15 patriots!*

# Lafayette punch (cold)

*This is an extremely simple champagne punch, and there's enough here to serve 20 people.*

## Ingredients:

1 block ice
6 oranges, sliced
sugar (enough to cover the orange slices)
1 bottle dry white wine
(750 ml or 1¼ pints)
4 bottles champagne or sparkling white wine
(3 litres or 5¼ pints)

# Punches, cups & toddies

## Method:

Slice the oranges and arrange them on the bottom of the punch bowl.

Sprinkle the orange slices with plenty of sugar. Pour in the white wine and let the oranges 'stand' for an hour or so.

Just before serving, add a block of ice and pour in the chilled champagne or sparkling white wine.

| method: | PUNCH BOWL |
| glass: | BALLON OR WINE GLASS |
| garnish: | ORANGE & MARASCHINO CHERRIES |

# Manhattan punch (cold)

*This Manhattan-style punch will serve around 12 people.*

## Ingredients:

1 block ice
(or some large chunks)
750 ml (1¼ pints) rosso
vermouth
1.5 litres (2⅔ pints) whisky
600 ml (21 fl oz) iced water
½ teaspoon bitters
2 oranges, sliced thinly
12 maraschino cherries
(optional)

# Punches, cups & toddies

## Method:

Put the block of ice into the
punch bowl. Pour the
vermouth, bitters and
whisky over the ice. Add
the iced water and stir
thoroughly.
Garnish with the orange
slices and serve each glass
with a cherry.

# Royale coffee (hot)

*The most famous hot coffee and liqueur drink topped with
whipped cream is Irish coffee. This uses Irish whiskey, but there
are numerous variations. Try the royale, with cognac.*

## Variations:

Replace the cognac in the following:

tropical coffee: 1 measure golden rum and sprinkle with cinnamon;

Caribbean coffee: 1 measure dark rum and sprinkle with chocolate;

Gaelic coffee: ¾ measure Scotch and sprinkle with chocolate.

## Ingredients:

1 measure cognac
5 measures hot black coffee
(sweetened to taste)
1½ measures whipped cream
grated chocolate

# Punches, cups & toddies

## Method:

To the warmed glass, add
the hot coffee and the
cognac.
Gently float the whipped
cream on top and sprinkle
with grated chocolate.

| method: | JUG |
|---|---|
| glass: | BALLON OR WINE GLASS |

# Sangria (cold)

*Once again, there are numerous versions of this famous Spanish punch. This basic recipe will keep 12 people happy, and you can add a measure or two of a liqueur if you want to experiment!*
*Viva Espana!*

## Ingredients:

ice cubes
750 ml (1¼ pints) red wine
(preferably Spanish)
4 measures brandy
(Spanish if possible)
200 ml (7 fl oz) soda water
or lemonade
juice 1 lemon
juice 1 orange
1 orange, 1 lemon, sliced
1 lime, sliced
1 tablespoon castor sugar
(or to taste)

## Punches, cups & toddies

### Method:

Half-fill a jug or pitcher
with ice.
Add the orange and lemon
juices and dissolve the
sugar.
Pour in the wine and the
brandy. Add the sliced
citrus fruit, then the soda
or lemonade.
Stir and serve immediately.

# Somerset punch (cold)

*This is a wonderful, cider-based punch that's great for parties on a budget. Somerset, in the west country, is the heart of English cider-making. You could 'spike' it up with some Calvados or apple-jack, if you have some. To serve around 15 people.*

## Ingredients:

1 block ice

1 litre (1¾ pints) dry cider

150 ml (5 fl oz ) dry white wine

2 measures brandy (Calvados or applejack if desired)

300 ml (10 fl oz ) ginger ale

150 ml (5 fl oz ) orange juice

150 ml (5 fl oz ) apple juice

2 measures lemon juice

sliced strawberries or apple slices

# Punches, cups & toddies

## Method:

Put the block of ice into the punch bowl and pour in the lemon juice, apple and orange juice.

Add the cider and the brandy (optional) and the ginger ale.

Garnish with some strawberry slices or apple slices.

| method: | PUNCH BOWL – A VERY BIG ONE! |
|---|---|
| glass: | BALLON OR WINE GLASS |

# Toledo punch (cold)

*This is a punch devised by Harry Johnson in 1882. It's for a really big celebration and will serve 90 of your closest friends! Try this when you win the lottery!*

## Ingredients:

225 g (½ lb) sugar
(or more to taste)
1 litre (1¾ pints) soda water
juice of 2 lemons
500 ml (1 pint) cognac
1 small bunch mint sprigs
2 oranges, sliced thinly into
half rings
½ pineapple – diced
6 strawberries, halved

# Punches, cups & toddies

## Method:

Put all of the above in a large (very large!) punchbowl and dissolve the sugar. Now add:    3 litres (5.3 pints) water
500 ml (1 pint) ordinary brandy
2 x 750 ml (25fl oz) bottles claret
2 x 750 ml (25fl oz) bottles white wine
(Johnson's recipe called for German Rhine wine)
3 x 750 ml (25fl oz) bottles champagne
Add a block of ice and serve in ballon or wine glasses.

# Mocktails

Many people don't drink alcohol. It may be for medical or dietary reasons or because of religious beliefs. It may be because they are driving, or that they just don't like the taste of alcohol. Some people may be allergic to alcohol, some might be 'in recovery' and some might just not want a drink at that moment. Some might be under age. Whatever the reasons, if someone says 'no thanks' to a cocktail, then don't press one on them. There are lots of wonderful-tasting and good-looking 'mocktails' to be offered instead.

With many mixed drinks, mocktails included, it's almost impossible to tell whether there is alcohol in them or not just by looking at them. If you're providing drinks for a number of people, make sure you know your ingredients. Read the labels on the bottles: many so-called 'non-alcoholic' beers do, in fact, contain a small amount of alcohol. Adding a dash of bitters to a glass of tonic water also means you've added alcohol, even if it is only a very tiny amount.

Tail feathers
see page 487.

There are hundreds of delicious mocktails to be enjoyed: some were specially designed, others, like the Virgin Mary (a bloody Mary without the Vodka) a Virgin Colada (a Pina Colada without the rum) or a Virgin Bellini (a Bellini without the champagne) are non-alcoholic versions of famous cocktails and very easy to make.

If you serve mocktails, then they should look just as appealing as their alcoholic cousins. Take the same care over ingredients and the same time and effort over their presentation. After all, the non-drinkers have been invited and you want them to have as good a time as the rest of your friends!

Many of the recipes in this section are ideal for children to

Bora-Bora
see page 472.

Many of the recipes in this section are ideal for children to make. Kids are entranced by the bright colours, zany names, the mixing and, above all, the umbrellas associated with cocktails, so why not let them create a few of their own? Fruity drinks are certainly more healthy than sugar-filled, fizzy concoctions, but using 'diet' versions of cola and lemonade will reduce the sugar intake if that is something that concerns you.

It might be sensible to invest in some clear plastic beakers rather than using your finest cocktail glasses, and make sure you have plenty of straws and umbrellas!

## Virgin Bellini
see page 489.

| method: | BUILD |
|---|---|
| glass: | HIGHBALL |
| garnish: | SLICE OF ORANGE AND A CHERRY |

# Atomic cat

*It looks a little like a mimosa (page 198) and tastes just as good.*

## Ingredients:

ice cubes

4 measures orange juice

4 measures tonic water

1 slice orange

1 maraschino cherry

## Mocktails

### Method:

Almost fill a highball glass with ice cubes and pour in the orange juice.

Add the tonic water and garnish with the slice of orange and the cherry.

Add a stirrer and serve.

# Batman cocktail

*Because Robin's legs weren't
long enough to reach the pedals
of the Batmobile, the Caped Crusader had
to do the driving.*

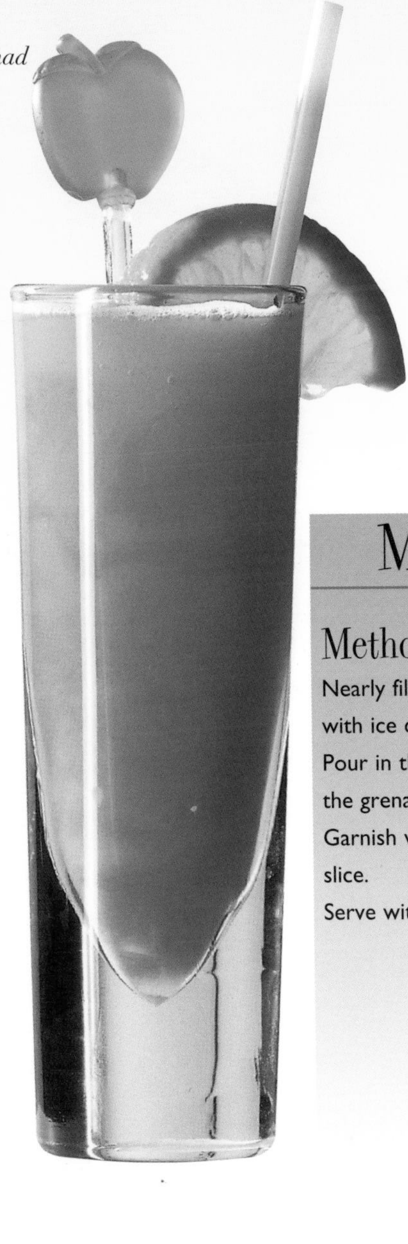

## Ingredients:

ice cubes

6 measures orange juice

½ teaspoon grenadine

1 orange slice

## Mocktails

## Method:

Nearly fill the Collins glass
with ice cubes.

Pour in the orange juice. Add
the grenadine and stir well.

Garnish with the orange
slice.

Serve with a stirrer.

| method: | SHAKER |
|---|---|
| glass: | BALLOON OR LARGE WINE GLASS OR GOBLET |
| garnish: | SLICE OF LIME AND A CHERRY |

# Bora-Bora

*Bora-Bora is in the Society Islands, part of French Polynesia in the Pacific Ocean, north west of Tahiti. Try this pineapple-flavour mocktail and conjure up images of swaying palm trees and tropical beaches.*

## Ingredients:

ice cubes

3 measures pineapple juice

3 measures dry ginger ale

½ measure grenadine

1 teaspoon lime juice

1 slice lime

1 maraschino cherry

## Mocktails

## Method:

Half-fill the shaker with ice cubes and pour in the pineapple juice, lime juice and grenadine.

Shake well and strain into an ice-filled glass.

Top with the dry ginger ale and garnish with the slice of lime and the cherry.

Serve with straws.

# Brontosaurus

*A long drink, as befitting the dinosaur with
the very long neck! The Greek word dinosaur means
'terrible lizard', and the
celery-stick garnish is a tribute to the herbivorous diet
of this long-extinct giant.*

## Ingredients:

ice cubes

3 measures grapefruit juice

½ measure lime juice

½ measure grenadine

3 measures lemonade

## Mocktails

## Method:

Half-fill the shaker with ice
cubes and pour in the lime
juice, grapefruit juice and
grenadine.
Shake well and strain into an
ice-filled highball glass and
top with the lemonade.
Garnish with the celery stick
(optional).

| method: | SHAKER |
|---|---|
| glass: | HIGHBALL |
| garnish: | SLICE OF LEMON |

# Cinderella

*This delicious, long, fruity drink is the real reason why Cinders stayed too long at the ball! You can drink it from a glass slipper if you want.*

## Ingredients:

ice cubes

2 measures orange juice

2 measures pineapple juice

1 measure lemon juice

½ measure gomme syrup

1 measure soda water

# Mocktails

## Method:

Half-fill the shaker with ice cubes and add the orange and pineapple juice, the lemon juice and the gomme syrup.

Shake well and strain into an ice-filled highball glass and top with soda.

Garnish with the slice of lemon and serve with straws.

# Cranberry cooler

*A great colour and a lovely, dry taste.*

## Ingredients:

ice cubes

4 measures cranberry juice

2 measures red grape juice

2 measures lemon-lime soda

1 lime wedge

## Mocktails

## Method:

Put some ice cubes in a highball glass and pour on the cranberry juice and red grape juice.

Top with the lemon-lime soda and stir well.

Garnish with the lime wedge and serve with a stirrer.

| method: | SHAKER |
| glass: | HIGHBALL |
| garnish: | LIME WEDGE |

# Flamingo

*Long, elegant and pink*
*– just like the bird.*

## Ingredients:

ice cubes

4 measures cranberry juice

2 measures pineapple juice

½ measure lemon juice

2 measures soda water

1 lime wedge

## Mocktails

### Method:

Half-fill the shaker with ice cubes.

Pour in the cranberry and pineapple juices and add the lemon juice.

Shake well and strain into ice-filled highball glass.

Top with the soda water and garnish with the lime wedge.

# Lassi

*Nothing to do with that incredibly clever dog, a lassi is*
*an Indian drink made with yoghurt. As well as being refreshing,*
*it's also very versatile. You can make it plain,*
*salted or sweet, or add fruit.*

## Ingredients:

ice cubes
2 measures plain yoghurt
6 measures cold water
pinch of salt
sprinkle of roasted cumin
seeds

## Variations:

Sweet lassi
Omit the salt and add 2
teaspoons granulated sugar
and 2 drops rosewater.
Whizz in the blender and
pour into an ice-filled
Collins glass.

Fruity lassi
Replace the water with 5
measures fruit juice and 1
measure lemon juice.
Try pineapple, cranberry,
mango or passionfruit
juice.

# Mocktails

## Method:

Place the yoghurt, water and
salt in the blender and blend
thoroughly.
Pour into an ice-filled highball
glass and add the cumin
seeds.
Stir well and serve with a
stirrer.

| method: | BUILD |
|---|---|
| glass: | HIGHBALL |
| garnish: | 2 CHERRIES AND GRATED CHOCOLATE |

# Mickey Mouse

*More an ice-cream float than a mocktail, but if you a) can remember all of the words to the Mickey Mouse Club song; b) ever had a Mouseketeer's hat with your name on it; or c) are a man who still has dreams in which Annette Funicello plays a major part, then you have every right to enjoy this!*

## Ingredients:

5 measures cold cola
1 scoop vanilla (or your favourite flavour) ice cream
1 measure whipped cream
2 maraschino cherries
grated chocolate

# Mocktails

## Method:

Put the cold cola into the highball glass and float the ice cream on top.
Add the whipped cream and garnish with the two cherries. Liberally dust with grated chocolate.
Add straws and a spoon.
Lock the door, take the phone off the hook and vow that you will go to the gym one day soon!

# Pink lemonade

*This is so easy to make – you can make a jugful
and play around with the ingredients as well.*

## Ingredients:

ice cubes
1½ measures lemon juice
1½ measures gomme syrup
⅓ measure grenadine
4 measures ice-cold water

## Variations:

For fizzy pink lemonade,
replace the cold water with
cold soda water. Add the soda
to the glass after the other
ingredients have been shaken
and strained.

For limeade, simply replace the
lemon juice with lime juice.

For orangeade, replace the
lemon juice with orange juice.

# Mocktails

## Method:

Half-fill the shaker with ice
cubes.
Pour in the lemon juice,
water, grenadine and gomme
syrup and shake well.
Strain into an ice-filled
highball glass and garnish with
the lemon slice and cherry.

| method: | BUILD |
| --- | --- |
| glass: | HIGHBALL |
| garnish: | SLICE OF LIME AND A CHERRY |

# Pomola

*Very simple to make and a welcome change from a 'straight' iced cola.*

## Ingredients:

ice cubes

5 measures cold cola

1 measure lime juice

⅓ measure grenadine

1 slice lime

1 maraschino cherry

# Mocktails

## Method:

Put some ice cubes in a highball glass.

Pour in the cold cola, the lime juice and the grenadine. Stir gently and garnish with the slice of lime and cherry. Serve with straws and a stirrer.

# Prohibition punch

*This is a great party drink, especially if there are a lot of people and it's a mixed crowd. This recipe will serve around six people.*

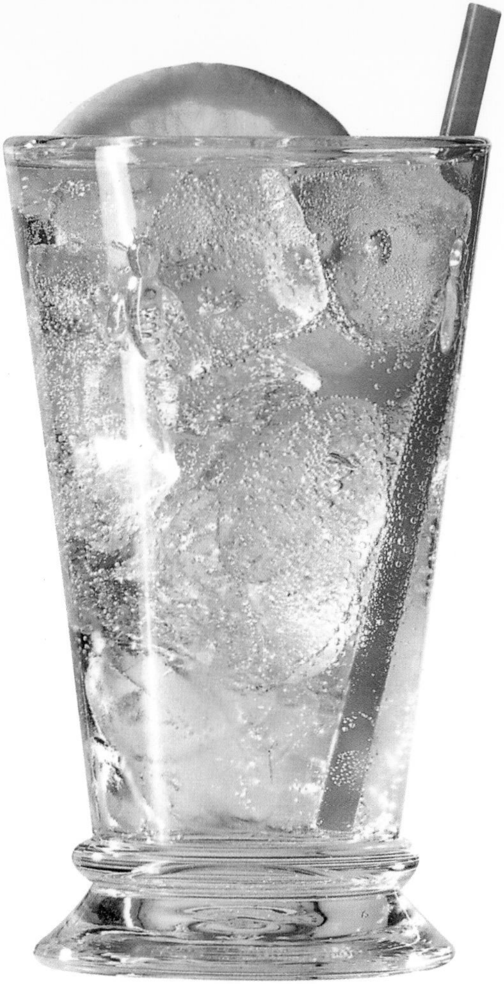

## Ingredients:

ice cubes
3 measures lemon juice
1 measure gomme syrup
225 ml (½ pint) apple juice
500ml (1 pint) ginger ale
orange slices

## Mocktails

## Method:

Put some ice cubes in the jug or pitcher.
Pour in the lemon juice, apple juice and gomme syrup and stir gently.
Pour in the ginger ale.
Serve in ice-filled highball glasses and garnish with an orange slice.

| method: | BUILD |
| glass: | HIGHBALL |
| garnish: | SPIRAL OF LEMON PEEL |

# Rail splitter

*A good Prohibition cooler.*

## Ingredients:

ice cubes

1 measure lemon juice

¾ measure gomme syrup

4 measures ginger ale

# Mocktails

## Method:

Put some ice cubes in a highball glass.

Pour in the lemon juice, gomme syrup and top with the ginger ale and stir gently.

Garnish with a spiral of lemon peel.

# Roy Rogers

*Named after Hollywood's most famous singing cowboy, whose real name was, in fact, Leonard Slye.*

## Ingredients:

ice cubes

4 measures ginger ale

2 measures lemon-lime soda

I teaspoon grenadine

I orange slice

I maraschino cherry

## Mocktails

## Method:

Put some ice cubes into a highball glass and pour in the ginger ale, lemon-lime soda and grenadine.
Stir well and garnish with the cherry and orange slice.

| method: | BUILD |
|---|---|
| glass: | CHAMPAGNE SAUCER OR HIGHBALL |
| garnish: | MARASCHINO CHERRY, SLICE OF ORANGE |

# Shirley Temple

*A number of celebrities have given their names to mixed drinks and cocktails: novelist Ernest Hemingway, actresses Rosalind Russell and Marjorie King (the Margarita), artist Charles Gibson and the millionaire Colonel Cornelius Vanderbilt are just a few. Some people think that all mocktails are called 'Shirley Temples' after the child star (and later American diplomat). For purists (and film buffs) however, there is, and only ever will be, one Shirley Temple.*

# Mocktails

## method:

**Champagne saucer:** Fill the chilled saucer with the cold lemon-lime soda or ginger ale. Add the grenadine and garnish with the cherry and orange slice.

**Highball:** Place some ice cubes in the highball glass. Pour in the lemon-lime soda or ginger ale. Add the grenadine and stir well. Garnish with the cherry and orange slice

## Ingredients:

ice cubes (if served in a highball)
5 measures cold lemon-lime soda
or 5 measures cold ginger ale
1 teaspoon grenadine
1 maraschino cherry
1 slice orange

# Southern ginger

*A non-alcoholic version of the mint julep.*

## Ingredients:

broken ice

5 measures dry ginger ale

½ measure gomme syrup

½ measure lemon juice

2 sprigs of mint (1 for garnish)

## Mocktails

## Method:

Put one sprig of mint into the highball glass and gently crush it to squeeze out some juice. Two-thirds fill the glass with broken ice and pour in the lemon juice, gomme syrup and ginger ale.
Mix gently.
Garnish with the remaining sprig of mint and serve with straws and a muddler.

| method: | BUILD |
|---|---|
| glass: | HIGHBALL |
| garnish: | SLICES OF ORANGE AND LEMON |

# St Clements

*'Oranges and lemons, say the bells of St Clement's'.*

## Ingredients:

broken ice

2 measures orange juice

2 measures sparkling bitter lemon

1 slice orange

1 slice lemon

# Mocktails

## Method:

Two-thirds fill the highball glass with broken ice.
Pour in the orange juice and add the sparkling bitter lemon.
Garnish with the orange and lemon slices and serve with straws.

# Tail Feathers

*This Prohibition highball uses ginger beer.*

## Ingredients:

ice cubes

I measure orange juice

5 measures ginger beer

(not ginger ale)

I sprig mint

I lime slice

# Mocktails

## Method:

Put some ice cubes in the highball glass.

Pour in the orange juice and add the ginger beer.

Garnish with the sprig of mint and the lime slice.

| method: | BLENDER |
|---|---|
| glass: | HIGHBALL |
| garnish: | SLICE OF ORANGE AND A CHERRY |

# Tarzan's juicy cooler

*Another great mocktail that makes excellent use of yoghurt.*

## Ingredients:

3 measures orange juice

3 measures pineapple juice

¼ measure grenadine

½ measure lemon juice

2 measures yoghurt (plain or fruit flavoured)

I teaspoon (or more to taste) clear honey

I orange slice

I maraschino cherry

# Mocktails

## Method:

Put half a glassful of crushed ice into the blender.

Pour in the orange juice, pineapple juice, grenadine, lemon juice, yoghurt and honey.

Blend briefly and pour into a highball glass.

Garnish with the orange slice and the maraschino cherry.

Serve with straws.

# Virgin Bellini

*You can make this with peach nectar or by 'crushing' a*
*peeled and de-stoned peach in a blender.*

## Ingredients:

3 measures peach nectar
(or crush 1 large, ripe
peach – peeled and
de-stoned – in a blender)
1 teaspoon grenadine
1 measure lemon juice
4 measures chilled soda water

# Mocktails

## Method:

Into a chilled champagne
flute, pour the peach nectar.
Add the grenadine and lemon
juice and top with the chilled
soda water.
Stir well.

# Yellowjacket

*A yellowjacket is a type of wasp, so be prepared for quite a sharp 'sting' of a drink!*

## Ingredients:

ice cubes

2 measures pineapple juice

2 measures orange juice

1½ measures lemon juice

## Mocktails

### Method:

Half-fill the shaker with ice cubes.

Pour in the lemon juice, orange juice and pineapple juice and shake well.

Strain into an ice-filled old-fashioned glass.

# Bibliography

Salvatore Calabrese, *Classic Cocktails*, Prion, 1997

Gary Regan, *The Bartender's Bible*, HarperCollins, 1993

*Harry's ABC of Mixing Cocktails*, Harry MacElhone with Andrew MacElhone, Souvenir Press, 1986

Gino Marcialis & Franco Zingalis, *The Cocktail Book*, MacDonald, 1983

Michael Jackson, *Michael Jackson's Pocket Bar Book*, Mitchell Beazley, 1981

David A. Ebury, *The Fine Art of Mixing Drinks*, Faber, 1963

Ambrose Heath, *Good Drinks*, Faber, 1939

# Credits and Acknowledgements

Additional photography by
STEPHEN BRAYNE.

Special thanks to
NICK LAWES.

All glassware and cocktail equipment supplied by:
GILL WING,
Upper Street, Islington, London.